Global Strategy in the Service Industries

Global service-based firms are often 'born global,' and these organizations have developed integrated global strategies based on industry relationships, in order to thrive in new environments.

Focusing on these global strategies, this textbook explores the workings of modern service businesses, presenting theoretical management concepts alongside illustrative examples. Original case studies from a range of global sectors, including Starbucks and Facebook, as well as broader studies, such as healthcare in Japan, provide practical insights into the art of thriving as a global business.

Written by a leading expert in the field, this multidisciplinary text is a vital read for all scholars and students wishing to view strategic relationships from the focal point of service industries.

Mario Glowik is Professor of International Strategic Management at the Berlin School of Economics and Law, Germany. His research centers on issues related to internationalization and innovation processes, with a particular focus on global industry networks and its relevant actors.

'Despite the increasing importance of the service sector for advanced economies as well as emerging markets, the focus of business education and research has been primarily on manufacturing. This book offers a comprehensive, insightful look at the international strategies of firms in service industries including up-to-date cases and examples. It is a valuable resource for academics and practitioners alike.'

—*Martina Musteen, Professor, San Diego State University, USA*

'With his new book, Mario presents a fascinating and substantial overview of the continuously changing landscape of global strategy. In particular, the carefully elaborated case studies provide us with a picture that is very much up-to-date and, thus, both reflects on the current challenges for strategists in the global economy and considerably contributes to our knowledge and understanding of the field. Students, academic scholars and practitioners from various disciplines will enjoy reading this book—as I did!'

—*Thomas Steger, Professor, University of Regensburg, Germany*

'The past decades since the late 1970s have shown a dramatic shift from the industrial, production-driven economy towards the service-driven economy. And in the years to come, this shift will accelerate even more through ongoing digitalization. Given that, the area of managing a service provider is so far not reflected with corresponding strength in scientific and study literature. Mario Glowik's new book helps to fill that gap and provides a comprehensive work on the strategic dimensions of leading a service company. It successfully applies strategic concepts specifically to the needs and particularities of that kind of industry. And, even more importantly, it has high practical relevance through its many case studies that bring "life" to theoretic concepts and make them very comprehensible. I therefore highly recommend Mario's book to both students and practitioners.'

—*Frank Oerthel, Professor, University of Applied Sciences, Kempten, Germany*

Global Strategy in the Service Industries

Dynamics, Analysis, Growth

Mario Glowik

Routledge
Taylor & Francis Group
LONDON AND NEW YORK

First published 2017
by Routledge
2 Park Square, Milton Park, Abingdon, Oxon OX14 4RN

and by Routledge
711 Third Avenue, New York, NY 10017

Routledge is an imprint of the Taylor & Francis Group, an informa business

British Library Cataloguing-in-Publication Data
A catalogue record for this book is available from the British Library.

Library of Congress Cataloging-in-Publication Data
A catalog record for this book has been requested

ISBN: 978-1-138-92792-6 (hbk)
ISBN: 978-1-138-92793-3 (pbk)
ISBN: 978-1-315-68216-7 (ebk)

Typeset in Bembo
by codeMantra

Contents

Figures

Tables

Preface

Modern service industries indicate promising growth potentials. Electronic commerce, information technology, lifestyle and healthcare firms take advantages in light of digitalized trade pattern as well as emerging countries in the Far East, on the one hand, and an aging population worldwide, on the other hand. At the same time, advanced information and data storage technologies provide optimal prerequisites for individual customer treatments, which raise the issue on how ethical and social responsible companies and data and information accumulating firms behave in reality. This textbook combines classic management contents with realistic and updated business cases with a particular focus on global strategies in modern service industries. Theoretical management concepts are combined with firm case studies to enhance the understanding of modern service businesses dynamics in a globalized world.

This textbook is divided into four main chapters. The *first part*, following this preface, serves as an introductory to global business dynamics. Macro-economic data concerning global trade developments, national debts, and currency reserves are discussed. Particular attention is paid to electronic (e-) commerce and ongoing digitalization, which, for sure, is entirely changing not only global business but also the societal life of people. The reader is invited to review opportunities and threats in terms of digitalization for the future based on the information provided in chapter one.

The *second part* introduces the strategy finding process and describes elements of the firm's environmental analysis on macro-, industry, and micro level including relevant scanning and analysis methods. The *third part* deals with the integrated strategy building on corporate, competitive, and functional firm levels. In light of globalized business dynamics, international and intercultural management topics are discussed. Part three presents an introduction to organization's structures, strategy implementation, and control concepts.

The *fourth part* is devoted to case studies that allow the reader to apply in practice and thus exercise what was discussed in theory in chapters one to three of this textbook. Adhering to the objectives of this book, the case studies focus on modern service industries, such as e-commerce, data and information technology business, lifestyle and healthcare, which make this publication unique and novel compared to other textbooks currently available in the markets. Relevant, important, and updated topics, such as corporate social responsibility, are not only introduced '*as it should be*' but also reviewed against relevant case studies, for example, of *Alibaba (China)* and *Facebook (USA)*. The case studies are developed to provide insights aimed to allow the reader to create his/her own opinion about corporate social responsibility in theory against business practice. The author believes that in times of increasing medial, financial, and lobbying power of large multinational enterprises through their access to a broad range of information and data sources, critical thinking becomes more important than ever.

Additional case studies, such as the economic analysis of *Russia in light of economic sanctions*, repeat environmental analysis methods introduced in part two against constraining but relevant global dynamics. The case study named *healthcare business in Japan* applies international macro and industry analysis techniques in terms of modern service industries. Japan belongs to the group of countries leading in the healthcare industries, and therefore, serves as an interesting benchmark that will be discussed in this textbook.

The case study of *Alphabet (USA)* illustrates how the firm, rather not through developing internal resources but through gaining valuable (external) knowledge resources by various acquisitions, strategic alliances, and joint ventures has made the firm what it is today. Alphabet's management instinct for promising future businesses indicates an industry benchmark related to 'big data.'

The topic of diversification strategies, as discussed in part three, is applied using the *case study of Philips (The Netherlands)*. The Dutch multinational firm was known in the past for its consumer electronics, electric household devices, and audio products. In recent years, Philips has considerably changed its business focus towards healthcare business. The case study does not indicate Philips's diversification strategy away from the consumer electronics industry. However, it does show how Philips gained access to the healthcare industry by competently acquiring specialized firms.

The *case study of Starbucks (USA)* illustrates the global market entry strategy concepts of the global lifestyle coffee house. Exploring the case content, answers to the questions are found regarding why, as commonly expected, Starbucks does not favor franchising but favors other strategies as their preferred global market entry mode. Additionally, the case study provides room for strategic reasoning as to why Starbucks is very successful in the US but tends to perform below expectations in some markets such as Germany.

The *case study of Fresenius (Germany)* illustrates the application of business practice in terms of concentration strategies in service industries. The healthcare firm owns and controls significantly important value added activities ranging from dialysis-focused research and development, to medical devices and dialysis treatments, up to the company's owned hospitals. The vertical integration of Fresenius serves as an industry benchmark and, therefore, is developed and selected for this textbook as a case study.

Pharmaceuticals are known as an industry where research and development knowledge properties are crucial for long-term business success. Leaving the mainstream, the German pharmaceutical firm Boehringer Ingelheim frequently applies market entry through license contracts followed by cooperative agreements, such as strategic alliances and joint ventures. The *case study of Boehringer Ingelheim (Germany)*, as discussed at the end of this book, illustrates opportunities and risks related to the pharmaceutical firm's global strategic concepts.

I would like to thank Yael Kishon (Facebook case study), Corinna Hlozek (macro environmental analysis in Russia), Constantin Wendlandt (healthcare industry in Japan), Snezhana Savova and Irina Fensky for their tremendous support and contributions to the content of this book. I thank Dr. Arndt Schmitz for his outstanding expertise, valuable comments, and pharmaceutical industry insight. I thank the anonymous reviewers who helped, through their valuable comments and proposals, to improve the textbook manuscript. For their professional expertise and ongoing support in realizing this publication, I thank Terry Clague, Izzy Fitzharris, and Miriam Armstrong from Routledge Taylor and Francis Publishers and Francesca Monaco from CodeMantra.

Global Strategy is developed for international business, international and strategic management, international marketing, and services and business lectures at the Bachelor, Master and MBA levels. I am convinced that this textbook, through its interdisciplinary approach, is suitable for business ethics, communication and intercultural management classes.

Mario Glowik
January 2017

1 Global business dynamics

Mario Glowik

Chapter learning objectives

- To compare current global business frameworks with those of the 1950s and 1960s;
- To explain the meanings and variances of tariff and non-tariff barriers in global business;
- To assess why non-tariff barriers became more important and learn what the challenges are of providing evidence in the case of non-tariff barriers;
- To consider how digitalization will change global business in the future and which industries will win and which conventional industries may disappear in the future; and
- To describe from the reader's perspective the major characteristics of successful firms doing international business in light of service-driven, digital, and liberalized global trade patterns.

Global trade pattern: history and today

The international trade of commodity products as well as the corresponding exchange of gold and silver over larger distances looks back on a long history. Merchants have walked, rode, and sailed on international trade routes for thousands of years. The most famous international trade path is probably the Silk Road, dating back to the first century *Before Christ*, stretching over 4,000 miles and connecting China to the Middle East, North Africa, and the Mediterranean. Because overland travel was slow and risky, mainly products with high value-to-bulk ratio yielding significant returns, such as luxury and spices, e.g. silk, satin, amber, porcelain, pepper, myrrh, and others, were traded. The Silk Road lasted for hundreds of years until the 15th century when maritime trade by the Spanish, Portuguese, Dutch, and British significantly increased its importance (McKenzie, 2013).

So, what are the main differences between today's global business and international trade and trade conducted in the past? The answer to this question considers the following major aspects, which will be discussed in the subsequent sub-chapters:

- Liberalized global trade pattern;
- Industry digitalization and electronic (e-) commerce;
- Globally spread value added activities and operations;
- Importance of corporate social responsibility; and
- Increasing economic power of the Asian continent.

One of the reasons for the Great Depression at the end of the 1920s was the sharp increase of import customs, such as for steel, cotton, watches, and other products, because of protectionist government policies on both sides of the Atlantic, namely, in the US and Europe. Consequently, worldwide trade dropped tremendously and accelerated the global economic downturns. Worsening economic conditions contributed to emerging nationalistic parties in Europe at the beginning of the 1930s. Learning from history that worldwide trade has a tremendous impact on the national economies, the General Agreement on Tariffs and Trade (GATT), signed on October 30, 1947, provided the basis for tariff reductions through a series of multilateral negotiations also named 'GATT rounds' (Holtfrerich, 1991; World Trade Organization, 2010b). Today's *liberalized global trade pattern* is a result of reduced *tariff barriers* (e.g. import duties and customs) in the last decades.

However, at the same time, so-called *non-tariff barriers* increasingly became an issue in global business. These non-tariff barriers contain, among other things,

- subsidies or tax benefits when provided for local firms only;
- escalating bureaucracy in terms of documentation when difficult to manage by foreign firms, such as approval procedure for product safety, hygiene certificates;
- accusation of dumping; or
- so-called *buy national campaigns* aimed at favoring local firms relative to products or services by foreign companies.

Compared to tariffs, the variations of non-tariff barriers are wide and more difficult to prove as 'unfair' by the foreign party. Additionally, the protection of intellectual property rights, which are of particular importance in services industries, had not been covered appropriately by GATT. Consequently, against the background intensified and more multifaceted global business concepts, such as in various service industries, the eighth GATT round, named the Uruguay Round of 1986–94, finalized the substitution of GATT by the World Trade Organization (WTO), which launched on January 1, 1995 (WTO, 2010a). Whereas GATT had mainly dealt with tariff barriers of manufactured commodity products, the WTO focuses on non-tariff barriers and the protection of intellectual property rights that are of particular importance in services industries. Furthermore, a dispute settlement system was established by the WTO. The main purpose behind the dispute settlement process in the WTO agreement and valid for all member nations is to settle conflicting interests through a neutral procedure before unilateral national legal actions are launched (World Trade Organization, 2010b).

The most recent negotiations of WTO were launched in Doha (Qatar) in November 2001. The agenda of the Doha Round is broader than past GATT agreements and is specifically targeted at addressing the needs of developing countries. The focus of negotiations has been to reform the agricultural subsidies of WTO member countries. In addition, the Doha Round addresses the improving access to global markets for firms originated in emerging countries and aims to ensure that new liberalization in the global economy respects the need for sustainable economic growth in developing countries. At the Bali Ministerial Conference in December 2013, ministers made several decisions, which addressed aspects of the Doha Round. Among others, it was decided that member countries need to provide transparent and non-discriminatory information on import and export procedures in their country, as well as ensure the establishment of risk management systems for customs control, and enhance transparency with regard to export competition. Furthermore, in dedication to supporting the development of least-developed countries, guidelines are established to allow members to support less developed countries through preferential treatment of their goods and services if this will be economically beneficial for the developing countries. As of January 2014, however, there are no further developments related to the Doha Round (World Trade Organization, 2015a).

Global trade flows

Over the years, except for more liberalized trade pattern, international trade has been influenced by various factors, including advances in information technology, financial crises, growing membership in the WTO, natural disasters, and geo-political tensions. These factors have led to volatility in commodity prices, changes in the leading traders and their trading partners, and the growing importance of services trade. According to the statistics, global trade experienced strong growth from 1995 to 2001, followed by a boom from 2002 to 2004 accompanied by rising commodity prices. The 2008 financial crisis, triggered by the subprime lending crisis in the United States, led to a global recession. As a result of the financial crisis, trade decreased dramatically in 2009 before rebounding strongly in 2010 and 2011. The volume of world exports plunged 12 percent in 2009 while world gross domestic product (GDP) dropped 2 percent. From 2011 to the present, trade growth has been stagnating (World Trade Organization, 2015b) (Figure 1.1).

China's accession to the WTO in December 2001 paved the way for its economic rise and contributed significantly to increasing world trade from 2002 to 2008. Another noteworthy event in the early 2000s was the introduction of euro coins and notes in 2002. Strong Chinese demand for natural resources contributed to increasing prices for crude oil and other primary commodities between 2002 and 2008 (World Trade Organization, 2015b). Already in 2009, China took over the position of a world export champion, which it successfully holds thus far, followed by the United States, Germany, and Japan. Figure 1.2 illustrates the ten leading merchandise export countries as of 2014.

Considering the fact that China and the United States are among the world leading trade nations, it is interesting to compare the trade flows between those two countries. China is among the largest US trading partners (Morrison, 2015). Indeed, statistics show that the imports from China account for a substantial amount of all its imports from Asia-Pacific regions (Figures 1.3 and 1.4). Exports from China to the United States show a steady increase between 2010 and 2014 (United States International Trade Commission, 2015).

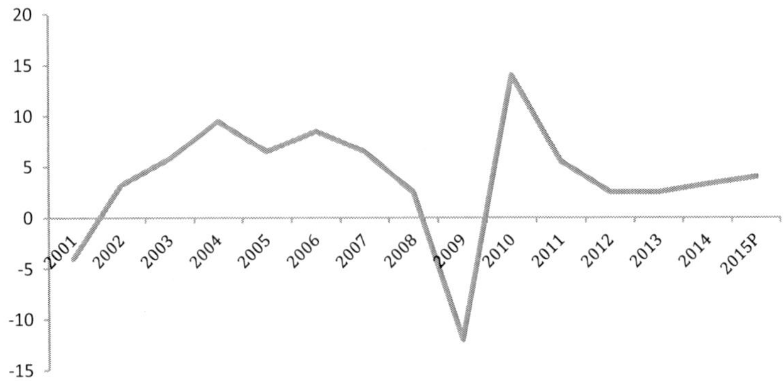

Figure 1.1 World trade development for the period 2001–2015 (annual change in percentage) (2015P = estimated).

Source: International Trade Statistics (World Trade Organization, 2010a, 2014, 2015c).

Note: 2015P–Estimates for 2015.

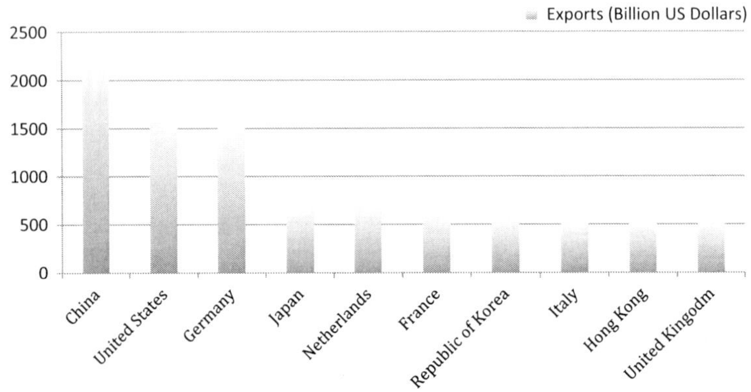

Figure 1.2 Leading exporters in world merchandise trade (Status 2014).

Source: International Trade Statistics 2015 (World Trade Organization, 2015b).

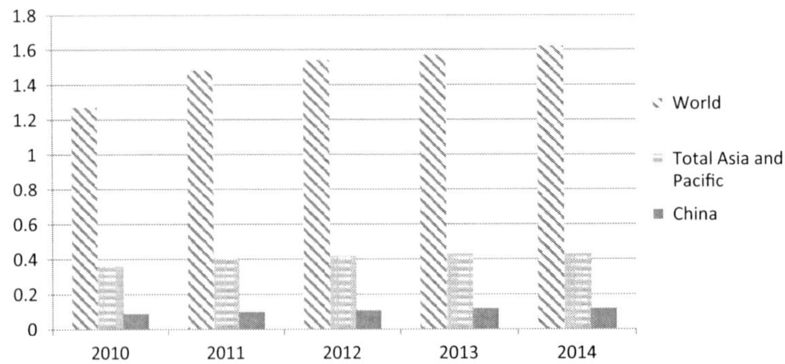

Figure 1.3 Annual US merchandise exports (in billion US dollars).

Source: United States International Trade Commission (2015).

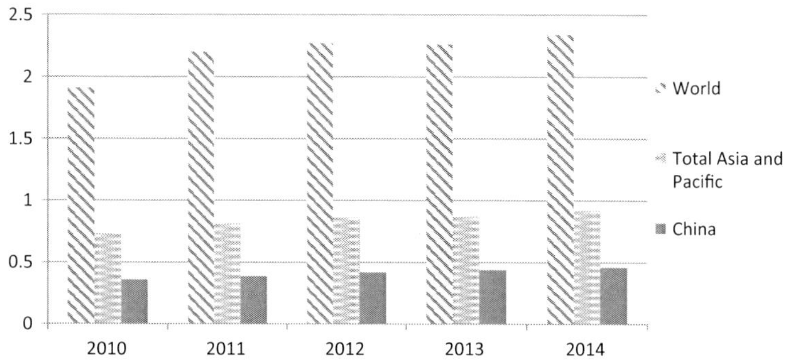

Figure 1.4 Annual US merchandise imports (in billion US dollars).
Source: United States International Trade Commission (2015).

Statistics deliver empirical evidence that the European Union (EU) and China also maintain intense trade relations. Except for the drop recorded in 2009 following the financial crisis, the value of European Union imports of goods from China has increased significantly in the last decade, from Euro 129.2 billion in 2004 to a peak of Euro 302.5 billion in 2014. EU exports to China, which did not decline during the financial crisis, have more than tripled from 2004 to 2014 up to Euro 164.7 billion last year (Figure 1.5). The EU trade deficit with China, which continued during the entire period, decreased between 2010 and 2013 before growing again in 2014, reaching an amount of minus Euro 137.7 billion. China became the second most important EU trading partner behind the United States, accounting for 14 percent of total EU trade in goods in 2014 (compared with 9 percent in 2004). In this 10-year time period, the share of Chinese imports increased from 12.6 percent in 2004 to 18.0 percent in 2014, and its share in exports nearly doubled (5.1 percent in 2004 versus 9.7 percent in 2014) (EU China Summit, 2015).

EU trade in goods with China is clearly dominated by manufactured goods, which accounted in 2014 for 97 percent of total EU imports from China and 86 percent of

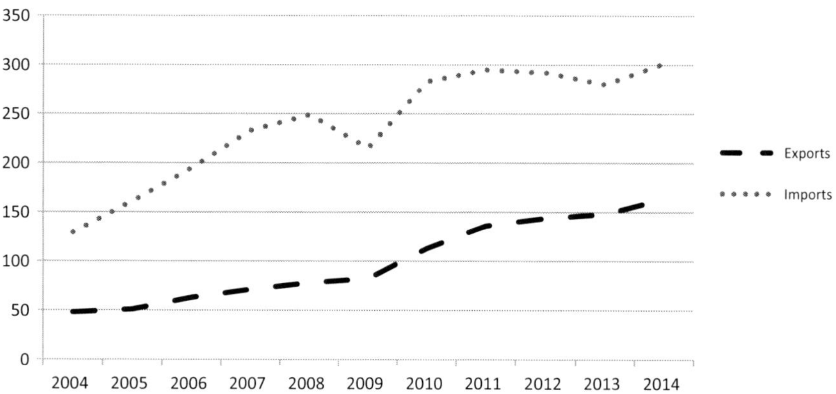

Figure 1.5 EU imports and exports with China during the period 2004–2014 (in billion Euro).
Source: EU-China Summit (2015).

EU exports to China. Among the EU Member States, Germany (Euro 75.0 billion or 46 percent of EU exports of goods to China) was by far the largest exporter to China in 2014, followed at a distance by the United Kingdom (Euro 19.6 billion or 12 percent), France (Euro 16.2 billion or 10 percent), and Italy (Euro 10.5 billion or 6 percent). Germany (Euro 60.9 billion or 20 percent of EU imports of goods from China) was also the largest importer from China in 2014, ahead of The Netherlands (Euro 57.3 billion or 19 percent), the United Kingdom percent (Euro 45.8 billion or 15 percent), France (Euro 25.4 billion or 8 percent), and Italy (Euro 25.1 billon or 8 percent). Every EU Member State recorded a deficit in trade in goods with China in 2014, except Germany (surplus Euro 14.1 billion) and Finland (surplus Euro 0.7 billion) (EU China Summit, 2015).

Electronic (e-) commerce, services industries, and digitalization

Commerce is the fundamental mechanism supporting economic activity of each village, city, region, and finally, the entire national economy. Technological improvements that facilitate commerce reduce transaction costs, or provide more information to participants lead to efficiency gains for the entire economy. Significant advances in commerce throughout time have led to large efficiency improvements for societies. The most significant is arguably the introduction of money thousands of years ago to replace a trade and barter system that required significant resources just to match the participants on both sides of a potential trade. More recently, the introduction of e-commerce and corresponding payment and credit systems contributed to intensified commercial relationships worldwide (OECD, 2013).

In general, e-commerce describes the sale or purchase of goods or services conducted over the Internet or other computer networks. An e-commerce transaction can be between enterprises, households, individuals, governments, and other public or private organizations. E-commerce involves goods and services crossing borders electronically (World Trade Organization, 2013).

The 2009 OECD definition of e-commerce further specifies that such transactions need to be conducted over computer networks by methods specifically designed for the purpose of receiving or placing of orders (OECD, 2013; World Trade Organization, 2013). E-commerce belongs to the tertiary sector of a national economy named services, which include segments such as trading, logistics, healthcare, tourisms, education, hotel, restaurants, financial and other businesses (e.g. insurance) (Hoffman et al., 2009). The main differences between conventional tangible goods and services lie in the fact that services are intangible or immaterial and that they cannot be stored. Service outputs are inseparable from their provider (Vaštiková, 2012). Services industries compared to agriculture (primary sector of an economy) and manufacturing industries (secondary sector of an economy), contribute the highest portion to the gross domestic products (GDPs) in modern national economies (Figure 1.6).

Considering the time from the 1950s until today, the United States are among the countries that have experienced the highest growth in services, mainly due to the utilization of information and digital data storage technologies (Eichengreen and Gupta, 2009: 13). Google and Facebook, introduced in case studies in this book, serve as representative firms, originated in the US, which are global leaders in 'big data' business. Japan and Germany, known for their conventionally manufacturing industries'

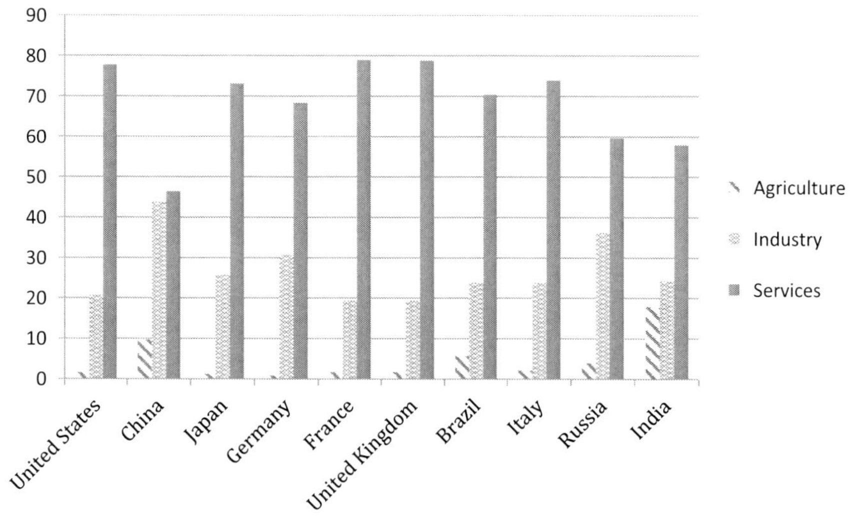

Figure 1.6 GDP by sector and country (status 2014 in percent).
Source: The World Factbook (2014).

strengths, increased the importance of its service sectors within their national economies in recent years. In both countries, the service sector expanded mainly due to its healthcare and medical expertise (Eichengreen and Gupta, 2009). The case studies of the German healthcare firms, namely Fresenius and Boehringer Ingelheim, as well as the case study chapter devoted to the development of the Asian medical device market published in this book, provide valuable insight to emerging service industry dynamics.

E-business is multifaceted and occurs between actors involved in business to business (B2B), business to private costumers (B2C), or between business to government transactions (B2G). E-commerce has increased rapidly over the last two decades for both professional business representatives and private households that are looking to realize timely and affordable transactions over the Internet. Customers benefit from an extraordinary large product portfolio and the convenience of purchasing goods and services from wherever they want and whenever they wish to do so. Not only large multinationals but also resource-limited smaller and medium-sized firms are able to realize higher sales volumes, and thus, economies of scale effects, without being physically present in the foreign markets (Maamar, 2003).

According to the Digital-Social-Local-Mobile (DiSoLoMo) trend, we witness that firms that ignore emerging web-based product and service developments face the risk of being logged out from its future markets (Kreutzer, 2014). An increasing number of 'physical' products becomes digitalized (e.g. music and video streaming). 'Social' addresses communication and relationship networks and corresponding social media platforms. 'Local' as in localization of business allows smaller-sized firms, for example, niche suppliers, to make use of e-business platforms, and thus become better able to raise international attention than in the past. 'Mobile' addresses the phenomenon that the exchange of information as well as purchase decisions are increasingly performed from mobile devices rather than conventional computers. In other words, every business which can be digitally commercialized will be digitally commercialized (Kreutzer, 2014). We witness an increasing complexity of horizontally, vertically, and conglomerate industry network relationships of the focal firm and its suppliers, service provider, customers, etc. (Kreutzer and Land, 2016). Modern e-commerce business environments require multifaceted and lifelong qualification and training of the firm's employees. The firm's international, digital, and service-driven company culture necessarily requires the following important aspects:

- multilevel expertise and cross-functional way of thinking of firm employees to better meet the increasing complexity of products (e.g. autonomous car driving) and corresponding production processes against the background of worldwide value added activities;
- international openness due to the firm's worldwide value added activities;
- 'on-demand' relationships between the firm and its customers to promptly meet the clients' incoming orders in terms of product and service delivery timing;
- intensified ties of the firm and its relevant stakeholders, such as logistics companies, hardware and software providers, (adventure) capital investors, universities, are of vital importance to better manage shortened product and technology life cycles; and increasing involvement of robotics not only in manufacturing but also in customer service.

Initially, e-commerce solutions were limited to communications between larger firms or multinational enterprises. It has only been about two decades since the benefits of e-commerce were extended to smaller or medium-sized firms with a World Wide Web presence, allowing them to complete transactions with end customers located anywhere in the world. A new wave of e-commerce growth is underway, supported by the rapid increase in mobile phones and portable devices, and has substantially contributed to new economic potential (OECD, 2013). The increased use of e-commerce by consumers leads to structural changes in commerce and industries, where a number of traditional intermediaries have found themselves bypassed or at least in need of adaptation, across retail sectors, from clothing to creative content. Today, mobile phone users can conduct global searches for information on products, compare prices internationally, and complete an order from any location and at any time. The full ramifications of this wave of mobile commerce are just starting to be understood (OECD, 2013).

Nevertheless, there is still room for improvements. In a survey by the Swedish National Board of Trade, enterprises engaged in cross-border e-commerce still face several barriers to e-commerce transactions. Some of them have their origin in national regulations, while others are of a technical or logistical nature. The most commonly cited barriers were lack of information on laws and regulations, differences in consumer laws, specific requirements on website content and customs-related matters. Currently, major e-commerce barriers identified were grouped into the following eight categories (OECD, 2015):

- lack of information about relevant laws, regulations, and common methods;
- burdensome customs procedures, high customs duties on returns, and corruption at the border;
- differences in national consumer and sales laws;
- requirements for specific payments solutions and differences in tax regulations;
- weak protection of intellectual property rights;
- limitations in the right to store and transfer information and data;
- requirements to have a local presence to register top-level domains, Internet censorship, and the need to use specific encryption technologies; and
- other barriers, including high roaming charges, problems in obtaining insurance, and slate subsidies (OECD, 2015).

Despite these challenges, the growth of e-business markets continues and allows companies, which established e-commerce channels, to benefit from an increasing international customer base. For example, in 2015, 674 million Chinese people used the World Wide Web, followed by 402 million users in Europe and 300 million users in the United States (Statista, 2015). Among the EU countries, the United Kingdom, Germany, and France together account for 60 percent of the European B2C e-commerce market volume. The USA, China, and the United Kingdom account for more than 50 percent of the total e-commerce market volume worldwide (Ecommerce Foundation, 2015). As of June 2015, there are approximately 3.2 billion WWW users registered, and there is no end in sight (Internet World Stats, 2015).

In 2014, 15 percent of all individuals in the EU-28-member countries purchased goods and services through the World Wide Web from sellers outside their country of residence, but within the EU-28. This is an increase of 25 percent compared to 2013. Major reasons for shopping abroad included competitive prices or a wider availability of goods and services.

Cross-border EU purchases by individuals were highest in either smaller member states with a limited availability of domestic online offers, such as Luxembourg (65 percent) and Malta (39 percent), or in EU member states with strong regional or linguistic ties to neighboring countries, such as Austria (40 percent), Finland (36 percent), Denmark (36 percent), and Belgium (34 percent). Given the fact that in nearly all countries cross-border e-commerce grew significantly last year, one can safely conclude that cross-border will be one of the major drivers of e-commerce in Europe and around the world (Ecommerce Foundation, 2015).

Country debts and international assets reserves

General government debt-to-GDP ratio, which is the amount of a country's total gross government debt as a percentage of its GDP, is an indicator of an economy's health and a key factor for the sustainability of government finance. 'Debt' is commonly defined as a specific subset of liabilities identified according to the types of financial instruments included or excluded. Debt is thus obtained as the sum of the following liability categories: currency and deposits; securities other than shares, except financial derivatives; loans; insurance technical reserves; and other accounts payable. Changes in government debt over time reflect the impact of government deficits (OECD, 2016). In general, we can witness that countries located in the Western hemisphere and Japan have tremendously increased its general government debt-to-GDP ratio since 2010 (Figure 1.7). Interpreting the figures and taking the case of Japan as an example, we note that the debt of Japan is approximately two and a half times higher than the country's yearly economic power expressed as its GDP. Among the 'top leading global debtors,' related to their national GDPs, there are seven countries located in Europe. According to the OECD definition, the economic health of various European countries has worsened in recent years.

In terms of accumulated current accounts, the United States, with far distance holds the leading positioning worldwide, followed by the United Kingdom, Brazil, Canada, Turkey, India, France, and Mexico (Figure 1.8). The current account can be expressed as the difference between the value of exports of goods and services and the value of imports of goods and services. A deficit then means that the country is importing more goods and services than it is exporting. The current account also includes net income (such as interest and dividends) and transfers from abroad (such as foreign aid), which are usually a small fraction of the total. The current account can also be expressed as the difference between national (both public and private) savings and investment. A current account deficit may, therefore, reflect a low level of national savings relative to investment or a high rate of investment or both. The United States runs a persistent balance of current account deficits and use foreign capital to finance the difference between domestic investment and domestic savings (Gosh and Ramakrishnan, 2016).

On the one hand, the largest accumulated country debts are found in Western countries (Figure 1.9). On the other hand, it is worthwhile to note which countries hold the largest international assets reserves as an indicator for their financial strength. A country's international reserves refer to those external assets that are readily available to and controlled by the country's monetary authorities for meeting the balance of payments financing needs, for intervention in exchange markets to affect the currency exchange

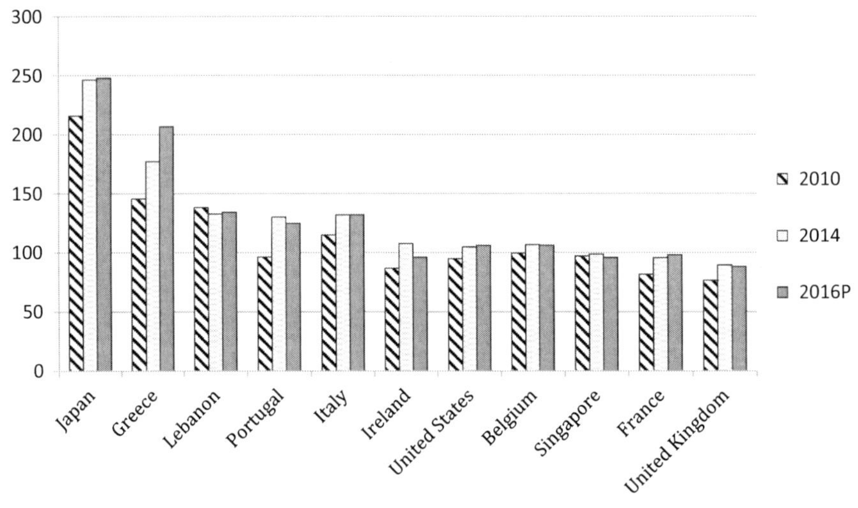

Figure 1.7 General government gross debt by country (in percentage of GDP). Comparison of the 'debt leading countries' for the years 2010, 2014, and 2016.

Source: International Monetary Fund. World Economic Outlook Database (2015).

Note: 2016P–IMF estimates for 2016.

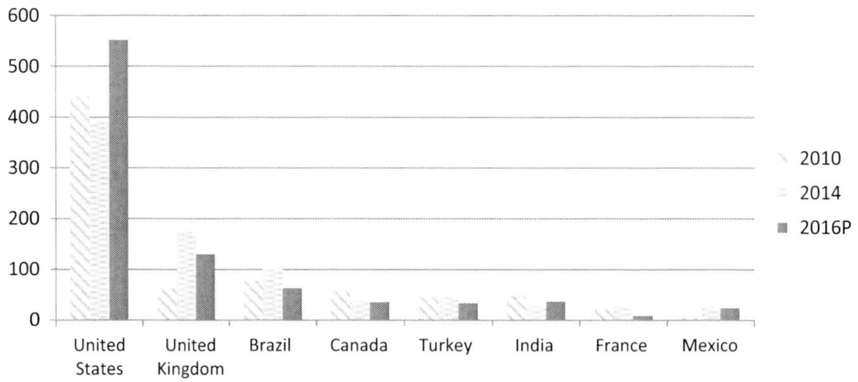

Figure 1.8 Country account deficit development 2010–2016P (in billion US dollars).
Source: International Monetary Fund. World Economic Outlook Database (2015).
Note: 2016P–IMF estimates for 2016.

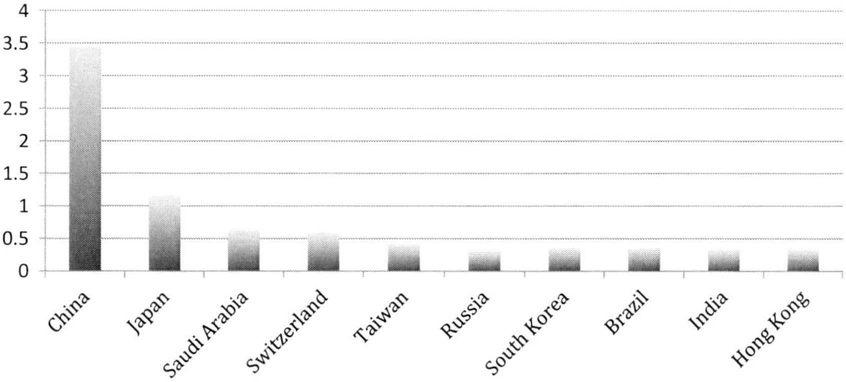

Figure 1.9 International assets reserves by country (status 2015) (in trillion US dollars).
Source: International Monetary Fund (2016a).

rate, and for other related purposes, such as maintaining confidence in the currency and the economy, and serving as a basis for foreign borrowing. The international assets reserves include monetary, gold, special drawing rights (SDRs), reserve position in the International Monetary Fund (IMF), and other reserve assets (International Monetary Fund, 2016a).

As shown in Figure 1.9 in 2015, China demonstrates the highest amount of around 3.2 trillion US dollars followed by a long distance by Japan (1.1 trillion US dollars), and Saudi Arabia (0.6 trillion US dollars). Among the ten global leading countries in terms of international assets reserves, half of them—namely, China, Hong Kong, Japan, Taiwan, and South Korea—are located in the Far East. Considering the countries' debts, at one side, and the financial reserves, on the other side, evidence indicates that the economic power has shifted in recent decades from the Western hemisphere towards Asia.

In contrast, in the Western countries, the national deficits are relatively high (Figure 1.8); however, the international assets reserves are comparatively nonexistent, except for Switzerland, (Figure 1.9). The financial crisis impacted the Western hemisphere more severely than Asia, and still Europe as a whole has not recovered although several years have passed since its outbreak in September 2008.

In September 2008, the US-originated Lehman Brothers posted a USD 3.93 billion third-quarter loss after USD 5.6 billion of write downs on so-called toxic mortgages. Facing a first but extremely severe loss for the first time since 14 years, Lehman Brothers heavily spread sale signs with plans to sell off assets to overcome the firm's crisis. As a result, private and institutional investors including governments (e.g. Island) witnessed rising home loan defaults. The US government took control of major lenders named Fannie Mae and Freddie Mac. Finally, Lehman Brothers went bankrupt and various investors primarily from Western countries lost their money (The Telegraph, 2008). Large banks, such as the German-based Commerzbank, could only survive through massive support by the German tax payers. The German government took control of the Commerzbank; in other words, speculative, private investments became 'collectively socialized.' The magnitude of the crisis, its extent, and negative domino effects to other industries (e.g. the US government was forced to temporarily take over General Motors) resemble the Great Depression of 1929. To overcome the negative effects of the 2008 crisis, in addition to governmental fiscal policy activities, various central banks, such as the US Federal Reserve Bank, the Bank of England, the Bank of Japan, and the European Central Bank, initiated 'quantitative easing' programs, which include extraordinary low interest rates as well as 'money flooding' initiatives of their national markets. The degree and the duration of extraordinary low interest periods and the number of internationally participating countries are unique in history. Therefore, experiences are rare and the long-term outcomes (e.g. risk of sharply increasing prices as already witnessed for the real estate market in Germany since 2015) of 'quantitative easing' programs are questionable.

Seller's Paradise: Companies Build Bonds for European Central Bank to Buy

The European Central Bank (ECB) had bought more than Euro 16 billion of corporate bonds as of 2016, August 12th according to the latest available data from the central bank. The lion's share has been already-issued bonds trading in secondary markets, but some has come in new debt sales, according to the ECB. Morgan Stanley has arranged for two private placements that have been bought by the ECB.

Private placements are private debt sales not open to the broader market, typically relying on a handful of investors that want to buy a company's bonds. Typically, there would not be a prospectus, there would not be any transparency; there would not be a press release. It is all done discreetly, said Apostolos Gkoutzinis, head of European capital markets at law firm Shearman & Sterling LLP.

The ECB executes bond purchases through the Eurozone's national central banks, which function like branches. The Bank of Spain holds some of a Euro 500 million private placement issued by Spanish oil company Repsol SA on July 1, and some of a Euro 200 million deal from Spanish power utility Iberdrola SA sold on June 10, two days after the ECB program got under way. Both deals were arranged solely by Morgan Stanley; since the start of the ECB's corporate buying program, they are the only private placements issued and have been bought by national central banks, according to the journal *Analysis*. Morgan Stanley declined to comment.

The ECB's corporate-bond program may well grow further. The bank is widely expected to extend quantitative easing beyond March 2017, at which time it is planned to end. Government bonds are growing increasingly scarce. The ECB can buy only bonds that yield more than its deposit rate, currently minus-0.4 percent. That rules out vast amounts of German government debt, and much else, too. More corporate bonds are one option, and the central bank could buy a greater proportion directly from companies.

Source: Whittall (2016).

On the one hand, due to liberalized trade patterns, advanced logistics and digital technologies, the prerequisites for launching global business activities are vast. On the other hand, there are various challenges for firms to perform international business activities in terms of societal, cultural, economic, and political issues. For example, in its recent April 2016 global financial stability report, The International Monetary Fund summarized its future outlook as follows:

International Monetary Fund: Future Outlook

In advanced economies, the outlook has deteriorated because of heightened uncertainty and setbacks to growth and confidence. Declines in oil and commodity prices have kept risks elevated in emerging market economies, while greater uncertainty about China's growth transition has increased spillovers to global markets. These developments tightened financial conditions, reduced risk appetite, raised credit risks, and stymied balance sheet repair, undermining financial stability.

Despite significant policy efforts to support aggregate demand and strengthen the financial system, the risks from slowing growth, remaining balance sheet vulnerabilities, and tighter and more volatile financial conditions have become more apparent. Increased political uncertainty related to geopolitical conflicts, political discord, terrorism, refugee flows, or global epidemics loom over some countries and regions, and if left unchecked, could have significant spillovers on financial markets (International Monetary Fund, 2016b).

Against the background of increasing global challenges, it is more than ever of vital importance to conduct a structured analysis of the firm's internal resources in light of the firm's external environmental surroundings needs before making any strategy decision. The strategy process should be well structured and should include stages ranging from the formulation of business objectives to environmental analysis to the development of strategy as explained in the following chapters.

Bibliography

Ecommerce Foundation 2015, *European B2C E-commerce report 2015. Facts, figures, infographics and trends of 2014 and the 2015 forecast of the European B2C E-commerce market of goods and services* [Online]. Available from: www.ecommerce-europe.eu/app/uploads/2016/08/european-b2c-3-commerce-report2015-light-20150615.pdf. [December 21, 2016].

Eichengreen, B & Gupta, P 2009, 'The two waves of service sector growth,' *Oxford Economic Papers,* vol. 65, pp. 96–123.

EU-China Summit 2015, *EU trade with China significantly up in 2014 for both goods and services* [Online]. Available from: http://ec.europa.eu/eurostat/documents/2995521/6893875/6-2606 2015-AP-EN.pdf/44d4c87c-98dd-4061-bdf6-b292884a5073. [June 17, 2016].

Gosh, A & Ramakrishnan, U 2016, *International Monetary Fund: current account deficits: is there a problem?* [Online]. Available from: www.imf.org/external/pubs/ft/fandd/basics/current.htm. [July 31, 2016].

Hoffman, KD, Bateson JEG, Wood EH & Kenyon AK 2009. *Services marketing. Concepts, strategies and cases,* South-Western Cengage Learning, London.

Holtfrerich, C-L 1991, *Wirtschaft USA.* Oldenbourg Verlag, München.

International Monetary Fund 2015, *World economic outlook database, October 2015* [Online]. Available from: www.imf.org/external/pubs/ft/weo/2015/02/weodata/index.aspx. [November 14, 2015].

International Monetary Fund 2016a, *International reserves and foreign currency liquidity: guidelines for a data template* [Online]. Available from: www.imf.org/external/np/sta/ir/IRProcessWeb/pdf/guide2013.pdf. [August 2, 2016].

International Monetary Fund 2016b, *Global financial stability report: potent policies for a successful normalization* [Online]. Available from: www.imf.org/external/publications/index.htm. [August 10, 2106].

Internet World Stats 2015, *Internet usage statistics. World internet usage and 2015 population stats* [Online]. Available from: www.internetworldstats.com/stats.htm. [November 15, 2015].

Kreutzer, RT 2014, *Praxisorientiertes online marketing. Konzepte-Instrumente-Checklisten.* Springer-Gabler, Wiesbaden.

Kreutzer, RT & Land, K-H 2016, *Digitaler Darwinismus,* Springer-Gabler, Wiesbaden.

Maamar, Z 2003, Commerce, e-commerce, and m-commerce: what comes next? *Communications of the ACM—mobile computing opportunities and challenges,* vol. 46, pp. 251–257.

McKenzie, F 2013, 'Introduction: the intersection of trade and conflict since 1500,' in *A global history of trade and conflict since 1500,* eds L Coppolaro & F Mckenzie, Palgrave Macmillan, Hampshire and New York.

Morrison, W 2015, *China-U.S. trade issues* [Online]. Congressional Research Service. Available from: www.fas.org/sgp/crs/row/RL33536.pdf. [June 17, 2016].

OECD 2013, *Electronic and mobile commerce* [Online]. Available from: www.oecd.org/officialdocuments/publicdisplaydocumentpdf/?cote=DSTI/ICCP/IE/IIS(2012)1/FINAL&docLanguage=En. [November 2, 2015].

OECD 2015, *Information economy report 2015: unlocking the potential of E-commerce for developing countries. Global and regional trends* [Online]. Available from: www.keepeek.com/Digital-Asset-Management/oecd/economic-and-social-development/information-economy-report-2015_b268ce04-en#.V6sqbvmLRD8#page4. [August 10, 2016].

OECD 2016, *General government debt* [Online]. Available from: https://data.oecd.org/gga/general-government-debt.htm. [August 1, 2016].

Statista 2015, *Number of internet users worldwide from 2005 to 2016* [Online]. Available from: www.statista.com/statistics/273018/number-of-internet-users-worldwide/. [November 15, 2015].

The Telegraph 2008, *The collapse of Lehman Brothers* [Online]. Available from: www.telegraph.co.uk/finance/financialcrisis/6173145/The-collapse-of-Lehman-Brothers.html. [September 10, 2016].

The World Factbook 2014, *GDP—composition by sector of origin* [Online]. Available from: www.cia.gov/library/publications/the-world-factbook/fields/2012.html. [December 16, 2016].

United States International Trade Commission 2015, *U.S. trade by geographic regions* [Online]. Available from: https://dataweb.usitc.gov/scripts/Regions.asp. [November 13, 2015].

Vaštiková, M 2012, Global economic crisis and marketing defence of the tertiary sector, *Acta Academica Karviniensia*, vol. 4, pp. 163–172.

Whittall, C 2016, *Seller's paradise: companies build bonds for European Central Bank to buy* [Online]. Available from: www.wsj.com/articles/sellers-paradise-companies-build-bonds-for-central-bank-to-buy-1471815100. [September 10, 2016].

World Trade Organization 2010a, *International trade statistics 2010* [Online]. Available from: www.wto.org/english/res_e/statis_e/its2010_e/its2010_e.pdf. [February 05, 2016].

World Trade Organization 2010b, *Understanding the WTO: basics: the GATT years from Havana to Marrakesh* [Online]. Available from: www.wto.org/english/thewto_e/whatis_e/tif_e/fact4_e.htm. [October 5, 2010].

World Trade Organization 2013, *Briefing note: electronic commerce* [Online]. Available from: www.wto.org/english/thewto_e/minist_e/mc9_e/brief_ecom_e.htm. [November 15, 2015].

World Trade Organization 2014, *International trade statistics 2014* [Online]. Available from: www.wto.org/english/res_e/statis_e/its2014_e/its2014_e.pdf. [December 21, 2016].

World Trade Organization 2015a, *Bali package and November 2014 decisions* [Online]. Available from: www.wto.org/english/thewto_e/minist_e/mc9_e/balipackage_e.htm#part2. [November 12, 2015].

World Trade Organization 2015b, *International trade statistics 2015* [Online]. Available from: www.wto.org/english/res_e/statis_e/its2015_e/its2015_e.pdf. [June 17, 2016].

World Trade Organization 2015c, *International trade statistics 2015* [Online]. Available from: www.wto.org/english/res_e/statis_e/its2015_e/its15_ e.pdf. [February 6, 2016].

2 Environmental analysis

Mario Glowik

Chapter learning objectives

- To assess why an environmental analysis is important before strategy decision;
- To explain market entry and market exit barriers;
- To describe the elements of macro analysis and their impact on the strategy-finding process;
- To explain the major factors of the firm's industry environment;
- To determine how the micro analysis and SWOT are linked in terms of strategy finding; and
- To describe the necessity of conducting regular updates in terms of the environmental analysis.

The strategy-finding process

First, the management sets the company mission. The corporate purpose or mission of the company usually is built on fundamental reasons that explain the firm's existence. These reasons are usually derived from the company's product and service offerings of which there is a current or potential 'desire' in the markets. Based on the firm's long-term business objectives, the management sets its value proposition to the market and how to build, organize, and sustain a competitive business system (Lasserre, 2012). During the course of setting the main business objectives, such as turnover targets and profit margins, the management determines business objectives, for example, turnover and profits, and addresses corresponding target markets (Figure 2.1).

The term 'strategy' indicates a long-term perspective to realize the business objectives. In light of consistently changing external environment surroundings of the firm, the process from formulating business objectives to strategy decision must be regularly updated. The management periodically needs to question whether there is in fact a strategic fit between the firm's mission and business objectives (e.g. turnover, profits), on the one hand, and the selected strategies, on the other hand. If this question cannot be answered satisfactorily, the management may take corrective measures.

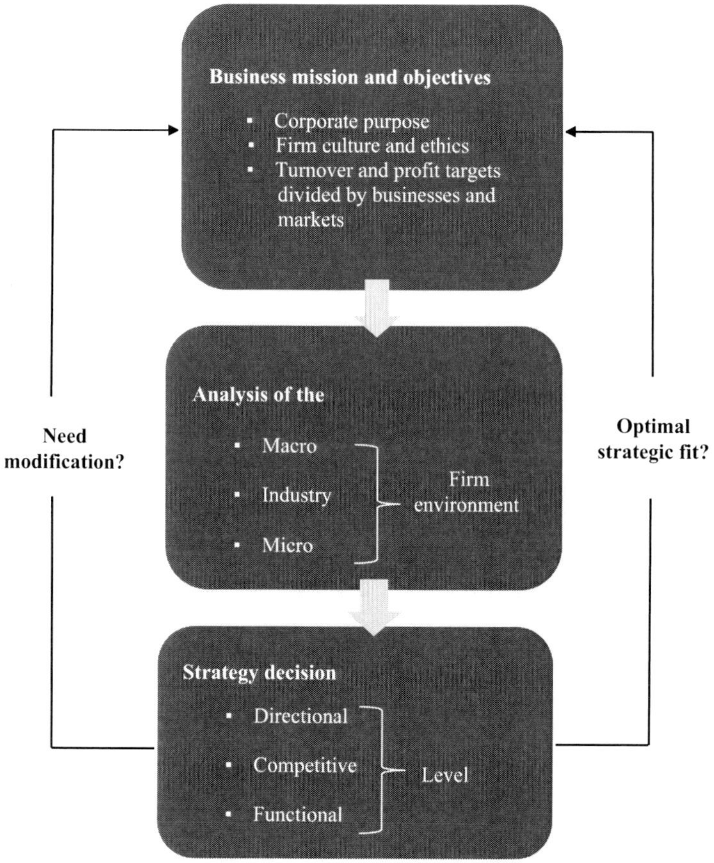

Figure 2.1 The process from the formulation of business objectives to strategy decision.

Who wants to voluntarily admit that the strategy is wrong?

The realization and the acceptance that a strategy decision in the past was wrong and needs to be corrected often is temporarily ignored and is, thus, usually delayed by the management. The time gap indicates one of the most important market exit barriers. The longer the time spent until corrections are launched, the more costly it is for the firm.

A profound and structured market analysis, which includes filtering relevant information from less relevant data, is of vital importance for the firm's strategy decision. The management undertakes the environmental analysis, which is segmented in three levels:

1 macro analysis (e.g. society, ecology, economy, law, and expertise);
2 the firm's industry environment analysis (e.g. technology and product life cycle, suppliers, and customers); and
3 the micro analysis of the firm (e.g. internal resource assets and limitations).

The information selection and evaluation are implemented using a stepwise orderly process from the top level (macro data and industry data) to the bottom level that addresses the firm's resources and indicates the micro level of analysis. In other words, the process of the environmental analysis reassembles a funnel where rather general country market data (e.g. gross domestic product and ecology standards) are studied first (top level of the funnel). Industry information, which are more specific (e.g. number of customers and suppliers) and narrow than country data, are evaluated at the industry level. Finally, there is the micro analysis, where the firm's tangible (e.g. real assets and financials) and intangible resources (e.g. technological or market knowledge) are examined (Figure 2.2).

In the final step, the strategy decision is made by the management based on the results of its environmental analysis. The orderly process in which the environmental analysis is performed first and the strategy decision second is of vital importance. Firms that

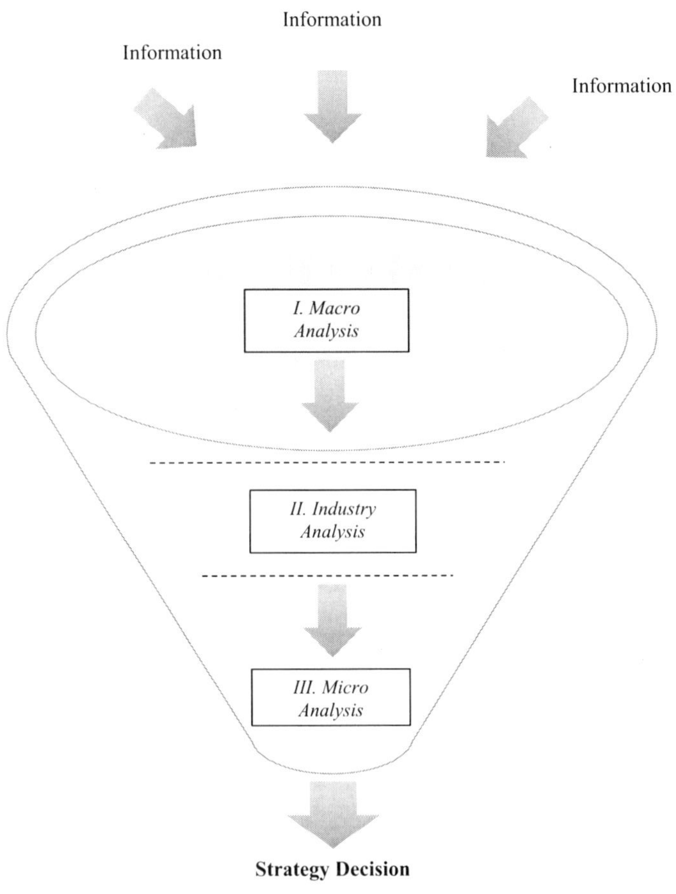

Figure 2.2 The funnel approach: from environmental analysis to strategy decision.

make the strategy decision without analyzing the firm's internal resources against the background of its external environmental factors risk either delivering unsuccessfully the firm's strategy results or appearing to be unrealistic. In the next section, the elements of the macro analysis are explained.

The environmental macro analysis

The environmental analysis provides informational evidence for the management's international target market selection. The discussion about the organization's resources and strategies, and their interface with its market environment is also found in the literature as 'institutional theories of organizations.' The institutional theory serves as a framework for identifying and analyzing the characteristics of organizations. In general, macro-economic factors include societal, economic, ecologic, and legal regulations, as well as an organization's traditional values and structures. With the aim of improving their competitive positioning, firms should adhere to rules such as regulatory structures and practices (Bruton et al., 2010; Glover et al., 2014).

Institutional voids are a result of the external uncertainties embodied in the macro environment of the firm's international target market. In many developing countries, people are living in poverty and, thus, are unable to participate in markets because of institutional voids. Institutional voids are described as situations when institutional arrangements that support markets are absent, weak, or unsuccessful. For example, political-legal uncertainties arise from instability in the political system or from policies of the local government, such as those concerning private ownership (e.g. expropriation and intervention), operational risk (e.g. price control and local content requirements), and transfer risk (currency inconvertibility and remittance). In developed countries, national governments have the authority to fill institutional voids by regulation, laws and governance structures, and other methods of monitoring and control concerning tax payments (Mair and Marti, 2009; Pan and Tse, 2000).

Aspects of the institutional environment have a direct impact on a firm's market entry strategy in a foreign target market. For example, legal restrictions on foreign ownership of domestic enterprises establish definite limits on foreign equity holdings. Country uncertainties regarding the protection of intellectual property rights further contribute to environmental risks and can result in a firm's reduced investment activity (Delios and Beamish, 1999; Sirmon et al., 2007).

One of the most representative and well-known tools for scanning macro-environmental factors of a firm is called PEST (political, economic, social, technology) analysis. In some sources, PEST is supplemented by ecological and legal factors; thus, the acronym becomes PESTEL or PESTLE (Koumparoulis, 2013). One drawback of PEST analysis is that originally less attention was paid to ecological issues. However, ecology has become an increasing challenge related to the global pollution of water and air as well as exploitation of natural resources. Current global business behavior should be viewed in light of, hopefully, an increasing public awareness regarding ecological challenges. Another weakness of PEST comes along with the acronym 'S,' which stands for social. Criticisms arise because 'social' includes insufficiently various factors of the country's 'society,' which is normally complex. In comparison, S.E.E.L.E. (society, ecology, economy, law, expertise) emphasizes societal (not narrowly 'social' according to PEST) and ecological issues and better considers modern service industry-driven societies ('expertise' instead of technology in case of PEST).

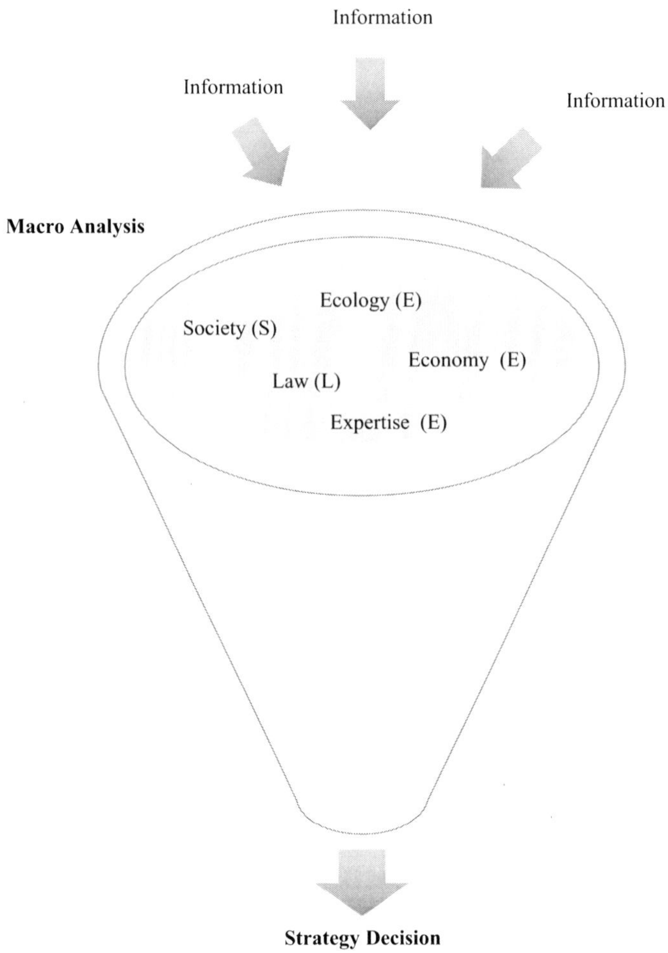

Figure 2.3 Elements of the macro analysis (S.E.E.L.E.).

The firm, for example, while preparing for an international market entry in a foreign target market, considers following elements of the macro-environmental scan when applying S.E.E.L.E. (Figure 2.3).

Society (S)

Within the societal category of the macro analysis, there are elements to be studied like work ethics, average daily and weekly working hours, and national and job-related holidays. For example, in many firms originated in Japan, Taiwan, or South Korea, managers commonly have less than one working week holiday per year. Additional issues related to the societal analysis are attitudes towards handicapped people, the diversity of religions and their impact on daily life, overall acceptance of equal human rights and gender rights, the acceptance and integration of immigrants, average household sizes, family life preferences, preferred activities during leisure times, and materialistic (e.g. symbols like a prestigious car brand) versus non-materialistic (e.g. living in a safe and healthy environment) priorities in life. Scandinavian countries, e.g. Sweden, emphasize non-materialistic values like family-friendly working environments flanked by gender equality and an equal opportunity educational system. Additional elements within the societal analysis of the foreign target country are crime rates, social security including healthcare, unemployment and pension systems, the embedding of children and pensioners' care in the society, marriage and divorce rates, birth and deaths rates, age distribution of the society, and others. Demographic changes in the target market do not only result in lower demand for a certain technology but also in modification and adaptation of existing technologies (Davidson and McFetridge, 1985; Moffat and Auer, 2006).

Ecology (E)

Despite prosperity, global business growths come along with drawbacks, such as ongoing pollution of the earth in terms of global water resources, ground conditions, and air that, among others, caused the extinction of animal species. Meanwhile, the decrease of environmental pollution indicates one of the biggest challenges for mankind. As a consequence, ecology aspects become increasingly important and move into the center of the firm's macro-environmental scan. On the one hand, the firm collects information about the ecological characteristics of the foreign target market. On the other hand, based on the information acquired by analyzing the ecology, the management can better position the firm in terms of its corporate social responsibility policy and shared value concepts to better achieve a sustainable business in the foreign target market.

The analysis of the ecology within the macro analysis includes elements such as climate condition; the risk of natural events like thunderstorms, earthquakes, drought periods, rain seasons; the availability of natural resources such as conventional fossils like oil and gas; or alternatives like wind, water, and sun to be applied for regenerative power generation. The ecology analysis also includes attitudes of the population regarding exhausting versus protecting their environment, which results in a differentiating quality of air and water and consequently the people's health and life (expectancy). Furthermore, the ecology analysis includes the evaluation of environmental standards for traffic intensity and traffic flows, industry emission standards, noise disturbance, and recycling procedures. Particularly for firms involved in agriculture and power generation business, the ecology analysis should include attitudes of the people in the target market concerning the acceptance or refusal of chemical material, or genetically manipulated animals and plants attitudes. For example, the majority of European customers tend to reject gen-manipulated plants and animals for food consumption. Additional issues to be considered when performing an ecology analysis are attitudes towards renewable energies and the acceptance or non-acceptance of nuclear power generation (which is, for example, planned to be terminated in Germany and Italy). Denmark, for example, is known for its traditional country preference towards eco-friendly power generation and, over decades, has built up an outstanding wind power generation expertise.

Economy (E)

The economic analysis targets financial indicators of the foreign target market. First, it is important to determine the influence of the government concerning the market (e.g. liberalized market economy such as in the United Kingdom or 'state planned economy' in China). Additional indicators of the economic health of the target country are gross domestic product trends, stability of the banking and finance system, unemployment rates, average wage and salary levels, purchasing power per capita, saving rates from disposable income, average household debts, social security withholdings, country account surplus versus account deficit, national trade balances (export versus imports), inflation versus deflation rates, currency policy and the currency exchange system. In countries that indicate relatively large state deficits and corresponding higher inflation rates, there is a risk that the local currency exchange rate depreciates related to other currencies. Thus, the management should be aware of this situation and should take the necessary precautions to avoid currency exchange losses (e.g. invoicing in rather stable currencies like British Pounds, Swiss Francs, Euro, or US Dollars).

OECD Income Inequality Report: The Gap between Rich and Poor

For much of the 20th century, the gap in incomes between the well-off and less well-off is generally thought to have narrowed in much of the world. In effect, the rich did not get much richer while the poor caught up a bit. According to research based on The World Top Incomes Database, this decline in inequality began in North America and much of Europe in around the 1920 and 1930s and a little later, perhaps the 1950s, in some developing countries. But then, in the 1970s and 1980s, the pattern began to reverse, and inequality began to rise again. This rise in inequality over recent decades is evident in most—but not all—rich economies. It has affected not just economies with a history of relatively high inequality but also countries where traditionally there was less inequality, like Denmark, Germany, and Sweden.

Since the 1980s, income inequality has risen in most OECD countries. The shift was even more pronounced over roughly the same period among the top 1 percent of earners, especially in English-speaking countries. In the United States, for example, the share of pre-tax income going to the richest 1 percent more than doubled, reaching almost 20 percent in 2012. The rise in inequality in many countries since the 1980s (and even earlier) underlines a significant economic trend. In simple terms, the benefits of economic growth have tended increasingly to go to a smaller segment of society. In the United States, for example, between 1975 and 2012 around 47 percent of total growth in pre-tax incomes went to the top 1 percent. The share was also high in several other (mostly) English-speaking countries: 37 percent in Canada and over 20 percent in Australia and the United Kingdom.

What accounts for these variations? Several factors play a role, but two are of importance. The first is the wage gap (or 'wage dispersion')—that is, the gap between the wages of high- and low-income workers. In some countries, this gap is much wider than in others. The second is the role of the state, which takes income in the form of taxes and hands it back in the form of transfers. Taxes and transfers reduce income inequality in all OECD countries but far more in some than in others.

These factors can be seen at work by comparing the inequality record of different countries. At the low end, the Nordic countries (Denmark, Iceland, Norway, and Sweden) and Switzerland all have below-average inequality and below-average poverty. Unemployment is low and the wage range is relatively narrow—very high wages are relatively rare. Most people receive cash transfers from the state, and income taxes are strongly progressive—in other words, higher earners lose a bigger share of their income in tax.

At the other end of the scale are a group of countries such as Chile, Israel, Mexico, Portugal, Turkey and the United States, which have relatively high income inequality. Several factors are at work—the wage range is relatively wide, with some people on very high wages, and the state often provides less in the way of cash transfers.

Since the late 1990s, the engine of the world economy has moved from the traditionally wealthy OECD countries to developing and emerging economies—a phenomenon sometimes called "shifting wealth." China and India are the most famous examples, but they are not alone: In the 1990s, only 12 developing economies saw their GDP per capita grow at more than double the rate of OECD countries; in the 2000s, that number soared to 83. Many developing countries are seeing considerable numbers of people escaping poverty and the emergence of a new middle class. But, many also are seeing widening income inequality, although the factors behind this are not always quite the same as in developed countries. Many factors have contributed to that decline, but the most important is the rise of China—it alone accounted for around half a billion people moving out of extreme poverty.

Source: OECD (2015).

Law (L)

Stable environments in terms of legal and political systems of the target country are of vital importance for sustainable business success in the target market. The protection of intellectual and private property rights is, among others, a crucial point to be studied by the management before entering the market. As a result of the legal analysis, the management is better able to answer the question as to whether the firm's patent holdings or trade mark rights are respected and whether the business concepts are safe or copied. The macro-environmental scans of legal and political surroundings include important elements that secure stable financial and banking systems in the target market. For example, the International Monetary Fund has outlined the following:

Banks in advanced economies face substantial challenges in adapting to the new regulatory and market environment. Regulation has improved capital and liquidity buffers at most banks and instituted better protections for taxpayers in systemic events. However, legacy problems of excess capacity, high levels of nonperforming loans, and poorly adapted business models continue to depress bank profitability, which could erode bank resilience over time. These legacy problems

(Continued)

> became more apparent in late 2015 and early 2016 as sharp downward pressures on bank equity and debt prices drove valuations down to levels that could impair their ability to tap capital markets. Actions taken by the European Central Bank in March 2016 have supported a rebound in valuations. Policymakers are urgently needed to address long-standing structural issues to prevent the return of systemic stress and enhance monetary transmission (International Monetary Fund, 2016).

Additional important factors of the law-related analysis are the corruption, the overall protection of human rights, free democratic voting and election systems, single or multi-political party systems, freedom of individual opinion and corresponding demonstration rights, free or censored mass media, and legally protected freedom for authors, writers, and correspondents.

Expertise (E)

Within the last category of the S.E.E.L.E. analysis, Expertise (E), the management scans the quality of the education system (e.g. literacy level, graduates from vocational schools, and university graduates) in the target country. The expertise part of the macro analysis questions whether specific knowledge is utilized in particular industries in the target market (e.g. Japan is known for its earthquake-proof construction method expertise). Furthermore, expertise analysis considers the populations' willingness to utilize new and complex technologies, methods, and techniques. For example, China is known as a country where the people favor electronic payments via smartphone instead of cash. In comparison, in Germany, people tend to hesitate using electronic payment systems due to security reasons, which are perceived as less developed than in the case of conventional bank transactions, cash, or credit card payments. Additionally, the expertise analysis should include research on the infrastructure such as density and quality of road and railway networks, airports, water routes, the regional connectivity to the World Wide Web, and corresponding data speed. Another interesting factor to be scanned is the average plant utilization and industry efficiency as well as the quality consciousness of the population in the target market.

As a result of the firm's research activities, data from the S.E.E.L.E. analysis are collected, analyzed, and summarized for the management. Through the application of S.E.E.L.E, opportunities and risks of different regional foreign target markets are comparable. The results serving as the decisional basis for the management can be illustrated in a country risk analysis as a simplified example (Figure 2.4). In this example, target country B provides more attractive macro surroundings than country A.

To summarize, the macro environment describes general environmental factors that have an impact on all organizations involved in business in the selected target markets (Johnson et al., 2009). To make the right strategy decision, it is of vital importance to acquire suitable and updated information by using macro-analysis activities. Usually free information sources for gaining valuable macro-environmental data are found, for example, in the websites of the International Monetary Fund (IMF), the Organization for Economic Co-operation and Development (OECD), the United Nations, and the chambers of commerce of relevant target countries. Additional sources to gain country-specific market information are professional market research firms. Businesses,

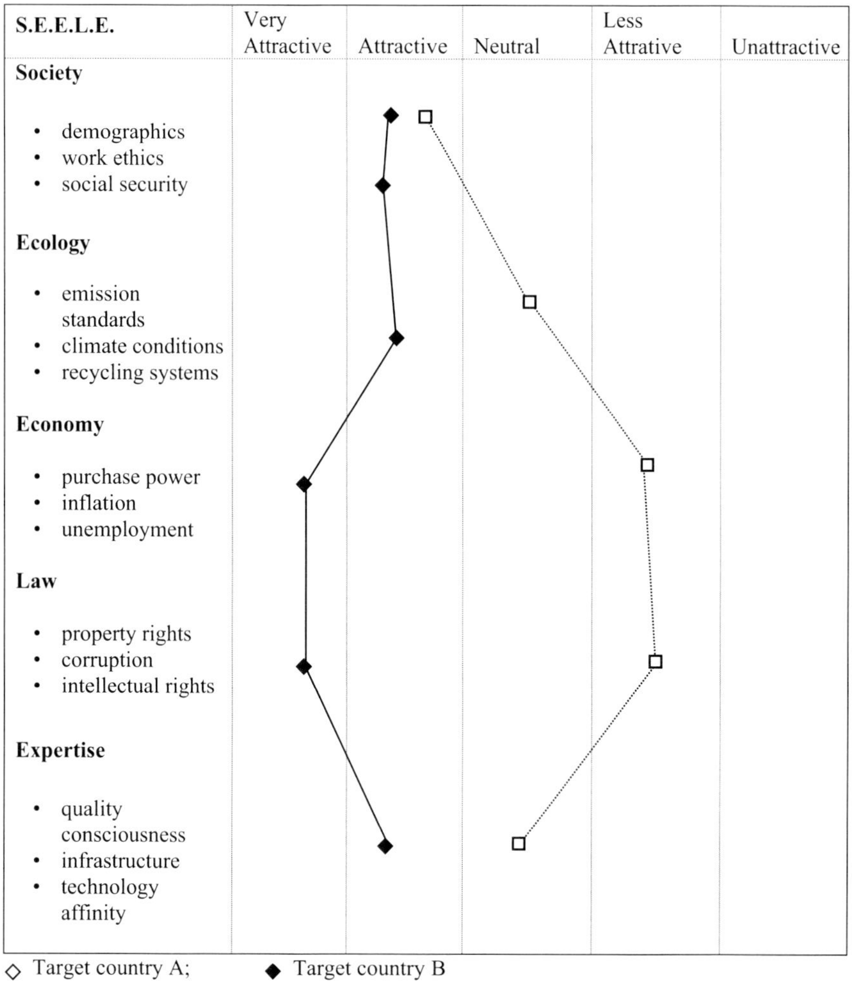

Figure 2.4 An illustration of country risk analysis.

industries, and corresponding markets naturally differ. Therefore, in a next step and following the macro analysis, the firm's management conducts an industry analysis as introduced in the next section.

The industry analysis

The industry analysis is methodologically connected to the market-based view (MBV) of a firm, which emphasizes the product and service market positions and corresponding firm's market competitive and bargaining power as a major input for above average margins, and as a result, higher firm value (Tallman, 1991). According to the MBV, the sources of value for the firm are embedded in the competitive positioning characterizing its external product and services markets (Makhija, 2003). Competitive advantage is achieved because of barriers for entry to competition result from the structural configurations of the target market or industry (Makhija, 2003).

There are three sources of power as emphasized by the MBV: monopoly power; barriers to entry; and bargaining power (Grant, 1991: 117–118; in Makhija, 2003: 437). A market or an industry that indicates high tariff or non-tariff entry barriers indicates higher returns—in the short run—as the existing companies have to face less competition. In the long run, innovativeness and efficiency of firms doing business in 'protected markets' shrink. A higher bargaining power in comparison to suppliers and customers also suggests that a firm might achieve higher margins compared to other firms that have less favorable sourcing and delivering alternatives within the industry (Makhija, 2003). The market power of a firm that is associated with higher profitability does not disappear quickly. Thus, greater market power is associated with greater firm value. The competitive dynamics and structural configurations of an industry do indeed change but over a certain period of time (Geroski and Masson, 1987). Compared to the past, we witness shortened technology and product life cycles that result in faster market reconfigurations as it is particularly the case in the electronics and information technology industries. The MBV model is originated from the Porter's 'five forces' approach, which states that a firm's performance is limited by specific industry properties and is a result of the bargaining power of suppliers and buyers, potential entrants, substitute products, and the current competition within a market (Porter, 2004; Peters et al., 2011).

Consequently, a firm's industry analysis (Figure 2.5) aims to endeavor industry-specific dynamics of the targeted business segmented by

- market attractiveness,
- product life cycles,
- intensity of competition,
- market entry barriers,
- market exit barriers,
- threat of product or service substitution,
- influencing power of shareholders and stakeholders,
- bargaining power of suppliers, and
- bargaining power of customers (Porter, 2008; Porter, 1999).

The amplitude of market attractiveness is mainly driven by market volume and market growth rates, which differ among industries. For example, due to demographic changes (relatively low birth rates cause an increasing aging of the population) as witnessed in many European countries, Japan, and South Korea, healthcare services industries indicate promising market potentials and margins are relatively high. Innovative firms enjoy favorable market conditions and are better able to meet their business objectives. Products and services, which are positioned at the beginning of the product life cycle, target innovativeness seeking customers who are usually willing to pay higher prices than market average prices (Vernon, 1972). However, challenges in terms of often rare supplier availability and limited experience curve effects, as well as low economies of scale effects, appear when products and services are sold at the beginning of its life cycles (Figure 2.6).

The demand for the product increases during the growth stage of the product life cycle. The higher the market demands because more customers are willing to buy the product, relative to the existing supply capacities, the more attractive is the industry environment of the firm. Attractive markets, in terms of growth rates and sales volumes, imply further entries by other competitors, which finally increase the competition on the market. During the maturity and saturation stages of the product life cycles, the demand of the product or services shrinks and competition intensifies, which is usually focused on the price (Vernon, 1966).

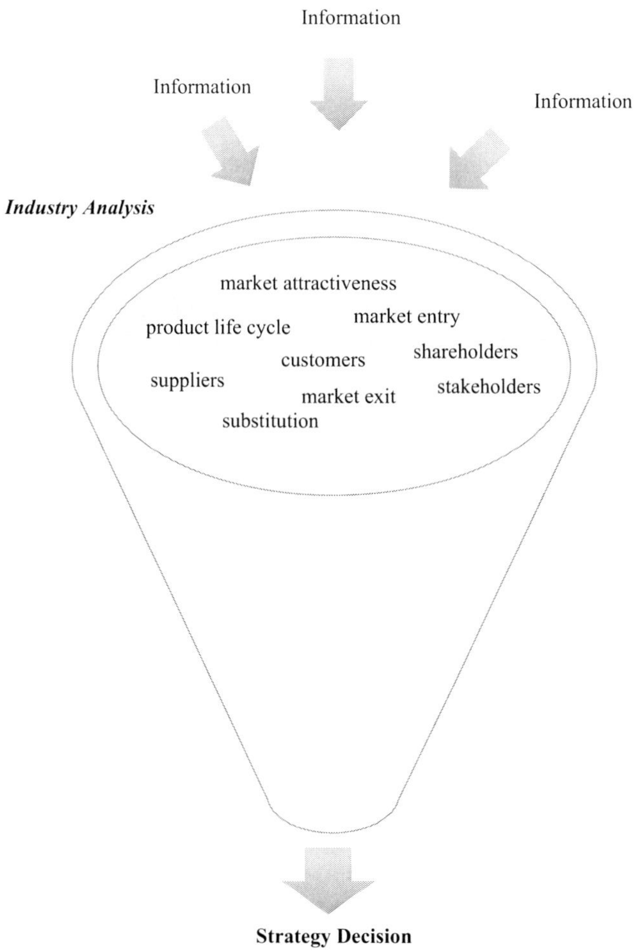

Figure 2.5 Elements of the industry analysis.

As a part of the industry analysis, the capacity utilization of the target market should be necessarily analyzed. Operational overcapacities usually appear at later stages of the product life cycle. Industry overcapacities, when not noted by the firm before entering the business, create the risk of too optimistic forecasts.

In general, against the background of global competitive forces, we witness ever shortened product life cycles combined with large investments. High investments in operations in order to start the business in a particular industry serve as further example of a market entry barrier.

In the course of the industry scan, the firm analyzes further market entry barriers, such as tariff barriers (e.g. import customs) and industry-specific non-tariff barriers. Non-tariff barriers are necessary investments to build up the business as well as import quotas, hygiene and safety standards when linked with non-reasonable bureaucratic paper work, which is difficult to manage for new market entrants. Important market exit barriers are sunk costs (lost money when giving up the market), the 'ego of the management,' which describes a delayed market exit when it becomes obvious that the market

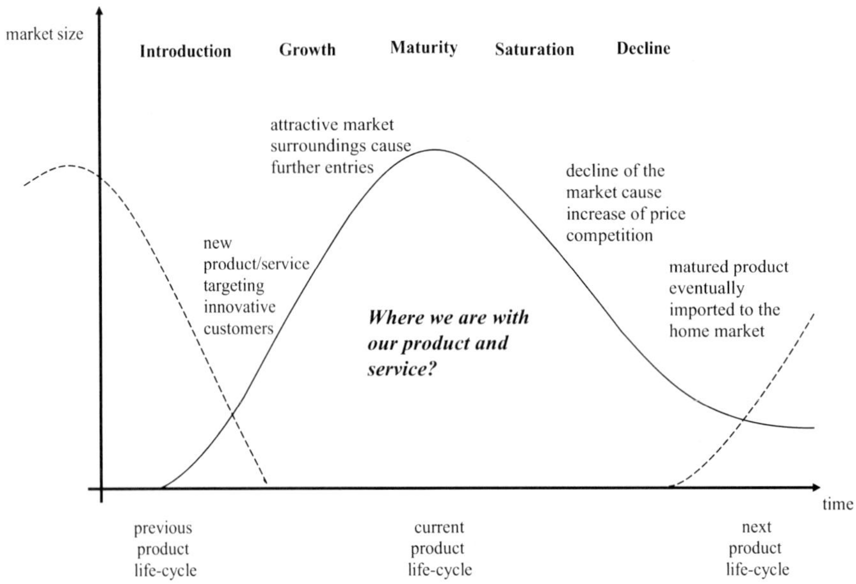

Figure 2.6 Phases of the product life cycle.

entry was a wrong decision by the management. Further exit barriers are signed agreements with local governments to pay back subsidies when leaving the market earlier than agreed. Finally, market exit barriers exist in connection with a package offer. For example, the firm must continue offering a product even it generates losses because this particular product is a part of a package offer (e.g. notebook device and notebook case).

The dynamics of changing societal lifestyles serve as a further important element of the industry analysis. Shortened product and technology life cycles accelerate the threat of substitution and provide another influencing factor for competitive rivalry in the industry. The faster the product and technological changes in the industry, the lesser time firms have available to gain back their investment returns on research and development, operations, and services with profit. In some cases, as a negative consequence of shortened product life cycles, some firms use materials and components indicating only minimum product lifetimes. Such policy is finally not ecologically friendly because it generates more waste and creates more pollution and energy use.

Changes in customer lifestyle provoke potential risks for intensified competition not only in one industry sector (conventional car concepts by electricity or hydrogen cars) but also in non-related industries. There are examples of cross-industry product impacts, such as digital cameras by smartphones or alarm clocks and smartphone. Further examples of well-known product modifications with an impact on different industries are city maps by digital navigation, and x-ray photographs by digital screen photo technology.

Another part of the industry analysis is devoted to shareholders and stakeholders. Institutional and private investors, banks and national governments belong to shareholders. Stakeholders are individuals or groups that have particular interests in the firm's mission, business objectives, and policy. There are internal and external stakeholders. Internal stakeholders are individuals who work for or own the business. This category includes employees, entrepreneurs, managers, and stockholders. External stakeholders are, for example, workers' unions, non-government organizations (NGOs) such as associations for consumer health protection or Greenpeace, Human Rights Watch, policymakers, and local communities where the firm operates. In other words, firm-related stakeholders represent the public in general (Hill, 2012).

Probably the most important external stakeholders are the firm's suppliers and customers. Suppliers as embedded in their industry networks represent driving forces in the firm's industry environment. The value of supplier relationships is associated with the access to knowledge, such as supplier's ideas concerning industry developments, market forecasts, and technological changes. Knowledge transfer and learning based on trustful supplier relationships are important elements of technological development in general and product improvements specifically (Forsgren et al., 2005). The supplier's bargaining power is not only a result of its technological expertise and the suppliers' firm size. Supplier's regional availability, reputation, product quality, order flexibility, delivery reliability, and alternative procurement sources contribute to their bargaining power and serve as important elements of the firm's industry analysis (Porter, 2008; Gobble, 2012).

Another important aspect of the industry analysis is evaluating the customers' role and their bargaining power in the target markets. The bargaining power is a result of the number of customers, their regional density and size. The characteristics and attitudes of intended customer groups are as important as the suppliers' influences on the product adaptation decision. Physical and behavioral characteristics of the customer have an impact on the firm's product and service adaptation. As a result of the industry analysis, depending on the target market, products and services are differentiated in terms of product performance, design, and service packages. The pricing policy is influenced by the customers' purchasing power and their product affinity in the foreign target country (Czinkota et al., 2011). For example, in Japan, Taiwan, and South Korea, the people have an affinity towards sophisticated consumer electronics products. They are ready to pay higher prices for state-of-the-art electronics compared to the Europeans. Therefore, these Asian countries provide better market surroundings regarding the sales of advanced consumer electronic products than other regions of the world.

The process of identifying, attracting, differentiating, and retaining customers where firms focus their efforts disproportionally on their most lucrative clients is defined as customer relation management (CRM). Conventional concepts focus on the effective combination of the firm's marketing mix instruments targeting a purchase decision of the customer. Modern concepts in terms of relationship marketing understand customer relationships as a series of interdependent purchase episodes. These purchase episodes, therefore, become the basis for the firm-customer relationship, which is beneficial for both sides. Uncertainty linked with the purchase decision is reduced when the customer is convinced to have a stable and competent partner who can improve the customer's current positioning. Relationship-focused management reduces inefficiencies created by generating one-off transactions, each of which requires a greater amount of effort and resources than is needed for encouraging repeat business and long-term retention. Long-term customer satisfaction is gained by becoming familiar with the customer's needs and expectations, increasing individual service, and promoting honest communication instead of using stereotyped advertisement slogans (Hoffman et al., 2009).

Institutional theory suggests that a firm's ability to exploit or enhance its capabilities varies across institutional contexts in diverse national and industry environments. Firms adopting entry modes that conform to institutional considerations, as well as transaction cost efficiencies, gain competitive advantages and, therefore, perform better in business than firms using other entry modes (Brouthers, 2013; Brouthers and Hennart, 2007).

To achieve sustainable competitive positioning, the management takes the information gained from the macro and industry analysis. To optimally combine external opportunities with the firm's strategies, the firm needs to analyze its resources through a micro analysis as introduced in the next section.

The firm's micro environment

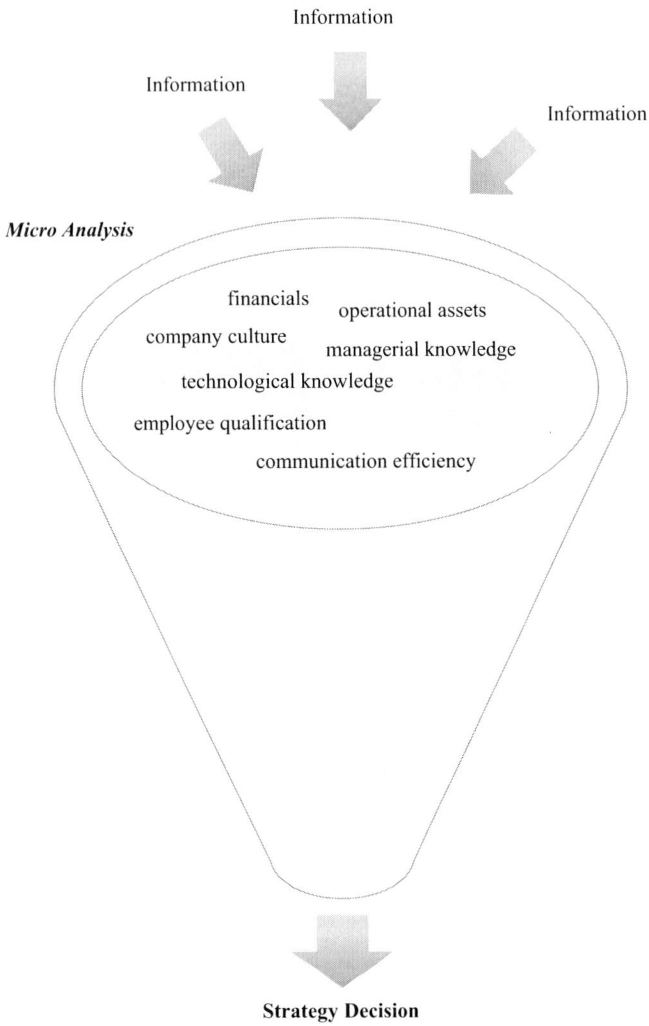

Figure 2.7 Elements of the micro analysis.

The micro analysis goes back to the resource-based view, which claims that a firm gains sustained competitive advantages if it holds resources that are valuable, rare, and difficult to imitate as well as non-substitutable by its competitors (Barney, 1991). Resources are valuable when they contribute to generate products and services of which there is a demand in the markets. Valuable resources enable the management to develop and implement strategies that maximize the firm's business performance, for example, through the sales of state-of-the art products and services or the improvement of organizational efficiency. Resources can be categorized as rare when current and potential competitors cannot rely simultaneously on similar resources, for example, managerial and technological knowledge. Sustained competitive advantage can be reached if valuable and rare resources can only be imperfectly imitated and not substituted adequately by the firm's current and future competitors (Grant, 2000; Penrose, 1995).

Resource dependence theory (RDT) states that companies are not independent with regard to strategically important resources because other firms provide them with these resources. Therefore, firms lacking resources and seeking to reduce the uncertainty surrounding their operational activities need to develop relationships with others, including customer and supplier relationships (Carter and Rogers, 2008; Cao and Zhang, 2010; Sarkis et al., 2011). Consequently, a firm's performance depends on its capability to manage this dependency (Ulrich and Barney, 1984). According to the RDT, companies need to collaborate to achieve a better performance in the long term instead of seeking short-term benefits at the cost of other firm stakeholders, for example, suppliers. The interdependency of supply chain partners as well as the quality and effectiveness of their relationships to the focal firm determines the business performance that can be reached (Sarkis et al., 2011).

Firm resources are categorized as tangible resources and intangible resources. Tangible resources are the firm's operational assets, real estate and grounds, financials, literally spoken 'everything which is physically touchable.' In contrast, intangible resources include technological knowledge (eventually protected by a 'tangible' and 'physical touchable' patent certificate) and managerial knowledge, the company culture that results in a lower or higher degree of loyalty and motivation of the employees. The managements' and the employees' certification serve as another important element of the micro (resource) analysis. Regular training and certification, which is of course not costless, is of vital importance in order to develop the firm's knowledge base in light of permanently changing external firm surroundings and globalized business patterns. The management's communication efficiency flanked by efficient internal information flows serve as fundamental resource properties and thus, if implemented properly, indicate important strengths of the firm (Grant, 1991; Grant, 1996; Barney and Arikan, 2006).

The well-known (resource) strengths–weaknesses–opportunities–threats (SWOT) analysis serves as a pragmatic tool to figure out the firm's resource configurations against its external environmental background (Armstrong and Kotler, 2011). An example of the SWOT analysis taking the case of Samsung Electronics (status 2016) is shown in Table 2.1.

In addition to SWOT, portfolio models serve as an instrument for contrasting external market opportunities (attractiveness: growth rates and margins) against the firm's competitive product positioning in terms of its market share. Product positioning is a result of consumer's perception of a product brand compared with that of competitors' brands (Czinkota et al., 2011). The value of the brand is a result of the product performance (e.g. technical parameter, quality, lifetime, and design) as witnessed and experienced in the markets over time.

One of the best known and pragmatic portfolio analysis models is the 'market growth/ market share matrix,' which goes back to the 1970s as introduced by the Boston Consulting Group (BCG). The BCG consists of two axes illustrating the market attractiveness and the market share and, thus, helps the operating management to navigate

Table 2.1 SWOT analysis taking the example of Samsung Electronics [status 2016]

Internal part (micro analysis)	*External part (macro analysis: S.E.E.L.E. and industry)*
Strengths • highly motivated employees • strong company culture • diversified business risk (e.g. consumer electronics, semiconductors, hotel, heavy industries, and financials) • economies of scale through large operations • strong brand reputation	**Opportunities** • increased share of electronics in various kinds of products • 'digitalization' of business and e-commerce • quasi-monopoly positioning in various industries in South Korea • market penetration of electricity cars (which mainly use electronic components) • healthcare as a new business field
Weaknesses • high fixed costs due to large plant utilizations • nebulous core competence of the firm • usually 'second fastest' instead of true technological innovator	**Threats** • fragile emerging economics in Brazil and Russia • economic slowdown in China • globally emerging competitors from China and Taiwan • policy of the North Korean government

the firm's products and services in its relevant markets (Henderson, 1971). The market attractiveness represents one vital element of the firm's industry environment and the relative market share indicates the competitive position of the firm's products (as a result of internal resource strengths or weaknesses). The BCG matrix is further divided into four sub-segments: poor dogs; question marks; cash cows; and stars. The relative strategic importance of the firm's product for the overall firm success is illustrated through varying circle sizes categorized as A, B, C, D, and E in Figure 2.8. As illustrated, a larger circle size such as 'A' means a higher strategic importance for the firm than, for example, a small circle like 'D,' which indicates rather less importance in terms of the overall firm performance.

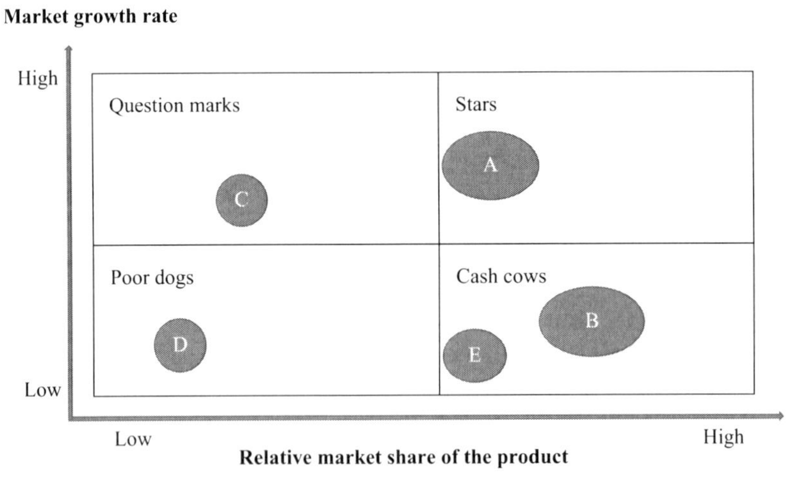

Figure 2.8 Example of a portfolio analysis.

According to the BCG matrix, question marks (Figure 2.8: product C) are products where market growth rates are promising but the firm's relative market share is low. Question marks are usually newly developed products in new markets where the firm needs to bind financial resources such as for promoting the product, investing in operational capacities, and further gaining experience curve effects. Assuming the market continues to develop successfully and internal firm resources are efficiently applied to meet the market demands and the customer's expectations, question marks become the firm's cash cows in the future.

Cash cows (Figure 2.8: products B and E) are products located in saturated markets where the firm holds relatively high market shares. Due to advanced experience curve and economies of scale effects, the products and services are operated at efficient costs. The sales of cash cow products contribute highest liquidity incomes to the firm (Glowik and Smyczek, 2011). Product life cycles in cash cow markets are normally positioned at mature or declining stages. Therefore, a firm's today cash cow market may disappear in the future because product substitutions are likely.

According to the BCG portfolio matrix, stars (Figure 2.8: product A) are products where the firm holds relatively strong market shares in promising markets with expected substantial growth rates. A new and innovative product invention, difficult to assimilate by the firm's competitors, provides the most optimal preconditions for a firm's star product. The stars of today's business should be continuously further developed, improved and, depending on the changing demand conditions, modified to become the cash cows of the firm's future business.

Products categorized as poor dogs (Figure 2.8: product D) are not located in attractive growth markets and the firm does not hold a satisfactory market share. Previous failures in market research or wrong management decisions in the past contribute to the undesirable outcome of poor dogs products. Because poor dogs generate losses, the firm's management should terminate corresponding businesses. The management's self-assessment and the acceptance that a decision in the past, which led to the poor dog, and therefore, obviously was wrong, usually serve as challenges. Management executives often hesitate and delay making essential decisions to give up business segments.

To summarize, the product portfolio of a firm ideally ensures that the net income generated by cash cows and stars outbalance the losses caused by the poor dogs and provide financial cushions for the development of the question marks (Hedley, 1977; Müller-Stewens and Lechner, 2011). Question marks and stars are located in promising markets at the beginning stage of their product life cycles, whereas cash cows and dogs are positioned in saturated and declining markets.

During the course of strategy development, the firm's management is aware that external business opportunities on the markets are combined optimally with inner resource strengths in order to gain sustained competitive advantage. The variables of the firm's macro environment (S.E.E.L.E) belong to the category of which the firm's management has no direct control. The industry environment of the firm consists of semi-controllable variables. For example, in government lobbying (stakeholder), the firm can influence industry standards, which occurs commonly in pharmaceuticals. Furthermore, through customer relationship management, the firm can actively influence the purchase behavior of its customers. However, the final procurement decision is on the customer's side (therefore, 'semi-controllable'). The firm's micro environment consists of the firm's resources (e.g. employee qualification). Here, the firm has full control over the corresponding resource variables and, thus, can actively develop them (Figure 2.9).

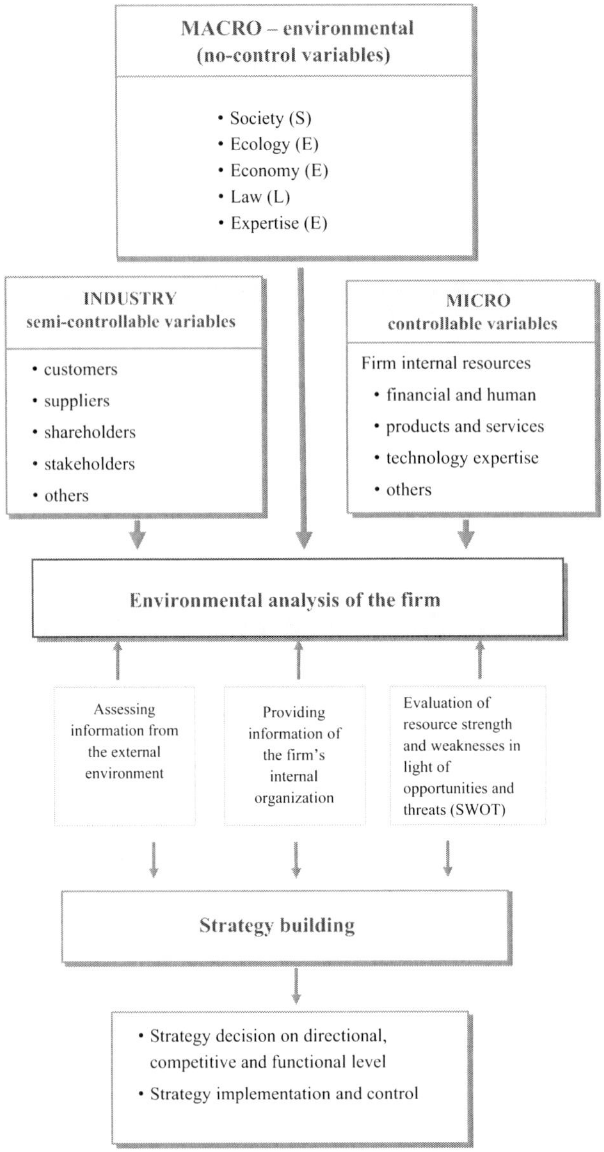

Figure 2.9 No-controllable, semi-controllable, and full-controllable variables of the firm's environment.

Naturally, no firm in this world can rely always on resource strengths. A worst-case scenario serving as an external market threat—for example, a firm's supplier does not meet ethical working standards, which is communicated in the media and linked with the firm's brand name—comes up against firm internal weaknesses: relatively high degree of added product value by the non-ethical supplier, which finally harms the firm's own reputation. Such a combination causes the firm's worsening performance and provokes even the risk of bankruptcy. In this case, the firm

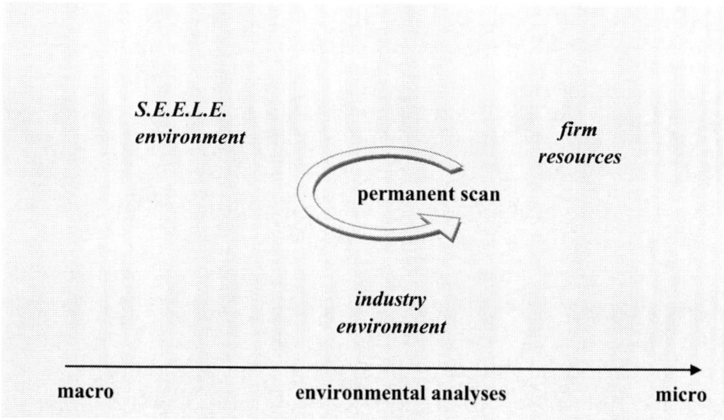

Figure 2.10 Mutual influencing elements of a firm's macro, industry, and micro environment.

has to improve its supplier selection processes, which require firm resources (full-controllable variable).

As a result of the environmental analysis of the firm's macro environment, the industry environment and the firm's micro level, the management is able to decide the firm's overall strategy building on cooperative, competitive, and functional levels. The environmental analysis also provides the informational basis to determine whether it is worthwhile to consider an international market entry and in which markets the entry should take place. In general, there are five main incentives for an international market entry as illustrated in Figure 2.10 (Dunning and Kundu, 1995; Dunning, 2001).

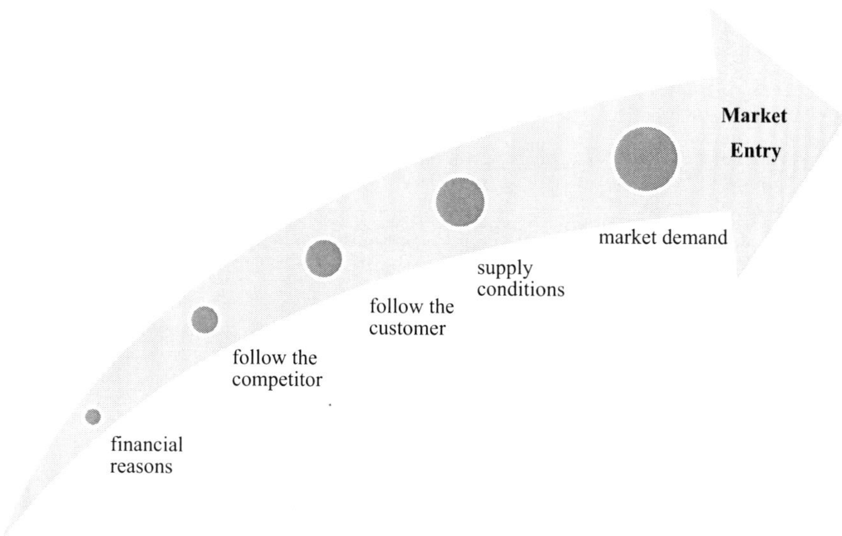

Figure 2.11 Market entry motives of a firm.

First, there are demand-oriented factors. In this case, a foreign market entry is considered because of the market's attractiveness in terms of market volume and growth rates, which provide further sales volumes, in addition to (often) saturated home markets.

Second, supply-oriented factors: access to rare and valuable resources available in foreign target markets, such as qualified and motivated employees, raw materials, knowledge, technological expertise, infrastructure, and others.

Third, follow-the-customer necessity: To avoid the risk of being dropped from the procurement list of an important customer, the firm needs to follow its customer, which is also doing business in the foreign target market.

Fourth, follow-the-competitor necessity: To avoid leaving the competitors either with all the sales opportunities or all the investment benefits provided in a regional industry cluster in foreign markets, the firm joins the business in the foreign markets.

Fifth, there are financial reasons such as advantages of foreign markets because of regional investment incentives (tax reductions, subsidies). For example, there are less costly debt financing sources because of lower interest rates, and a higher liquidity in the foreign markets. In addition, large multinationals can make use of cross-stock listing.

In light of globalized trade pattern, shortened product and technology life cycles contribute to accelerated market dynamics and promising market configurations today may change towards becoming a threat tomorrow (e.g. product substitution because of changing lifestyle). Thus, the management's major task is to scan, analyze, and forecast permanently and appropriately its industries and markets in order to adjust appropriately the firm's inner resource allocations according to changing environmental circumstances to achieve sustainable, competitive survival. A well-developed environmental scan of the firm's surroundings and resources is of vital importance for the strategy development on directional, competitive, and functional levels, as described in the following chapter.

Bibliography

Armstrong, G & Kotler P 2011, *Marketing: an introduction*, Pearson Education Limited, Harlow, Essex.

Barney, J 1991, Firm resources and sustained competitive advantage, *Journal of Management*, vol. 17, pp. 99–120.

Barney, JB & Arikan, AM 2006, 'The resource-based view: origins and implications,' in *The blackwell handbook of strategic management*, eds MA Hitt, RE Freeman & JS Harrison, Blackwell Publishing, Oxford.

Brouthers, KD 2013, Institutional, cultural and transaction cost influences on entry mode choice and performance, *Journal of International Business Studies*, vol. 44, pp. 1–13.

Brouthers, KD & Hennart, J-F 2007, Boundaries of the firm: insights from international entry mode research, *Journal of Management*, vol. 33, pp. 395–425.

Bruton, GD, Ahlstrom, D & Li, H-L 2010, Institutional theory and entrepreneurship: where are we now and where do we need to move in the future? *Entrepreneurship: Theory and Practise*, vol. 34, pp. 421–440.

Cao, M & Zhang, Q 2010, Supply chain collaborative advantage: a firm's perspective, *International Journal of Production Economics*, vol. 128, pp. 358–367.

Carter, CR & Rogers, DS 2008, A framework of sustainable supply chain management: moving toward new theory, *International Journal of Physical Distribution & Logistics Management*, vol. 38, pp. 360–387.

Czinkota, MR, Ronkainen, IA & Zvobgo, G 2011, *International marketing*, Cengage Learning, Andover, Hampshire.

Davidson, WH & McFetridge, DG 1985, Key characteristics in the choice of international technology transfer mode, *Journal of International Business Studies*, vol. 16, pp. 5–21.

Delios, A & Beamish, PW 1999, Ownership strategy of Japanese firms: transactional, institutional, and experience influences, *Strategic Management Journal*, vol. 20, pp. 915–933.

Dunning, JH 2001, The eclectic (OLI) paradigm of international production: past, present and future, *International Journal of the Economics of Business*, vol. 8, pp. 173–190.

Dunning, JH & Kundu, SK 1995, The internationalization of the hotel industry—some new findings form a field study, *Management International Review*, vol. 35, pp. 101–133.

Forsgren, M, Holm, U & Johanson, J 2005, *Managing the embedded multinational. A business network view*, Edward Elgar Publishing Limited, Cheltenham.

Geroski, PA & Masson, RT 1987, Dynamic market models in industrial organization, *International Journal of Industrial Organization*, vol. 5, pp. 1–13.

Glover, JL, Champion, D, Daniels, KJ & Dainty, AJD 2014, An institutional theory perspective on sustainable practices across the dairy supply chain, *International J. Production Economics*, vol. 152, pp. 102–111.

Glowik, M & Smyczek, S 2011, *International marketing management. Strategies, concepts and cases in Europe*, Oldenbourg Verlag, München.

Gobble, MAM 2012, Innovation and strategy, *Research Technology Management*, vol. 55 (3), pp. 63–67.

Grant, RM 1991, The resource-based theory of competitive advantage. Implications for strategy formulation, *California Management Review*, vol. 33, pp. 114–135.

Grant, RM 1996, Toward a knowledge-based theory of the firm, *Strategic Management Journal*, vol. 17, pp. 109–122.

Hedley, B 1977, Strategy and the business portfolio, *Long Range Planning*, vol. 10, pp. 9–15.

Henderson, BD 1971, *Construction of a business strategy. The Boston Consulting Group. Series on corporate strategies*, The Boston Consulting Group, Boston.

Hill, CWL 2012, *International business: Competing in the global marketplace*, McGraw-Hill/Irwin, Boston.

Hoffman, KD, Bateson, JEG, Wood, EH & Kenyon, AK 2009, *Services marketing. Concepts, strategies and cases*, South-Western Cengage Learning, London.

International Monetary Fund 2016, *Global financial stability report: potent policies for a successful normalization* [Online]. Available from: www.imf.org/external/publications/index.htm. [August 10, 2106].

Johnson, G, Scholes, K & Whittington, R 2009, *Exploring corporate strategy*, Pearson, Harlow.

Koumparoulis, DN 2013, PEST analysis: the case of E-shop, *International Journal of Economy, Management and Social Sciences*, vol. 2, pp. 31–36.

Lasserre, P 2012, *Global strategic management*, Palgrave Macmillan, Basingstoke.

Mair, J & Marti, I 2009, Entrepreneurship in and around institutional voids: a case study from Bangladesh, *Journal of Business Venturing*, vol. 24, pp. 419–435.

Makhija, M 2003, Comparing the resource-based and market-based views of the firm: empirical evidence from Czech privatization, *Strategic Management Journal*, vol. 24, pp. 433–451.

Moffat, A & Auer, A 2006, Corporate environmental innovation (CEI): a government initiative to support corporate sustainability leadership, *Journal of Cleaner Production*, vol. 14, pp. 589–600.

Müller-Stewens, G & Lechner, C 2011, *Strategisches Management. Wie strategische Initiativen zum Wandel führen*, Schäffer-Poeschel, Stuttgart.

OECD 2015, *Income inequality: the gap between rich and poor* [Online]. Available from: www.keepeek.com/Digital-Asset-Management/oecd/social-issues-migration-health/income-inequality/what-s-happening-to-income-inequality_9789264246010-4-en#page6. [December 17, 2016].

Pan, Y & Tse, DK 2000, The hierarchical model of market entry modes, *Journal of International Business Studies*, vol. 31, pp. 535–554.

Penrose, E 1995, *The theory of the growth of the firm*, Oxford University Press, Oxford.

Peters, M, Siller, L & Matzler, K 2011, The resource-based and the market-based approaches to cultural tourism in alpine destinations, *Journal of Sustainable Tourism*, vol. 19, pp. 877–893.

Porter, ME 1999, *Wettbewerbsstrategie. Methoden zur Analyse von Branchen und Konkurrenten*, Campus Verlag, Frankfurt/Main.

Porter, ME 2004, *Competitive advantage: Creating and sustaining superior performance*, Free Press, New York.

Porter, ME 2008, The five competitive forces that shape strategy, *Harvard Business Review*, vol. 86, pp. 78–93.

Sarkis, J, Zhu, Q & Lai, K-H 2011, An organizational theoretic review of green supply chain management literature, *International Journal of Production Economics*, vol. 130, pp. 1–15.

Sirmon, DG, Hitt, MA & Ireland, RD 2007, Managing firm resources in dynamic environments to create value: looking inside the black box, *Academy of Management Review*, vol. 32, pp. 273–292.

Tallman, SB 1991, Strategic management models and resource-based strategies among MNEs in a host market, *Strategic Management Journal*, vol. 12, pp. 69–82.

Ulrich, D & Barney, JB 1984, Perspectives in organizations: resource dependence, efficiency, and population, *Academy of Management Review*, vol. 9, pp. 471–481.

Vernon, R 1966, International investment and international trade in the product cycle, *Quarterly Journal of Economics*, vol. 80, pp. 190–207.

Vernon, R 1972, International trade: the product life cycle approach, in *The product life cycle and international trade*, ed LT Wells, Harvard University, Boston.

3 Strategy building

Mario Glowik

Chapter learning objectives

- To discuss the meaning of corporate social responsibility in terms of the firm's global strategic positioning;
- To explain important elements of the firm's strategic decision finding process;
- To describe the strategic alternatives on the directional firm level and corresponding reasons behind each strategy;
- To explain the variants of concentration strategies and diversification strategies and discuss the advantages and disadvantages of each strategic alternative;
- To compare the advantages and disadvantages of forward integration through conventional distribution and e-commerce platforms and challenges when implementing both in parallel;
- To discuss the motives for establishing international joint ventures and potential international joint venture failure reasons;
- To assess why organizational structures do not always follow the firm strategy on time;
- To explain major elements of an export contract and introduce the meaning of international commercial terms as well as common export payment modes;
- To describe the meaning and contents of 'cultural dimensions' and maintain a critical perspective in terms of their applicability in business practice; and
- To explain strategy implementation and performance measures, such as balanced scorecard.

Strategy development

Strategy development is a systematic and planned approach in order to realize the management's long-term business objectives. The process includes the adoption of courses of action by the firm and the allocation of tangible and intangible resources necessary for implementing these objectives (Chandler, 1962). Before the strategy decision is made, the management evaluates external opportunities in and threats to its market environments in light of the firm's resource strengths and weaknesses (Wheelen and Hunger, 2010). Ideally, external business opportunities endeavored in the firm's markets (e.g. demand for ecologically sustainable products) are connected to the organization's internal resource strengths (e.g. engineering knowledge, how to create these innovative, ecological-sustainable products). However, no company in this world can rely on resource strengths only. Competition is dynamic and customers' lifestyles change. The organization's management should always be prepared for external threats that may emerge in the global markets, particularly against the background of short technology and product life cycles.

Although strategy is necessarily characterized as a long-term process, competitive advantages can often not be realized as planned, because upcoming changes in the market surroundings may occur on short notice. Thus, strategy development should consist of flexible elements, which, depending on the changing business dynamics, allow the firm's originally planned strategy to evolve towards the firm's realized strategy (Mintzberg et al., 2003). Successful managers provide a company atmosphere that reacts promptly to the changing market surroundings, which for example might include the process of changing internal weaknesses to become a firm's resource strength.

The strategy formulation addresses the following: (1) directional (corporate) firm level; (2) competitive firm level; and (3) functional level (Figure 3.1). In start-ups, micro, or small- and medium-sized firms, the strategy alternatives over the three segments are naturally limited (e.g. there is usually no competitive level due to the small firm size).

Strategic management is the process of specifying the firm's objectives, developing policies and plans to successfully achieve and sustainable attain these objectives (Raduan et al., 2009). The firm's quantitative business objectives, such as turnover and profits, should be consistent with its societal and ecological obligations to secure the firm's sustainable achievements, which are typically described as corporate social responsibility.

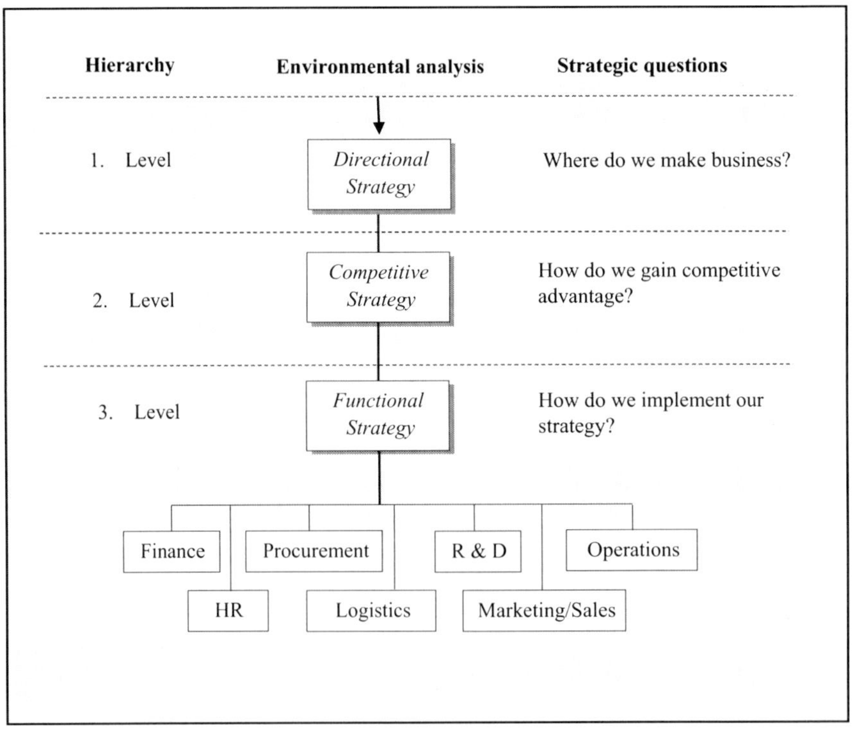

Figure 3.1 Strategies on the directional, competitive, and functional levels.

Corporate social responsibility

> One thing is for sure: If we continue the way we exploit and pollute water, air, land, and natural resources, this earth changes its face faster than expected and mankind will suffer more than imagined.

Corporate social responsibility (CSR) is a multifaceted concept, which is delineated as the dedication of organizations to operate ethically and responsibly towards their employees, the local community, the firm's societal and natural environment (Lindgreen and Swaen, 2010; Lindgreen and Wynstra, 2005). The development of CSR concepts dates back to the 1950s when the first CSR-related models, such as 'corporate social integrity,' launched discussion. The terminology was later expanded by 'business ethics' and 'corporate philanthropy,' to what is more recently described as 'sustainable development,' 'corporate citizenship,' and 'corporate sustainability' (Madrakhimova, 2013).

In the early 1990s, the so-called CSR pyramid, which contains economic responsibilities (located at the bottom of the CSR pyramid), legal, ethical, and philanthropic responsibilities (at the top of the pyramid), launched the literature (Carroll, 1991). Economic responsibilities consider the firm's obligation to maximize the shareholders' return on investments. Legal responsibilities describe the firm's obligations in terms of respecting national and international laws in terms of working hours, intellectual property rights, tax payments, and others. Ethical responsibilities embody those standards, norms, or expectations that reflect a concern for what customers, suppliers, employees, shareholders, and the community regard as fair, just, or in keeping with the respect or protection of the stakeholders' moral rights. Philanthropy encompasses those corporate actions that are in response to society's expectation that businesses be good corporate citizens, which includes engaging in acts or programs to promote human welfare or goodwill. Examples of philanthropy include business contributions of financial resources or executive time, such as contributions to the arts, sport events, education, i.e. everything that is in favor of the firm's community (Carroll, 1991).

All-in-all CSR represents a multifaceted concept formed as a result of various models and theories, such as institutional concepts, agency theory, the resource-based view of the firm, and the stakeholder theory (Lindgreen and Swaen, 2010). As a result, several opposing and controversial schools of thought exist, which sometimes are positioned at the extremes of either perceiving CSR as a means to maximizing a company's revenue or as the company's social, civic and moral obligation towards the growth of the general human welfare (Madrakhimova, 2013).

In light of accelerated cross-border value added activities, larger firms such as multinational enterprises (MNEs) globally spread their operations around the world. MNEs make use of their global networks, which enable them to gain competitive advantages against the background of shortened product and technology life cycles. Additionally, MNEs through their access to globally attractive markets in terms of growth rates and market volumes can, thus, quickly realize economies of scale effects. In this respect, growing concern has emerged in modern societies concerning ecological sustainable operations, safety, and working conditions of employees. Especially in emerging countries in the Far East, legal regulations regarding working standards and environmental pollution are less strict than, for example, in the EU countries (Smith et al., 2010). In various cases, CSR activities are implemented by the firms' management either due to legal regulations or to the development of a corresponding firm reputation, which aims to improve the profit. In general, more voluntary CSR-related measures are necessary. We need to understand CSR as a multidimensional concept, which improves everybody's daily life in terms of societal and ecological standards as well as in work and leisure times. CSR initiatives are important in establishing socially responsible practices to support the wider society and reducing the harmful environmental impact arising from manufacturing, packaging, and transportation of companies' products (Lindgreen and Swaen, 2010). When MNEs really want to fully commit to ethical behavior, they need to ensure that CSR is also applied across their entire supply chains (Ciliberti et al., 2008).

For implementation and control of CSR initiatives, firms are advised to implement CSR management systems, through which they clearly communicate their honest engagement in CSR activities, establish a written agreement addressing suppliers' ethical responsibilities, and regularly monitor suppliers' practices to ensure compliance. Finally, when truly implementing CSR as an entire philosophy, MNEs should provide training and education of their suppliers, contracted manufacturers, as well as distributers if required (Ciliberti et al., 2008).

Due to the various weaknesses in terms of global, legal enforcements, CSR indicates a largely voluntary behavior. Thus, it is often questioned why companies actually engage in responsible behaviors. In general, CSR appears to be increasingly valued by customers, employers, and other stakeholders. We, the customers, influence societal expectations and morals, and through our purchase decisions, we put substantial pressure on firms to rethink their CSR commitment worldwide. Consequently, those companies that fail to commit to socially responsible behaviors might suffer 'negative ethical consumerism leading to consumers' refusal to purchase their brands (Smith et al., 2010). CSR activities are perceived as a means to boost image, and revenues can, when ignored, actually weaken the firm's long-term business performance. Indeed, recent research shows that companies are becoming extremely careful in how they communicate their ethical working and company behaviors to avoid skepticism and criticism that CSR activities are only communicated as a way to boost their image (Du et al., 2010; Lindgreen and Swaen, 2010).

> We as the consumers through our purchase decision have the power. We can favor CSR standards and support those firms that implement CSR in their company culture. However, we must watch carefully whether CSR is done honestly by the firm or just communicated as to pretend to do so, similar as a marketing tool in order to increase profits.

It will never be completely excluded that some companies just communicate their CSR campaigns rather as 'impression management strategy' to paint a favorable picture on their own. Research has highlighted that customers tend to make two types of attributions regarding companies' CSR activities. The first type is called intrinsic attributions, leading the individual to perceive CSR as genuine attempts to serve the needs of society and the environment. The second type is named as extrinsic attributions, which is perceived as a revenue-generating strategy. As a consequence, either of them will lead an individual to an extreme attitude towards a company. However, if these two types of attributions are combined, consumers are more likely to accept if a company is using CSR to support its business case. Therefore, companies are advised to actually explicitly acknowledge and transparently communicate their motives for engaging in CSR activities, and emphasize the 'win-win' for all stakeholders of the firm's societal and ecological environment, such as customers, employees, suppliers, as parts of the entire population (Smith et al., 2010; Du et al., 2010).

CSR concepts have been further developed by the 'shared value' approach. While CSR tends to be rather reactive towards its societal responsibility, the shared value concept emphasized to actively search for societal and environmental challenges and integrate social issues more actively into the firm's business and strategy concepts (Porter and Kramer, 2014; Porter and Kramer, 2011b). Creating shared value represents a broader conception of CSR. It is not philanthropy but self-interested behavior to create economic value by creating societal value. When companies individually pursue shared value concepts connected to their particular businesses, society's overall interests are better served. In return, companies acquire legitimacy in the eyes of the communities in which they operate, which allow policymakers to set a regulatory framework that fosters and supports business. For example, the use of energy throughout the firm's value added chain needs to be re-examined in terms of operation processes, transportation, suppliers, target customers, and distribution. As a result, there are improvements in terms of more efficient energy utilization through better logistics, lower emissions, recycling systems, and numerous other practices—all of which create shared value (Porter and Kramer, 2011a).

However, the topics of CSR and shared value concepts are insufficiently developed in terms of small- and medium-sized enterprises (SMEs) (Lindgreen and Swaen, 2010). SMEs and their CSR activities, due to their firm sizes, which often follow up niche strategies, are usually less recognized than MNEs in the society. Accordingly, SMEs usually do not have the financial resources (for example, compared to multinational firms) to actively promote and inform the public (stakeholders) that they have implemented a CSR policy. Furthermore, most of the SMEs are not subject to publication requirements compared to large, resource-rich, stock-listed companies. There are potential drawbacks because SMEs tend to have little bargaining power for assuring that ethical CSR conforms to behavior from their business partners. For example, research of five Italian SMEs has demonstrated that even though most of their suppliers agreed to the firm's codes of conduct, these SMEs struggled to monitor their suppliers in terms of ecological damage as well as the working conditions of the suppliers' employees due to SMEs' limited resources and organizational constraints (Ciliberti et al., 2008). Despite these challenges, SMEs naturally should have a strong interest in CSR and shared value activities. This interest particularly emerged by that fact that SMEs are usually in close relationship with their stakeholders of their local communities (Danis et al., 2010).

Directional corporate level strategies

On the corporative level, the management makes the decision about the basic strategic positioning of the company (directional strategy). As illustrated in Figure 3.2, there are three alternatives on the directional level, namely, growth strategy, stability strategy, and retrenchment strategy. When implementing a growth strategy, as the term indicates, the management aims to increase its turnover and profits. The management can basically utilize two decisional alternatives. First, growth strategies can be realized by expanding the business activities in the firm's current markets (increases of sales volume in current sales regions and of current products and services) (Kotler and Armstrong, 2011). Alternatively, the firm expands in new markets (newly developed sales regions and new products and services). Related to its geographical expansion, the management decides to grow in the firm's domestic market or international markets or in both (Hitt et al., 2016; Wheelen and Hunger, 2010).

When internationalizing, the firm's operation in the foreign market depends on its choice of foreign market entry mode. An entry mode is described as 'an institutional arrangement chosen by the parent company in the foreign market' (Hollensen, 2014;

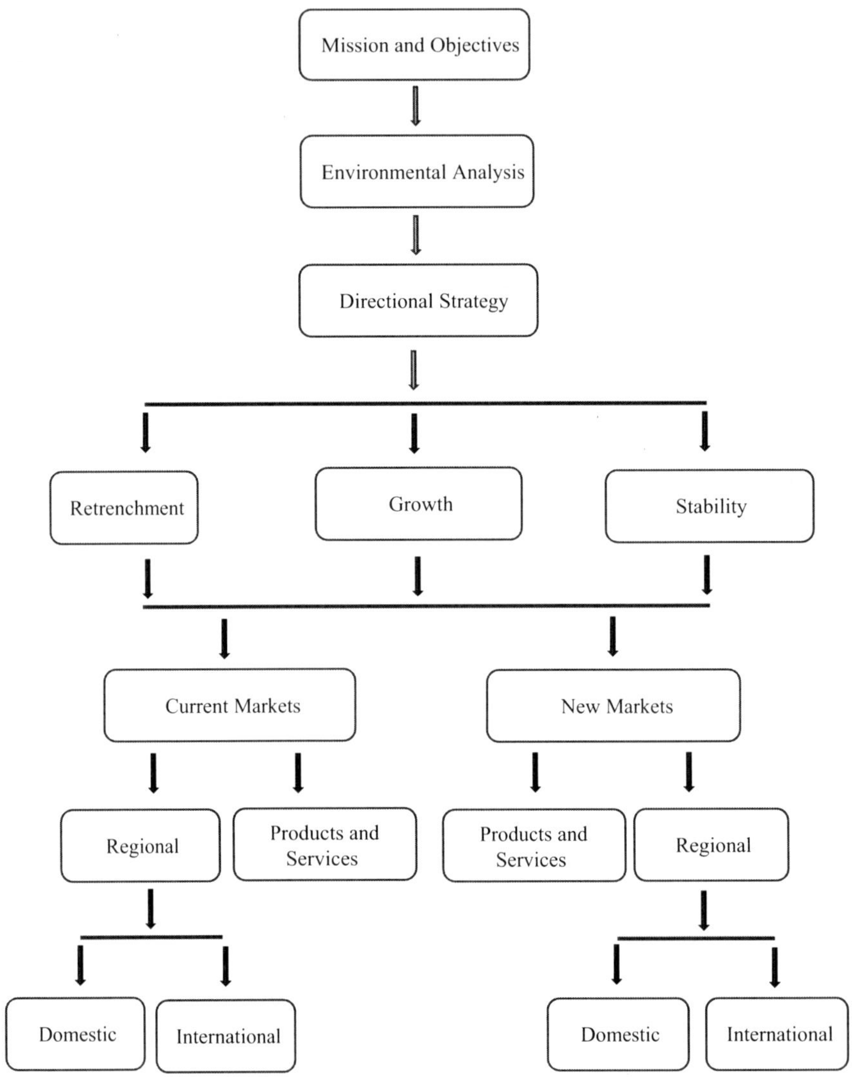

Figure 3.2 Strategic alternatives on the directional level.

Kumar and Subramanian, 1997). The decision regarding the foreign entry mode strategy is one of the most critical as it is often less efficient to change the mode of entry due to long-term consequences for the firm, once it is established (Brouthers and Hennart, 2007; Pedersen et al., 2002)

Market entry mode decisions comprise the essential choice of location and the level of control. Hence, resources might be located domestically or abroad and are controlled by the firm itself or through contracted firms. Consequently, in terms of the operational control of the firm's foreign business, there are mainly three entry mode categories to be distinguished, namely, high, intermediate, and low control modes (Hollensen, 2010; Hollensen et al., 2011).

High control modes comprise the firm's foreign direct investment in the form of wholly owned subsidiaries (WOS) full control over operations in the foreign market. The WOS (also called hierarchical market entry mode) provide the most control but also require a substantial commitment of resources, such as financial, human resources, international business knowledge, and experience of the operating staff and others (Sanchez-Peinado et al., 2007). Intermediate modes include mainly international strategic alliances and international joint ventures where the partners agree to share resources, such as technology and market knowledge. Low control modes include indirect and direct export. Export implies a minimal resource commitment and, thus, little or no control over the conditions under which the product or service is marketed abroad (Hollensen et al., 2011).

Transaction cost theory addresses international entry mode decisions stating that entry modes chosen based on the transaction cost model can result in the most efficient structure (Shrader, 2001; Brouthers, 2013). Transaction cost theory deals with the costs of integrating a firm relative to the costs of an external firm acting for the firm in a foreign market. Thereby, entry mode choices are influenced by costs occurring for finding, negotiating, and monitoring the performance of the contracted partner firm (Brouthers, 2013; Williamson, 1985). Additional costs in finding and negotiating incur due to 'difficulties of estimating and including all contingencies in the agreement' and due to information asymmetries. The more complex the product specifications, the higher the uncertainty and the more difficult it becomes to fix all of the relevant issues in a contract. Furthermore, the costs for monitoring and enforcing the contract can arise because of distance, communication difficulties, or lack of measurable performance outcome (Williamson, 1985; Brouthers, 2013). Several studies have proven that if transaction costs increase, firms tend to opt for more hierarchical modes, such as wholly owned subsidiaries (Taylor et al., 1998). In addition, firms with a high level of firm-specific technology employ higher control governance structures, such as WOS, to reduce opportunistic behavior, such as shirking, free-riding, or disseminating technology (Williamson, 1985; Brouthers, 2013). Hence, according to the transaction cost theory, firms need to select the entry mode that minimizes transaction costs (Hollensen et al., 2011).

The institutional theory may serve as an extension to the transaction cost theory as the institutional theory provides the structure to human interactions. Environmental uncertainty is a crucial factor influencing a foreign market entry mode decision and, therefore, institutional and cultural context variables should be combined with transaction cost variables to explain entry mode decisions (North, 1990; Hollensen et al., 2011; Nielsen and Nielsen, 2011). Thus, institutional theory suggests that a firm's ability to exploit or enhance its capabilities can vary across institutional contexts in different national environments. Firms adopting entry modes that conform to institutional considerations, as well as transaction cost efficiencies, should perform better than firms using other entry modes (Brouthers, 2013).

Stability strategies are launched when the firm's environmental surroundings (e.g. as a result of the subprime crisis in summer 2007) are rather uncertain and corresponding business forecasts are nebulous. As the term indicates, first, the management aims to 'stabilize' sales and profits. Stabilization is often successfully implemented by reviewing the firm's current value added activities directed at increasing operational efficiency and profitability. Stability strategies are recommended, for example, after the firm's acquisition of another company. The firm needs time to integrate the acquired assets and employees into its own structure and company culture. The integration and harmonization of the firm's cultures are particularly challenging and require time (Slater and Robson, 2012; Bushardt et al., 2011). In some cases, a stabilization strategy is implemented by reconfiguring the firm's assets, which include selling the current stake at one engagement (e.g. joint ventures), and reinvesting the available financial resources to increase the management's interests at other firms as the below joint venture case of Deutsche Telekom and Orange illustrates.

Deutsche Telekom and Orange sell their mobile *Joint Venture EE* to British Telekom for GBP 12.5 billion

Feb. 5, 2015

Deutsche Telekom will retain a 12 percent shareholding in BT, the prospective leading converged operator in the UK. Synergy potential with an estimated net present value of GBP 4.6 billion.

Value creation is achieved by optimizing the company's portfolio. Deutsche Telekom and the French telecommunications operator Orange SA have reached an agreement with the British telecommunications operator BT Group plc. on the sale of their UK joint venture EE. On closing the transaction, Deutsche Telekom will become the largest shareholder in BT with a stake of c. 12 percent.

Tim Höttges, Chief Executive Officer of Deutsche Telekom, highlighted the significant value creation for the Deutsche Telekom group and said: 'The transaction is much more than just the creation of the leading integrated fixed and mobile network operator in Europe's second largest economy. We will be the largest individual shareholder in BT and we are laying the foundations for our two companies to be able to work together in the future. This is another example of the consistent and successful execution of our portfolio optimization strategy.'

Gavin Patterson, Chief Executive Officer of BT, said: 'This is a major milestone for BT as it will allow us to accelerate our mobility plans and increase our investment in them.' Stéphane Richard, Chief Executive Officer of Orange, said: 'This is a landmark transaction for Orange and the next natural step in the evolution of BT and EE. We are confident the combined company will go on to provide new and exciting services to its customers as the demand for data and connected services continues to grow.'

Source: Deutsche Telekom (2015).

In contrast to growth strategy, a retrenchment strategy is launched when the management concludes from its environmental analysis that the current business performs less successfully than expected or even generates continued losses, and there is only marginal progress or even no hope for potential recovery. Retrenchment means that the firm partially or entirely gives up the business of certain products or services. The management decides to reduce or shut down capacities (e.g. operation and services, branches, and plants). Furthermore, the firm partially or entirely draws its presences from the existing, domestic, and international markets (regional, products and services). In the best-case scenario, there is another firm willing to buy operational assets that the management decided to cut off (sell-out). The following are primary reasons for implementing a retrenchment strategy:

- The questioned industry/market in which the firm operates is stagnant or is shrinking.
- The business operations, which have been acquired by another firm, could not have been implemented successfully in the firm's organization. The firm is too diversified and, thus, needs to return to concentrate on its core competencies (namely: What can we do best?).
- The product or service itself becomes outdated due to the customers' changing lifestyles.
- There is an operational and cultural misfit between the firm and a joint venture partner, or company where the firm invested capital that could not be solved ('expected synergies did not become true').
- There are emerging changes in technology life cycles (e.g. conventional cars versus electric cars).

As a result of reduced resources assets, the firm's turnover, in the short run, shrinks but hopefully the losses become profits in the medium and long run. The management, after terminating poor performing businesses, concentrates on attractive and promising markets (supposedly, the environmental analysis was performed accurately); this focus is also called turn-around strategy (Cavusgil et al., 2008; Hill, 2012).

Assuming the management decides to launch a growth strategy, there are basically two alternatives in terms of the firm's industry route, namely, concentration and diversification. The management's strategy decision to expand in current markets (industries) is defined as a concentration strategy. Concentration strategies are promoted if the management concludes from its environmental analysis that the firm is currently positioned in attractive markets (markets indicating promising volumes and growth rate). The firm's growth through concentration strategy can be implemented either in the form of horizontal industry concentration or vertical industry concentration (Figure 3.3).

In the context of horizontal concentration, the firm focuses on its current value added activities and expands its corresponding product and services offerings (e.g. antivirus software for conventional computers and, in addition, for smartphones). Horizontal concentration is implemented by expanding the current product model portfolio (e.g. various smartphone models by Samsung) (Freytag and Clarke, 2001).

Vertical industry concentration strategies can be segmented between vertical forward integration and vertical backward integration. The termination of backward and forward is set from the perspective of the firm's current value added activities. In the case of vertical backward integration, the management takes over value added activities, which

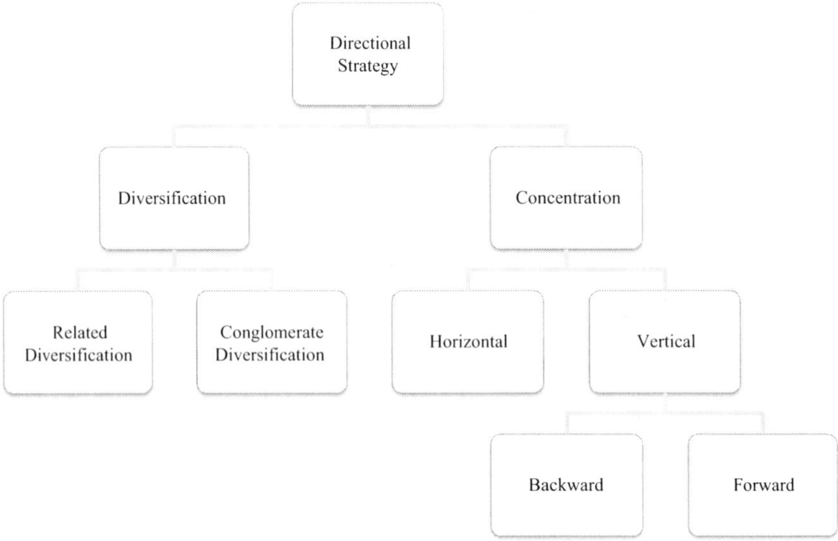

Figure 3.3 Modes of diversification and concentration strategies.

had been previously done by the firm's suppliers. Vertical forward integration implies that the firm expands its activities towards distribution on its individual value added chain to become closer to its customers, e.g. Amazon opens its own retail sales shops (Wheelen and Hunger, 2010; Mahoney, 1992). Vertical integration leads to a higher degree of continuity and efficiency in the relationship between research and development activities and operations and improved security from losing internal knowledge assets to outsiders. Vertical integration allows firm specific experience and economies of scale to be accumulated over repeated projects (Pisano, 1991).

In recent decades, due to emerging digitalization of business, vertical forward integration strategies have become multifaceted. As illustrated in Figure 3.4, the firm may use a multi-channel distribution concept, which consists of conventional sales (physical distribution via the wholesaler retailers) and e-commerce sales channels. In the case of e-commerce, the firm launches a webpage where the customer orders the product and service (vertical forward integration). The delivery from the firm's warehouse to the customer's destination is usually organized by a logistics firm (e.g. DHL, UPS, and others).

To conclude, concentration strategies make sense if the management is convinced that the firm's current business activities are well positioned in the right industry where the firm can make its 'core competencies alive.' However, the management must balance the advantages and disadvantages of concentration strategies. The major advantages include better quality monitoring mechanisms, direct access to the customers' wishes and expectations, and less dependency from suppliers that help to secure delivery punctuality. Concentration strategies aim to develop industry-specific expertise through involvement in a broad range of value added activities that serve as a market entry barrier for potential competitors. The challenges of vertical integration strategies

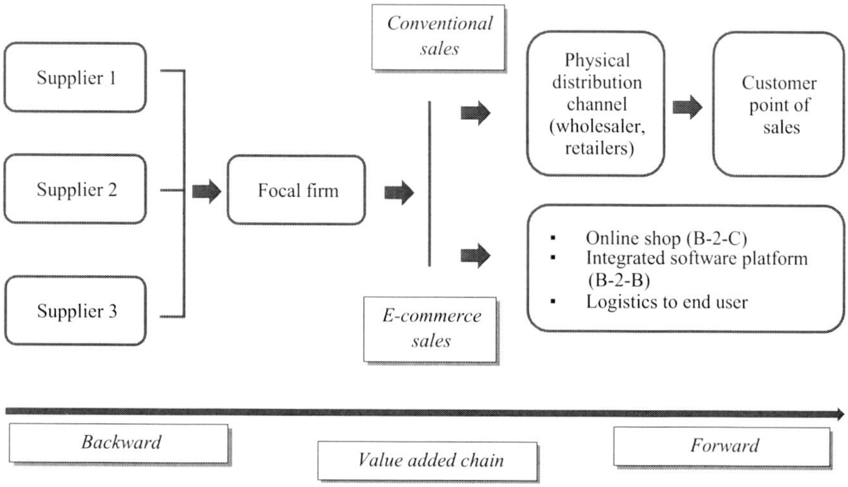

Figure 3.4 Value added chain: conventional and e-commerce forward integration.

Table 3.1 Advantages and disadvantages of concentration strategies

Advantages	*Disadvantages*
• Better quality control mechanisms of the value added chain • Knowledge is not lost to outsiders • Less supplier dependency (backward integration) • Better prerequisites for experience curve • Direct customer contact (forward integration) • Development of industry-specific core competencies and expertise	• Increases in operational capacities and fixed costs • Higher organizational and communication complexity • Less managerial flexibility • Higher industry dependency • 'Becoming blind' in terms of industry innovations outside the firm

evolve due to higher operational capacities, increased communication and information necessities, higher industry dependency that results in less managerial flexibility, and other factors. An overview of the advantages and disadvantages of concentration strategies is presented in Table 3.1.

Diversification strategies are launched when the management realizes from its environmental analysis that the firm has less attractive markets, which indicate low or even negative growth rates. To overcome the threat of industry stagnation, the firm, from the perspective of its current value added activities, expands in the direction of more promising industries. Diversification strategies are segmented between related diversification and non-related (conglomerate) diversification strategies (Figure 3.3). Related diversification strategy means that the firm launches operations that are familiar to its current value added activities (for example, a smartphone assembler starts operations and sales of tablets). In the case of conglomerate diversification, the firm becomes involved

Table 3.2 Advantages and disadvantages of diversification strategies

Advantages	*Disadvantages*
• Access to attractive markets • Serving different markets reduces the business risk • Sales balance of market specific seasonal effects (e.g. winter ski and summer surfboard) • Presence in different markets increases brand awareness among customers • Transfer of valuable brand to different markets	• Increase in fixed costs • Higher organizational complexity • Overestimation of market potentials • Increased communication efforts • Unfamiliar value added activities may cause difficulties, e.g. quality, innovation, and service • Risk of losing core competencies

in businesses that are non-related to its current value added activities. For example, a web-based company such as Google becomes involved in the automotive business assembling autonomous driving cars. In general, the risk momentum of conglomerate diversification strategies is higher than the related diversification strategies because of the firm's increased unfamiliarity in the new business field. The management needs to carefully balance the advantages and threats related to the firm's business diversification. The important advantages of diversification include, for example, the opportunity to move to more promising markets and the reduced business risk. The main drawbacks of diversification strategies are increased fix costs, higher organizational complexity, increased communication efforts, and a potential risk of overestimating market potentials of the new but non-familiar businesses (Müller-Stewens and Lechner, 2011; Wheelen and Hunger, 2010). A list of advantages and disadvantages of diversification strategies is provided in Table 3.2.

In general, whether the management aims to implement a growth strategy through concentration strategy or diversification strategy, there is always the question concerning whether the firm internally holds the necessary resources. For example, when expanding the business in non-familiar new industries using conglomerate diversification, usually new technological and market knowledge is required (Raduan et al., 2009). Suppose the management concludes that business expansion is possible by using internal firm resource assets. The firm's growth is realized, for example, by expanding the existing operational capacities (e.g. the new warehouse), and increasing firm asset efficiency (e.g. more efficient procurement, reorganization of value added activities). Another alternative of expanding using internally available firm resources is to build up and develop entirely new operational capacities, e.g. constructing new branches and plants (Penrose, 1995; Penrose, 1959).

As shown in Figure 3.5 in case the management concludes from its micro analysis that the firm does not hold the necessary internal resources for realizing its growth strategy, the management implements a second alternative, namely, expanding through external resource paths. Growth through external resource paths, for example, is implemented through equity participation of another firm, which holds the desired resources, e.g. technological or market expertise. Additional alternatives for external growth are national or international joint ventures and strategic alliances, mergers, and acquisitions.

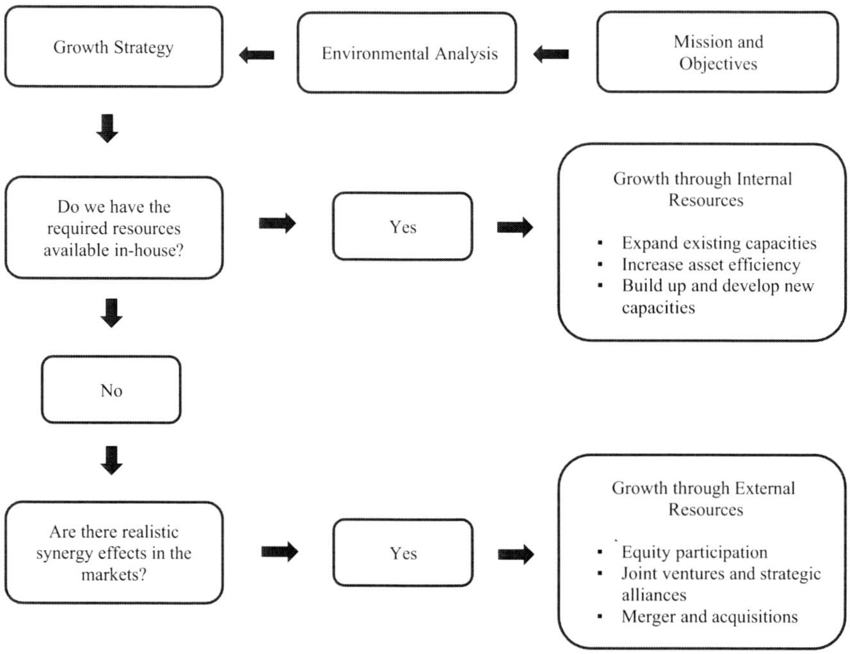

Figure 3.5 Growth through internal resource allocation or external resources (synergy effects seeking).

(International) joint ventures are defined based on two major characteristics:

- a joint venture indicates a third legally independent firm established by two or more firms, named joint venture parents (first differentiating factor compared to a strategic alliance)
- joint ventures become international joint ventures in the case of cross-border relationships of the joint venture stakeholders (e.g. different country origins of the joint venture parents, joint venture firm operations established in a third country from the perspective of the joint venture parent headquarters)
- legally independent means the joint venture firm takes over full liability for its contractual relationships with other firms, such as suppliers, customers, and service providers in terms of product performance, quality, safety, and environmental standards, delivery punctuality, etc.
- equity engagements (financial investment) is always a fundamental prerequisite for each joint venture parent firm (second differentiating factor compared to a strategic alliance)
- the equity ratio of each partner of total joint venture assets results in minority (less than fifty percent), equal (fifty-fifty), or majority (more than fifty percent) joint venture configuration
- the equity ratio influences the partner's management decision power and the share of earning as well as the financial and operational risk

There are various motives regarding why firms establish international joint ventures, such as,

- There are country cases, where market entry indicates a higher probability of being successful when cooperating with a local partner due to legal or socio-cultural requirements.
- For example, Japan is known for their close industry network configurations exclusively developed between Japanese firms. These 'inner-Japanese networks' serve as a considerable (non-tariff) market entry barrier for foreign firms. Cooperating in a joint venture with a Japanese partner helps to overcome these market entry barriers in Japan.
- Particularly in industries that indicate rather short-term technology and product life cycles, such as in consumer electronics, information technology as well as telecommunication equipment industries, the establishment of an international joint venture makes sense to share the partner's research and development efforts intended to expedite their market response times in terms of newly developed products and services (Ren et al., 2009; Hennart and Reddy, 1997).

However, international joint ventures belong to the most challenging market entry modes and the failure rate is relatively high (Larimo, 2007). The major reasons for the high failure rate are as follows:

- a wrong partner selection increases the risk of opportunistic behavior (e.g. one joint venture partner hides important information or does not contribute necessary resource commitments to the joint venture operations);
- in some cases, when the management realizes that a certain product or business generates losses, the business is transferred to an newly established joint venture—hoping that synergy effects developed with the partner will enable the recovery of the operating business;
- transferring operations to a joint venture is perceived more positively among the firm's stakeholders than communicating that a shutdown of operations is necessary due to poorly performing business;
- the involved joint venture partner firms concealed their own resource weaknesses to negotiate a maximum share and corresponding decision power in the newly established joint venture firm;
- diversified management styles due to differing cultural backgrounds (e.g. short-term versus long-term perspective in terms of realizing business objectives);
- different work ethics and communication styles (e.g. direct versus indirect communication); and
- attempt to renegotiate joint venture business aims and hierarchical structures after the joint venture establishment (Li et al., 2008; Park and Harris, 2014).

Foreign direct investment (FDI) serves as an alternative method to realize a firm's international growth strategy. FDI indicates long-lasting interests of the firm in the foreign target markets and represents the highest form of hierarchical control of the firm's foreign operations. Successful market entry through FDI requires considerable financial resource buffer because this form of market entry is time consuming and come along with the relatively high financial risks (López-Duarte and Vidal-Suárez, 2010). Furthermore, when the management considers market entry through FDI, foreign business experience is of vital importance. FDI can be realized through the use of internal firm resources, if available, for example, the establishment of new operational capacities, expanding existing capacities, or the increase of asset efficiency. Alternatively, the firm's growth strategy can be implemented through external resource paths, such as equity participation at another firm, or acquisition and mergers. Acquisitions that are not desired but not avoidable from the perspective of the acquired firm are named 'hostile takeovers' (Wheelen and Hunger, 2010). Through acquisitions the firm gains fast access to valuable resources outside the organization, such as regional market knowledge or technological expertise directly acquired from the target firm. Multinational enterprises (MNEs) own and hierarchically control value added activities in more than one country, which were often gained through acquisitions (Dunning and Lundan, 2008). The company's growths through acquisitions require not only strong financial but also organizational resources.

In the case of a merger involving two firms, usually of similar size, joining their assets, a new organization is established. The new organization's name usually is a combination of the previously separated firm names, for example, 'Dow Chemical' and 'Du Pont' merged and became 'DowDuPont' (De la Merced and Picker, 2015).

Dow Chemical and DuPont Set Merger and Plans to Split

Dec. 11, 2015

Over the last week, around a hundred people crammed into a law firm's offices high in the General Motors Building on Fifth Avenue, drafting plans to merge Dow Chemical and DuPont.

Yet, all the work of those bankers and lawyers aimed at combining two industrial titans, with a shared history of more than three centuries, will ultimately go towards a larger goal: breaking up the newly united chemical company.

As Dow and DuPont formally announced their merger, the two companies made clear that they intend to separate into three companies, a path expected to be littered with complex deals, thousands of job cuts, and months of government scrutiny. What the two devised is what they describe as a merger of equals, putting together DuPont, the 213-year-old inventor of Kevlar, with Dow, the 118-year-old maker of plastics and chemicals. The shareholders of each company are expected to own half of the newly combined business—to be called DowDuPont—while the combined corporation will maintain headquarters in both Wilmington, Delaware, and Midland, Michigan. In all, the companies plan to strip away more than $3 billion in costs from the deal and say there are potential growth synergies of 1 billion US dollars.

Under the terms of the merger, the Dow shareholders would receive one share of the new combined company for each of their shares, while the DuPont shareholders would receive 1.282 shares for each. Under the merger's exchange ratio, the DuPont shareholders would receive 68.43 US dollars a share, based on Friday's closing stock price, or a total of roughly 60 billion US dollars. The companies said the new company would have a combined market capitalization of 130 billion US dollars.

Source: De la Merced and Picker (2015).

The main motives for mergers are, for example, first, the desired access to rare and valuable resources, such as technological knowledge, market expertise, access to client data, and distribution channels of the target firm doing business in related and non-related industries (Qui and Wang, 2011). Second, there are business performance motives of the management, such as the increase of turnover and profitability, which results in higher cash flows and increased shareholder value (Napier, 1989). Third, there are potentials to realize monopoly-advantages through greater market dominance of the merged firms compared to when the firms continue to operate separately. Finally, there is the 'ego' of the management because managing a large multinational firm usually is interpreted as a symbol of being successful (Halpern, 1983).

Growth strategies through external paths, such as acquisitions, are usually linked with the term 'synergy effects.' When targeting synergy effects, the management hopes that their own resources, when combined with the external firm's resources, will result in disproportionately positive effects. However, synergies are often overestimated or even non-realistic (Charterina and Landeta, 2013).

While the value of all global merger and acquisitions amounted to 4.5 trillion US dollars in 2015, more than a half of them fail, meaning that the expected synergy effects in terms of costs, profitability, and market power have not been realized (IMAA Institute, 2015; Rottig et al., 2014). The reasons for the high merger and acquisition failure rate are, for example, instead of analyzing in depth the actors' resource strengths and weaknesses, which is naturally time consuming, pre-merger activities are often done too hastily. Either there is pressure from the shareholders to finalize the process (because one partner accumulates losses the more time goes by), or there is another candidate, usually a competitor, which is willing to bid or increase its previous offer. The diversified national and organizational culture backgrounds, which, for example, have an impact on differentiating time horizons of when profits should be realized, or contrasting quality consciousness and work ethics, serve as additional reasons for failed mergers and acquisitions (Qui and Wang, 2011; Ulijn et al., 2010).

Competitive strategies

Whereas the directional strategies involve decisions about the organization as a whole, the competitive strategies are related to particular business fields. Larger firms, such as MNEs, usually organize implementing competitive strategies in the firm's strategic business units (SBUs). An SBU is a part of the organization for which there are distinct markets for its products and services that more or less differ from another SBU of the firm. In larger firms, the middle management usually is responsible for keeping competitive strategies alive. Competitive strategies are linked with the main question regarding how to compete successfully in distinct markets (Johnson et al., 2009).

In general, among the portfolio of competitive strategies, we distinguish between differentiation strategies, cost leadership strategies, and niche strategy with differentiation focus, and niche strategy with cost leadership focus (Porter, 1980; Newbert, 2008).

Differentiation strategy means that the management targets to distinguish the firm from its competitors as being unique in the entire industry and its corresponding markets. The firm holds an exceptional positioning and, thus, receives customer loyalty, for example, through highly innovative products, large product portfolio, flexible order handling, reasonable transportation lead times, on-time delivery, outstanding quality, attractive design, prompt and non-bureaucratic after sales service, and others (Porter, 1999).

In comparison to differentiation, when implementing a cost leadership strategy, the firm aims to be one of the most efficient actors in the overall industries. Efficiency is, for example, achieved through economies of scale effects, access to raw material resources that others do not have, and learning and experiencing curve effects. Cost leadership does not mean to simply be the 'cheapest' in terms of its market prices offered. The firm's profitability is reached through large-scale operations of rather standardized products and services. These products and services are usually positioned at the growth or maturity stage of its product life cycle but never at the introductory stage (Vernon, 1966). When learning from the mistakes of others who have launched the market earlier, the cost leadership approaching firm is better able to manage its profitability even with lower unit prices. In other words, cost leadership implementing firms make use of the latecomer's advantages (Mathews, 2006; Christmann, 2000).

Small- and medium-sized enterprises, which naturally cannot make use of large resource endowments, may decide to combine differentiation and cost leadership in a niche market. When the firm implements a niche strategy with cost leadership focus, the firm makes use of the experience curve and scale production but, of course, should not forget the major characteristics of differentiation strategies, such as services. In comparison, when the small- and medium-sized enterprise implements a differentiation strategy, for example, innovation and services are vital to the firm's cost-efficient operations, which constitute a major characteristic of cost leadership. From here the criticism of Porter's generic strategies are deduced because it is not clear where exactly the 'borderline' between elements of cost leadership and differentiation is drawn. As a result, the categorization of differentiation and cost leadership and focus strategy initially appear to be logical; however, measurement and quantification of distinguishing variables that make up each generic strategy are difficult to generalize. In other words, the questions are left unanswered regarding 'how much differentiation characteristics,' for example, in terms of service is necessary for a cost leadership firm and, vice versa, how efficient should a differentiator be in terms of economies of scale (Gebauer and Kowalkowski, 2012; Porter, 1980)?

Functional strategies

At the functional (department) level, the organization's value creation activities actually take place, consistent with the business objectives and strategies decided and cascaded from the directional (corporate) and business levels. There is a strategic linkage between the corporate level, business level, and functional level strategies; however, their harmonization and implementation lack coherence and consistency in many firms (Daniel, 2015).

Procurement

Naturally, the procurement department, as a part of the firm's value chain, is closely connected to sales, operations, warehousing, and logistics functions. Global procurement integrates and coordinates sourcing requirements across worldwide business units of the firm applying unified processes, technologies, and sourcing standards and procedures (Trent and Monczka, 2003). Considering CSR and shared value concepts, sustainable sourcing has gained importance and hopefully is being taken seriously by more firms.

On the one hand, sustainable procurement policies create trust among the major stakeholders of the firm's societal networks and, as a result, contribute to a positive firm reputation. On the other hand, sustainable sourcing is not costless, among others, because it requires a corresponding mindset among the management and employees. Second, sustainable sourcing, which includes not only ecology standards but also ethical and moral criteria, assumes a well-developed and transparent supplier selection criteria, which is usually set in a code of conduct (CoC). The more globally spread the firm's procurement activities, the more complex is the process of setting CoC criteria and monitoring them (Goebal et al., 2012). Developing reliable CoC standards requires trustful and long-term oriented relationships, which include the exchange of technological, legal, and market knowledge between the firm and its suppliers (Chen and Paulraj, 2004).

Green Public Procurement (GPP) of the European Union is defined as procurement for a better environment as a process whereby public authorities seek to procure goods, services, and works with a reduced environmental impact throughout their life cycle compared to goods, services, and works with the same primary function that would otherwise be procured.

GPP is a voluntary instrument, which means that EU member states and public authorities can determine the extent to which they implement it. Public authorities are major consumers in Europe: They spend approximately Euro 1.8 trillion annually, representing around 14 percent of the EU's gross domestic product. By using their purchasing power to choose goods and services with lower impacts on the environment, they can make an important contribution to sustainable consumption and production.

Green purchasing is also about influencing the market. By promoting and using GPP, public authorities can provide industries with real incentives for developing green technologies and products. In some sectors, public purchasers command a significant share of the market (e.g. public transport and construction, health services, and education) and so their decisions have considerable impact.

Source: European Union (2016).

Procurement strategies on the functional level are distinguished between single sourcing, parallel sourcing, and multiple sourcing strategies. As the term indicates, in the case of single sourcing, the firm relies on one supplying company only. The major advantage of single sourcing comes along with higher bargaining power because large procurement volumes of the product are placed at one supplier, which, as a result, is probably more flexible when negotiating the prices. Single sourcing makes the firm heavily dependent on the selected supplier only. If the supplier is not willing (e.g. less order changing flexibility) or not capable (e.g. quality problems with regard to their own production), the impact on their own firm is severe, and may cause, in a worst-case scenario, a temporary stop of the 'production line' (Azambuja, 2014).

To reduce the supplier's dependency, the firm may implement a parallel sourcing strategy. The major part of the procurement volume (for example, around 70 percent) of the product is given to one 'preferred supplier' and the 'second supplier' takes over the remaining 30 percent. In the case of multiple sourcing strategies, the procurement volume for the product is divided between more than two suppliers. In this case, the dependency from the supplier is reduced as well as the firm's bargaining power. Multiple sourcing makes sense only for larger firms, such as multinational enterprises, because of their size and diversified value-added and, procurement, and supply chains (Song et al., 2012).

When implementing a multiple sourcing strategy, the firm may rely on one preferred supplier where, for example, 40 percent of the product's order volume is placed. The second supplier and, depending on the strategic importance of the product, a third supplier and fourth supplier are contracted 'for safety reasons.' These three suppliers make sure that the remaining procurement volume is delivered (for example, 20 percent each firm). However, the bargaining power of the firm is reduced because the procurement volume is divided between the preferred major supplier and the remaining supplying firms. In general, the more sophisticated and differentiated the product, the more challenging it is for the firm to find the proper supplying sources. Particularly, innovative firms, which bring their products at early stages of the product's life cycles into the markets, are usually confronted with difficulties to find similar supplying firms in terms of innovative capabilities. Therefore, the development of long-term relationships based on mutual trust and commitment provide better prerequisites for stable supply chains in terms of delivery timing and product quality than a policy of frequent new contracting and early terminating of the firm's supplier (Yeniyurt et al., 2013).

Human resource

The main responsibilities of the firm's human resource department are related to the timely disposal of suitable and qualified personnel, their continued qualification and training according to permanently changing environmental necessities. If necessary, the release of employees according to legal and societal-ethical standards indicates another obligation that requires psychological sensitive behavioral skills as well as solid legal knowledge. The more internationalized the firm, the higher the complexity in terms of cultural, societal, and legal environments where the firm, and consequently, its human resource department operate.

In accordance with the firm's overall strategic objectives, missions, and aims, the human resource department develops management by objectives standards and contractual agreements. There is a tendency that firms targeting economies of scale and economies of scope effects rather prioritize their management by objective targets on cost savings and operational efficiency. Creative, innovative, and technology-driven firms, often located in modern services industries, tend to focus their management by objective targets on the remuneration of ideas and innovative product and services solutions.

Modern human resource management necessarily includes gender aspects in terms of equal career opportunities of the firm's female and male employees, handicapped people, and minorities. The ongoing ageing population in most of the Western societies also requires the necessity to provide reasonable working conditions for elderly employees that contribute huge experience stock to the company.

The necessity of implementing a 'learning organization culture' in times of ever faster changing technology and product life cycles in a 'digitalized world' leads to increased challenges for the firm's employees, and as a result, for the firm's human resource department's daily work. The employee selection process becomes more multifaceted and includes, in addition to the evaluation of purely job-related qualifications, the assessment of whether the selected person is ready to become accustomed to the daily pressures and challenges. Job dissatisfaction naturally leads to higher employee fluctuations—which is costly—because in-house training and qualification programs go away as the person quits its job and starts working at another (competitor) company. All in all, searching and finding qualified personal at reasonable costs serves as the biggest challenge for the human resource departments due to the fact that the requirements for the employee's overall education is steadily increasing in times of globally and interconnected industries and services.

Finance and controlling

The finance and controlling department is responsible for the firm's internal and external liquidity flows, cost calculations and cost monitoring, revenues and cash, equity and debt management as well as tax payments. On the one hand, a conservative financial strategy makes independent from external donors, thus leads to a reasonable level of borrowing costs. On the other hand, when interest rates in the markets are lower than the expected margins realized through the expansion of operational capacities in the course of a growth strategy, it makes sense to increase the firm's debt up to a certain level. Monitoring the debt to equity ratio, in a most professional manner, belongs to another important responsibility of the finance and controlling department. In the case of exports, monitoring the payment security instruments, such as letters of credits, export insurances, and so on, is secured by the finance and controlling department, usually in close cooperation with the marketing and sales (export) department.

Functional strategies of the finance and controlling department follow the firm's strategy building on corporate and competitive levels. For example, manufacturing firms seeking to realize economies of scale effects in saturated markets pay particular attention to the lowest unit costs but most possible standardization and efficiency. In comparison, for example, firms with outstanding customer service concentrate their financial efforts on customer relations management concepts aiming to seek the most possible customer satisfaction, which, in return, provides higher margins and thus contribute to the overall financial performance of the firm.

Supply chain finance (SCF) is defined as the inter-organizational optimization of financing as well as the integration of financing processes with customers, suppliers, and service providers to increase the value not only of the own but all participating stakeholders (Pfohl and Gomm, 2009). SCF is an approach within the supply chain aiming to jointly create value through means of planning, steering, and controlling the flow of financial resources on an inter-organizational level. SCF, when implemented by the relevant actors without seeking opportunistic interests, promotes the stability and smooth capital flows within the entire supply chains (Lan and Hua, 2013). As a result, it improves the involved organizations' ability to put financial resources to their most productive use (Pezza, 2011).

The financial flows within a collaboration of supply chain actors are determined by strategic decisions about the payment conditions that require tracking and controlling of payments as an essential part of supply chain collaboration's day-to-day business. In collaborative financial supply chains, the constant tracing of cash flow figures and visibility are crucial (Hofmann, 2005).

Research and development

On the functional level, research and development either targets a technological leadership or technological followership strategy. As the term indicates, technological leadership strategy means that the firm targets to develop and launch earlier than its competitors innovative and state-of-the-art products. Particularly for service and technology leaders, close interaction between research and development (R&D) and the marketing department is of vital importance to determine emerging customers' requirements in order to develop state-of-the-art products for the markets (Dutta et al., 1999). Inaccurate anticipation of the customers' needs usually cause failed product and service innovations (Ram and Sheth, 1989).

Especially at the beginning of the product life cycle, the product itself may indicate some weaknesses in terms of performance or durability. Supplier selection is not easy at this stage because the more innovative the product, the more challenging it is to find appropriate suppliers at reasonable prices. Therefore, research and development efforts for innovative products positioned at the beginning of their life cycles usually focus on improving the products and service performance as the firms receive the customers' feedback from its marketing department.

In comparison, technological followership aims to learn from the mistakes of the (innovative) others (latecomer's advantages). Technological followership makes sense for products that are positioned at mature stages of the product life cycle (Mathews, 2002; Mathews, 2006). Research and development efforts concentrate on the products' and services' standardization aimed at increasing operational efficiency. Total quality management systems, Kanban, Kaizen and lean management systems, which aim to prioritize important sources for process improvement by minimizing resource wasting, are usually monitored by the research and development that closely cooperates with the firm's operations department on the firm's functional level (Ciliberti et al., 2008; Hung et al., 2011).

The more the product advances on its individual product life cycle, the higher the competitive power and corresponding price pressure. Therefore, cost-saving efforts through research and development proposals move into the center of the management's interest. The firm's research and development department is closely connected to the firm's purchasing, operations, and marketing and sales, logistics, and after sales services to secure the firm's sustained competitive positioning and its markets.

Operations

As the complexity of globally integrated value added activities has increased, varieties of operational strategies on the functional level have amplified accordingly. First, operational strategies are segmented between 'individual order,' serial production, and mass and production (Wheelen and Hunger, 2010). In the case of individual order strategy, each product and service are individually tailored based on the customer's request and are therefore unique. The more differentiated and individual the customer's expectations and wishes, the more recommendable it is for the firm to implement an individual order strategy. For example, the architecture, construction planning, and building of a house are always based on an individual customer order. However, in the case of an individual order strategy, standardization advantages are almost zero and finding an 'average market price' is more than difficult. Individual order strategies indicate an extraordinarily high dependency between seller and buyer and, therefore, increase the risk of opportunistic behavior (Das and Rahman, 2010; Williamson, 1975). On the one hand, high dependency is due to the fact that the product is made based on a customer's tailored specification and is therefore difficult to sell on the market by the firm in case the buyer finally rejects the product as agreed in the contract. On the other hand, the buyer is in difficulties because of rare or even non-existing alternatives when the seller rejects fulfilling its contract obligation, such as delaying the delivery or renegotiating the price (Hill, 1990).

Standardization advantages are realized when implementing a serial production strategy. A 'series' indicates a number of products with similar product features, for example, in terms of their technical performance, design, energy consumption, and so on. In other words, serial production allows a certain degree of product modifications within standardized but different 'series.' The maximum degree of standardization is reached when implementing a mass production strategy. Mass production strategy leads to maximized economies of scale effects through large and standardized outputs. While the unit cost efficiency is high, individual customer preferences are considered at least to a certain degree (Tan and Sousa, 2013).

Recently, the term 'mass customization' has emerged to describe a hybrid between product differentiation and mass standardization (Slamanig, 2011). In the case of mass customization, the basic structure (e.g. product components, device, and model chassis) of the product is always the same (modular product concept). As a result, the firm's value added activities aim to be efficient as possible due to large output volumes. In the second step, based on the customer order, some selected product features are added that make the product itself up to a certain degree differentiated and individual for the customer (Piller, 2005). For example, in the automotive industry, different car models are based on the same card chassis platform, such as the car chassis of Mercedes-Benz C-Class, which is the same as the Mercedes-Benz GLC-Class (Matzler et al., 2011).

International offshoring describes the partial or complete shift of operations (e.g. research and development, product assembly, and service operations) to company owned facilities abroad. Offshoring is realized through greenfield investments (e.g. building entirely new plants in the foreign target country) or through acquisitions of competitors' assets as a part of the firm's FDI strategy. The major reasons for offshoring are access to valuable resources abroad (e.g. qualified employees) that are attractive markets (e.g. in terms of market volume and growth rates). Offshoring does not necessarily presume that the firm's value added activities are terminated at home.

In the case of backshoring (reverse offshoring), the firm reduces or terminates its value added activities abroad and relocates them back to its home base. The reasons for backshoring are, for example, quality, efficiency, and cost issues that make the foreign activities less attractive relative to the firm's home base. In contrast to offshoring, in the case of international outsourcing, the firm shifts its value added activities to another contracted firm abroad. Generally, outsourcing is described as the procurement of value added activities from independent suppliers, in contrast to internal sourcing (within a firm) (Bertrand and Mol, 2013). Outsourcing is the process of employing an external provider to perform functions that could be performed in-house (Potkány, 2008). Operations at the home base are usually terminated.

Outsourcing consists of various benefits, such as (Caruth et al., 2012):

- Reduction of operational costs as the contracted firm abroad may perform the specific activities more efficiently and faster;
- Savings of management time and involvement that allow the company to focus on core competencies;

- Professional expertise of the contracted firm, enabling the company to perform tasks more effectively;
- Savings of logistics costs by directly serving the target markets from the facilities of the contracted firm; and
- Increase of order management flexibility and transportation lead time.

However, there some disadvantages related to outsourcing, such as:

- Decreased morale of employees at home who may ask: 'What will be the next step?' as a consequence of outsourcing;
- Poor product and service quality;
- Cultural and communicational misfit between the outsourcing firm and the contracted company abroad;
- Increase in communication complexity;
- Perceived loss of operational control leading to limited access of updated information concerning technological advances in operations, new or better supplier sources, market development, and others;
- Risk that the contracted firm abroad 'through learning' might become a severe competitor in the future; and
- The outsourcing firm's reputation harmed by different corporate social responsibility standards at the contracted firm (Garaventa and Tellefsen, 2001; Caruth et al., 2012).

In the case of international contract manufacturing, the firm (named original equipment manufacturer—OEM) expands its product and service output through another contracted firm located in a foreign target country. Contract manufacturing, in contrast to outsourcing, does not mean that the firm's value added activities at its home base are necessarily shut down (Chopra and Meindl, 2014). The firm continues its operation at home while expanding its output through plant facilities of the contracted firm in the foreign target market. Transportation lead time and logistics costs are reduced when the customers located in the foreign target market are delivered directly from the facilities of the contracted firm. Of course, there is the alternative that the products manufactured at the contracted firm abroad (which, for example, makes use of attractive manufacturing costs) are delivered and sold on the OEM's domestic markets.

Logistics

In the past, logistics simply described the timely and safe physical movement of goods between seller and buyer. In these days, logistics gained much more attendance since it has a vital impact on the firm's business performance to achieve sustained competitive advantages (Christopher, 2011; McKinnon, 2015). Modern logistics management takes an entire supply chain perspective and includes updated planning and on-time transportation that seeks to optimize the flow of materials, components, and services (Coyle et al., 2012; Waters and Rinsler, 2014). Logistics also includes activities such as packaging, materials handling, inventory forecasting, and the management of return goods from the customers. In a broader scope, logistics activities indicate types of services that provide customers with benefits in terms of time, place, possession utilities, and finally, costs (Coyle et al., 2012; Waters and Rinsler, 2014). Primary logistics describes inbound transportation activities from the suppliers, efficient warehousing, inventory management, and timely order processing. Secondary logistic activities target the transportation from the firm's warehouse facilities to its customers, and, if necessary, back to the firm's facilities, for example, in case of quality complaints raised by the customers (Waters and Rinsler, 2014).

Logistics has become an integrated process of strategically managing the procurement, in-house movement and storage of materials, semi-finished products, and finished inventory. Modern logistics focuses on physical organization of after sales services and ecologically friendly recycling conducted in such a way that the firm's reputation is positively spread in the markets and current and future profitability of the firm is secured (Christopher, 2011).

The increase of internationally shared value added activities and the necessity to exchange materials and products between different locations have resulted in the emergence of more complex cross-border business activities, which has amplified the meaning of logistics towards 'value chain management' (Baldwin and Lopez-Gonzalez, 2015). A value chain is defined as the full range of activities that firms conduct to transfer a product from its design and conception to its end use and beyond (Backer and Miroudot, 2013). The value chain is considered as 'global' when the activities are carried out by the firm within international industry networks. Relative to 'chain,' the term 'networks' considers the complexity of the interactions among global stakeholders, such as suppliers, logistics firms, policy decision-makers, marketing staff, and customers (Cattaneo et al., 2013).

One of the main rationales behind the firm's engagement in global value chains is the opportunity to identify and take advantage of most competitive supply sources of necessary operations inputs, which for example are not domestically available or at higher costs and thus reduce the competitiveness of the local firms. As a consequence, global competition is increasingly vertically, and particularly in oligopolistic industries, firms often supply components and services among each other while, at the same time, they are competitors (Cattaneo et al., 2013). It is increasingly more difficult for even purely domestic market-oriented companies to avoid taking part in or competing with global value chains, as they are highly likely, for example, to face the competition of imported goods and services, which have been created somewhere in the world. Nevertheless, the high degree of inter-connectedness between actors of the global value chain networks increases the risk that results from a certain negative outcome, such as natural events, political instabilities, or economic crisis at a certain location of the value chain, which significantly could have an impact on the rest of the industry network (Gereffi and Luo, 2015).

Marketing and sales

Due to its incremental importance throughout the entire value-adding process, marketing is now understood as a market-oriented business concept rather than a pure sales or advertisement function (Backhaus, 2003). Consequently, 'market orientation' and 'marketing orientation' should be understood as connected but yet distinguishable concepts. While the latter is restricted to actions of the marketing department, meeting customer needs should be perceived as the responsibility of all firm functions. As a result, the term 'marketing orientation' would overemphasize the role of the marketing department within a market-driven business culture and simultaneously degrade the potential of other firm units to create value for the customer (Kohli and Jaworski, 1990; Glowik and Bruhs, 2014). Market orientation indicates a customer-focused business culture that utilizes and effectively integrates all the given firm resources that are deployed in various business functions with the ongoing objective of satisfying customer needs and creating superior value by building customer relationships. The coordinated integration of different departmental resources is guided by the information gained from relevant market stakeholders (e.g. suppliers, customers, and competitors) analysis about existing market requirements (Slater and Narver, 1994). Efficient coordination across the various businesses requires open and cross-functional communication between marketing and sales, procurement, research and development, operations, and other firm functions (Glowik and Bruhs, 2014).

The marketing and sales department has a substantial influence on the product and services pricing, communication policy, and market timing of its products and services.

Pricing

High-technology products (e.g. advanced smartphones) can serve as a status and lifestyle symbol. Innovative customers, also named early adopters of new technologies, are willing to pay a higher price than market average prices for these products (Dey et al., 2016; Rogers, 2003). The suitable price strategy is 'skimming' where the firm launches the markets with relatively high prices targeting market segments characterized by state-of-the-art technology-seeking customers. The firm's marketing department assures that the value of the product and service innovation are communicated properly and sufficiently through their distribution channels addressing relevant stakeholders (e.g. customers, environmental protection organizations). In the course of the product life cycle, the firms incrementally reduces the price of the product and starts to address the early and late majority customers, and finally the laggards (Rogers, 2003).

In contrast to skimming, the firm decides to launch a penetration price strategy when it targets to enter its markets with rather large sales volumes. The product is usually positioned at later stages of its product life cycle (e.g. mature stage) and the firm utilizes the experience curve and economies of scale effects. As a result, the market is penetrated by the firm with rather lower prices aiming to sell maximum quantities (Smith, 2008).

Communication

In terms of the firm's communication strategy on the functional level, the marketing department can choose between pull and push strategy. A product-related communication implemented through a pull strategy means that the firm raises attention aiming to create a desire to buy the product and service among the target customers. Instead of focusing on the price, innovative or modern lifestyle product features, for example, are communicated by the firm. A pull strategy is recommendable when launching new products on the markets that are positioned at the beginning of its product and technology life cycle. In contrast, a push strategy is recommended for highly standardized products that are positioned at later stages of their product life cycle. Marketing communication rather focuses on attractive price and payment conditions, thus targeting to push larger quantities through the distribution channels that help to accelerate the economies of scale effects (Wheelen and Hunger, 2010).

Market timing

Related to the market entry timing, the marketing department chooses between shower strategy and waterfall strategy. In the case of waterfall strategy, the firm incrementally launches its markets. The waterfall strategy indicates strong similarities to the conventional internationalization concept named Uppsala, which claims that the firm accumulates knowledge through a stepwise market entry. As illustrated in Figure 3.6 taking the example of a firm located in Germany, neighboring countries, because of their regional closeness (lower transportation costs) and less perceived cultural and language differences in comparison to the firm's home market, should be entered first (Kotler et al., 2009; Johanson and Vahlne, 2009).

The waterfall strategy is recommended when the firm has less international experience and its target markets differ considerably in terms of customer expectations, such as product performance, design, and service configurations. In addition, management mistakes in one market are avoided in other markets due to the firm's learning curve, better market knowledge, and increased international sales experience.

However, in light of globalized value added and trade pattern and short product and technology life cycles, the most severe drawback of the waterfall strategy comes along with the stepwise and, therefore, delayed regional market entry. In this case, the firm's competitors, for example, serve the target markets faster and, therefore, take the market share. There is a risk that the product life cycle reaches its decline stage before the firm has entered all possible target markets (Vernon, 1972).

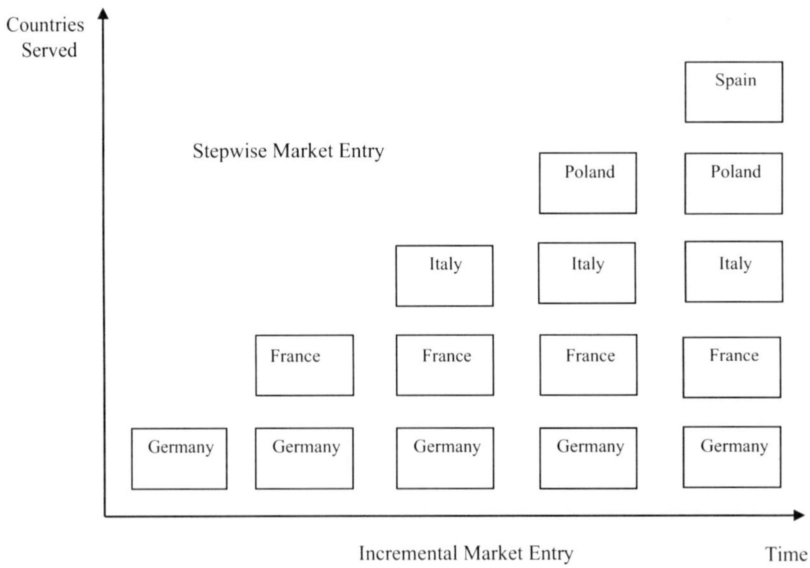

Figure 3.6 Incremental market entry when waterfall strategy is applied.

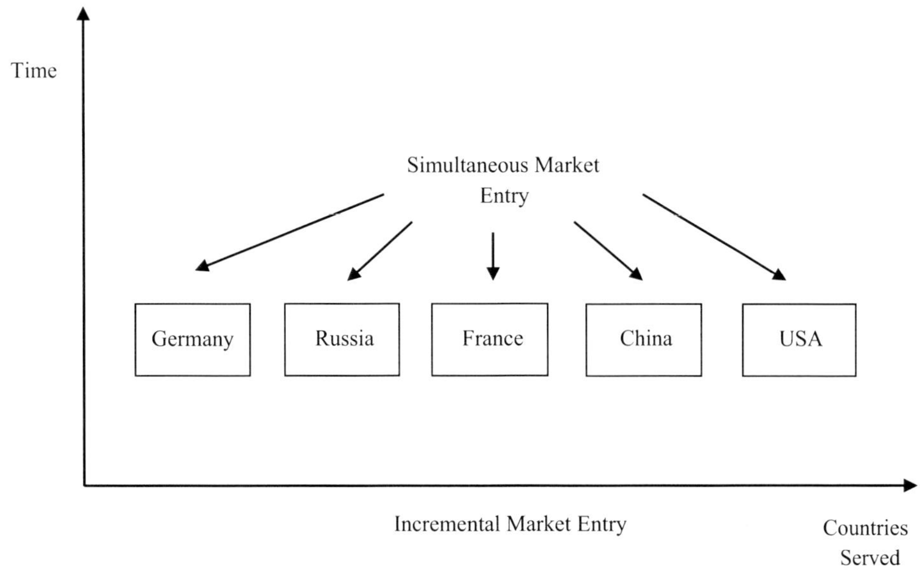

Figure 3.7 Incremental market entry when shower strategy is applied.

Therefore, in industries that indicate relatively short product and technology life cycles, implementing a shower strategy is recommendable. In this case, in the course of product introduction, the firm serves all markets simultaneously (Figure 3.7). To successfully implement a shower strategy, the firm needs considerable resource cushions in terms of its operational resources, proper distribution channels, and after sales service capacities (Kotabe and Helsen, 2008; Kalish et al., 1995).

Licensing and franchising concepts provide optimal prerequisites for fast market entry. Contractual licensing describes the transfer of knowledge between one licensor and usually various licensees. The licensor, as the owner of knowledge, needs to have a registered patent or trademark, which legally protects the licensor from illegal use of its intellectual property. The licensor, however, does not need to build up operational capacities. Instead, the licensor grants exclusive rights to a licensee located in the target market to use the intellectual property for a defined purpose for a certain period against the payment of royalties (Aulakh, Jiang, and Li, 2013: 700).

A further fast entry mode, for example, when implementing a shower strategy indicates franchising. Franchising is a contractual agreement between a franchisor, who sells its business concept to usually many franchisees that are legally and financially independent (Hendrikse and Jiang, 2007). The franchisor sells to the franchisees (typically small business owners) the right to commercialize goods or services under the franchisor's established brand name (market goodwill). During the contractual relationship, the franchisor provides ongoing commercial, administrative, and technical assistance. In return, the franchisee typically pays an initial start-up fee, royalties based on the sales, and advertising fees—all of which depend on the conditions agreed to in the franchising contract (Combs et al., 2004). The advantages and disadvantages from the franchisor's as well as franchisee's perspective are illustrated in Table 3.3.

Table 3.3 Advantages and disadvantages from the franchisor's and franchisee's perspectives

Franchisor Perspective	
Advantages	*Disadvantages*
• Clone of a proven business concept • Rapid international market entry • Company growth with limited financial resources • Sharing of entrepreneurial risk with franchisees • Use of franchisee's regional and cultural expertise	• Sharing knowledge combined with the risk of building up a new competitor • Likelihood that the franchisee may harm the reputation (e.g. quality and hygiene standards) • Limited organizational monitoring and control • The higher the likelihood of communication complexity with more franchises
Franchisee Perspective	
Advantages	*Disadvantages*
• Takeover of a proven business concept including operations, supplier selection, etc. • Helpful franchisor's brand-related market goodwill for reducing the business risk • Training and qualification by the franchisor • Franchisor's support concerning choice of branch location	• Dependency on the franchisor in terms of firm strategy, product, and marketing policy • Need to pay business start-up/running fees without having entrepreneurial freedom • Higher bargaining power of the franchisor • Franchise fees subject to change • Permanent monitoring by franchisor

Export

Foreign trade through exports indicates the oldest form of international business maintained for hundreds of years. Export indicates cross-border business of products and services, which are sold to consumers in countries that are different from the exporter's home country where the main part of the product and services value added activities took place. The buyer of the product and services, located in the foreign target country, is named importer. For example, compared to joint venture agreements or building up one's own plant operations through foreign direct investments, export indicates a fast and financially less risky market entry mode.

Basically, we distinguish between direct and indirect exports. Having no, or very little, experience in the business of foreign trade, it is desirable for the firm to initiate its first foreign engagement through so-called indirect exports. This market entry mode is called indirect export because an intermediator, with a commission, searches for potential customers (importers) in the target foreign country. The commission is subject to negotiation between the exporter and the importer. In the case of direct exports, the firm undertakes personal relationships with the importing customer abroad. Direct export requires more international business experience and resources relative to indirect business because of traveling as well as actively managing the negotiations and contracts. The advantages from direct market access and the benefits from gaining valuable first-hand customer information may easily exceed the costs of active export management (Hill, 2012; Glowik, 2016).

Exports applied as an international business strategy, despite its long tradition, enjoy an increased importance in recent decades, particularly for small Internet-based start-up firms. Smaller firms, which usually cannot rely on large financial resources cushions, are able to raise international attention, through their own firm webpage. Global firm presences became possible via the World Wide Web, which reduces the necessity to promote the firm and its product and services in international trade fairs. As a result, smaller and innovative firms are better able to a certain extent to save business traveling costs and trade boost fees, which have increased continuously in recent years. Liberalized trade pattern and improved and cheaper global logistics further support export potentials for smaller firms compared to the past.

In general, exporter and importer negotiate product and service characteristics in terms of their

- performance and design;
- quality parameters and quantity;
- delivery time;
- the unit price; and
- transportation method and corresponding shipping documents.

All of these factors are agreed on in the contract between exporter and importer. The shipping documents, as prepared by the logistics firm on delivery, are Bill of Lading (B/L) for the transportation by vessel, Convention Marchandise Routière (CMR) for road shipment by truck and Air Waybill in the event of air shipment. Further important elements to be fixed in the export contract are

- packing list contents;
- possibly certificate in terms of technical, hygiene, safety approvals, and environmental standards;
- eventually, a Certificate of Origin of the product, when requested by the buyer due to import customs requirements;
- possibly delivery insurance certificate;
- international commercial terms (Incoterms); and
- payment conditions.

The Incoterms and the payment conditions, because of their importance and general applicability for all types of export contracts, are explained below.

Incoterms

The International Chamber of Commerce first published in 1936 so-called international trade rules, which have been modified several times up to the latest version named International Commercial Terms 2010 (Incoterms, 2010). Various Incoterms revisions have been made in recent decades to ensure that the wording of the Incoterms rules clearly and accurately reflects present-day trade practices between exporter and importer. As a result, the Incoterms provide a commonly accepted basis on which to regulate the duties of the exporter (seller) and the importer (buyer) and divide the costs, such as transportation and border duties between both parties. Founded in 1919, the International Chamber of Commerce today is one of the largest and representative business organizations in the world with three main responsibilities: rules-setting; arbitration; and policy. The ICC has hundreds of thousands of member companies in over 120 countries conducting business in various industries (ICC, 2010). The Incoterms are internationally recognized standard trade terms used in export sales contracts. In general, they are used to make sure buyer and seller know:

- who is responsible for the cost of transporting the goods, including insurance, taxes, and duties;
- where the goods should be picked up from and transported to; and
- who is responsible for the goods at each step during transportation (Gov.UK, 2016).

More specifically, Incoterms define the point where the risk, such as damage, waste, and loss of the goods, is transferred from the exporter to the importer. Incoterms have an impact on neither the payment conditions nor the transfer of the property rights of the cargo. Incoterms are not applied automatically between the foreign trade partners. They are only applicable if seller and buyer specifically agree on Incoterms in their contract. In general, Incoterms are divided into codes as introduced below (Incoterms, 2010).

EX works (EXW) ... named place of delivery

EXW represent the minimum obligation for the seller, and the buyer must bear all costs and risks involved in taking the goods from the seller's premises. The seller fulfills his obligation, when the goods are placed at the disposal of the buyer at the seller's premises or another named place (e.g. factory warehouse) not cleared for export and not loaded on any collecting vehicle. The seller renders the buyer, at the latter's request, risk, and expense, assistance in obtaining export approval by official customs authorization necessary for the export of goods.

Free carrier (FCA) ... named place of delivery

FCA means that the seller delivers the goods, cleared for export, at his own risk and expense, to the carrier nominated by the buyer at the named place. If the delivery occurs at the seller's premises, the seller is responsible for loading the cargo.

Free alongside ship (FAS) ... named port of shipment

FAS indicates that the exporter fulfills his obligation when the goods are placed alongside the vessel nominated by the buyer at the named port of shipment. The buyer must bear all costs and risks of loss of or damage to the goods from that moment. The exporter obtains at his own risk and expenses any export approval or other official customs formalities necessary for the export of the goods.

Free on board (FOB) ... named port of shipment

FOB means the exporter fulfilled his delivery obligations when the goods pass the ship's rail at the named port of loading. This means that the buyer must bear all costs and risks of loss of or damage to the goods from that point. The vessel is nominated by the buyer. The exporter obtains at his own risk and expense any export approval or other official authorization of the exporter's border customs and carry out all customs formalities necessary for the export of the goods. The FOB term is used exclusively for sea or inland waterway transport but not for road or air shipment. In case of vessel shipments, FOB indicates the most commonly agreed term among the entire Incoterms portfolio.

Cost and freight (CFR) ... named port of destination

CFR defines that the exporter delivers when the goods pass the ship's rail at the named port of destination. The seller must deliver the goods on board the vessel and he pays the costs and freight necessary to bring the goods to the named port of destination. The exporter nominates the vessel for the transportation to the port of shipment. The importer bears all risks of loss of or damage to the goods until such time as they have passed the ship's railing at the port of shipment. The seller must obtain at his own risk and expense any export license or other official authorization and carry out all customs formalities necessary for the export of the goods. The CFR term can be used only for sea or inland waterway transport but not for road or air shipment (Gov.UK, 2016; Incoterms, 2010).

Cost, insurance, and freight (CIF) ... named port of destination

CIF is similar to CFR, except for the necessity of insurance: The exporter obtains at his own expense cargo insurance as agreed on in the contract, such that the importer is entitled to claim directly from the insurer if necessary. The seller provides the buyer with the corresponding insurance policy. The CIF term can be used only for sea or inland waterway transport but not for road or air shipment.

Carriage paid to (CPT) ... named destination

The exporter delivers the goods at his own expense to the agreed point of destination. The carrier is nominated by the exporter. The seller obtains at his own risk and expenses any customs approval or any further customs formalities if required for the export of the goods (named in business practice: 'to clean the goods for export.' If subsequent carriers are used for the carriage to the agreed destination, the risk passes from the seller to the buyer when the goods have been delivered to the first carrier. The CPT term is used irrespective of the mode of transport including multimodal transport.

Carriage and insurance paid (CIP) ... named destination

CIP is similar to CPT, except for the insurance requirement. The carrier is nominated by the exporter who also contracts for insurance, pays the insurance premium, and provides the insurance certificate on the request of the importer (Incoterms, 2010; Gov. UK, 2016).

Delivered at terminal (DAT) ... named terminal

The exporter delivers the goods at his own expense to the named terminal (e.g. railroad, airport, or container port terminal). The seller obtains at his own risks and expenses any certificates by customs authorities and bears all costs and risks of loss of or damage to the named terminal. The term is used irrespective of the mode of transport, including multimodal transport.

Delivered at place (DAP) ... named destination

DAP defines that the exporter supplies the goods at his own account to the named place of destination. The seller obtains at his own risk any customs formalities necessary up to the named place of delivery, which can be far from the exporter's home base. The exporter bears all costs and risks of loss of or damage to the goods until delivery to the named place. The term is used irrespective of the mode of transport, including multimodal transport.

Delivered duty paid (DDP) ... named destination

While the EXW Incoterm indicates minimum obligation for the exporter, DDP represents maximum responsibilities for the exporter. The seller bears all the costs and risks of transportation, including all customs formalities necessary for the export of the goods, eventually for their transit through other countries, and for their import to the final place of destination. The exporter places the goods at the disposal of the importer. The term is used irrespective of the mode of transport, such as vessel, truck, air, or railroad including multimodal transport combining previously mentioned transportation modes (Incoterms, 2010; Gov.UK, 2016).

Dependent on the Incoterm's mode, there are costs in terms of transportation and possibly insurance to be divided between the exporter and the importer. These costs must be considered by the seller when calculating its price offer. In the case of EXW, the buyer pays for the logistics and takes the risk of damage to or loss of the product. In contrast, DDP requires that the seller bears all of the costs, such as transportation and customs clearance. Table 3.4 shows the differences of costs (EXW Berlin, Germany versus DDP Seoul, South Korea) to be considered when calculating the export price, each calculated for the same product unit.

As a result of the below calculation (same profit margins assumed): The DDP export unit price offer has to be higher than the EXW unit price.

Table 3.4 EXW Berlin (Germany) price calculation versus DDP Seoul (South Korea) price calculation

EXW Berlin (Germany) Price Calculation	*DDP Seoul (South Korea) Price Calculation*
Net unit price (manufacturing costs + profit margin)	Net unit price (manufacturing costs + profit margin) + truck shipment from Berlin to Hamburg + vessel shipment Hamburg port to Pusan port + South Korea border customs clearance fees + truck shipment Pusan port to Seoul final destination
= **EXW export unit price**	= **DDP export unit price**

Payment conditions

Seller and buyer have various payment alternatives related to the sales contract. The safest payment term from the exporter's perspective is 'payment in advance' or 'pre-payment,' which is typically used when (1) the importer's firm is unknown, or (2) the credit worthiness of the importer is doubtful, or (3) potential payment restrictions within the country of destination may cause a considerable delay of money transfer (Cateora et al., 2009). From the importer's perspective, payment in advance is rather disadvantageous because it reduces the importer's liquidity before having the goods at his disposal. Moreover, the importer bears the risk that the payment is done but the shipment is delayed by the exporter or even canceled, e.g. due to exporter's bankruptcy. Another potential risk for the importer is that the cargo is shipped but on arrival, the importer recognizes that the quality standards, as agreed on in the product specifications of the contract, are not met (Glowik and Smyczek, 2011).

In contrast to pre-payment, the payment mode 'open account' transfers the risk from the importer to the exporter. Here, the exporter delivers his cargo to the importer, who pays the invoice amount on receipt of the invoice (shipment) within the contractual agreed period of time. Therefore, the exporter bears the risk in case the importer is unwilling or incapable of paying the shipment amount. The longer the payment term is agreed on, common periods in international business to business are 30, 45, 60, 90, and 180 days after invoice date, the higher is the risk for the exporter. Therefore, business contracts based on open account should be agreed on only when the exporter and importer know and trust each other. Another payment alternative is if the exporter sells his products and services against a draft issued by the importer. Suppose the draft issuer enjoys credit worthiness, the draft can be used by the exporter for his own debts. Alternatively, the exporter submits the draft to his bank and receives the (discounted) invoice (draft) amount payment by the bank. The bank's rate of discount depends on the importer's credit worthiness. In the worst-case scenario, the draft would not be accepted by the bank.

In case of factoring, a third company (factor) purchases the accounts receivable from the exporter. Ideally, the exporter meets the factor before any contract is signed and the shipment is procured to secure its willingness to buy the receivable. The factor acts as a credit approval agency as well as securing agent for the receipt of the outstanding payment to the exporter in case the importer is unable to pay his debts (Albaum et al., 2008). Factoring comes along with two major disadvantages from the exporter's position. First, the introduction of a factoring firm (third party) does not provide a trustful ground for long-term oriented business activities between the exporter and the importer since the factor directly contacts the importer in the context of the payment procedure. Second, depending on the importer's creditworthiness as well as the country risk of the importer's location, the exporter may receive only a marginal part of the total invoice amount pending. These potential disadvantages are minimized, when instead of factoring, a letter of credit as a payment term is agreed on between the seller and the buyer (Glowik and Smyczek, 2011).

The letter of credit (LC) indicates one of the oldest and most common worldwide applied instruments to secure the exporter's payment receipt by the importer. Exporter and importer have to agree on the LC payment method in their contract. If the importer does not pay, the LC issuing bank settles the claim to the exporter. In principle, it is possible to open an LC from one bank. Hence, the credit worthiness of the issuing bank as well as its geographical location (e.g. compare country risk analysis) is important. Thus, the involvement of a second LC confirming bank, often located in the exporter's home country is recommended. To summarize, the use of LC as a payment instrument provides the following advantages for the exporter and the importer:

1 The exporter secures his receipt of payment because the importer claims his debt to the issuing bank against the receipt of the original shipment documents (LC as payment security instrument).
2 The importer can be sure that the cargo has been shipped by the exporter on receipt of the original shipment documents by the issuing bank (LC as delivery security instrument).
3 When the contracting parties agree on a deferred payment LC, the importer receives the cargo but takes advantage of the delayed payment. Because the importer can take advantage of the credit, the exporter improves his competitive position being sure to receive the money from the bank (LC as a credit instrument). Even though there is a deferred payment agreed on between the contracted parties, the exporter may use 'forfaiting,' which means advancing the receipt of the amount pending by the confirming bank against payment of forfeiting fees, which depend on the period advanced, the foreign firm credit worthiness and the importer's residence's country risk (Glowik and Smyczek, 2011).

Trade credit insurance

Trade credit insurance also known as credit insurance, business credit insurance, or export credit insurance include products that cover the payment risk resulting from the delivery of goods or services of the exporter (Jones, 2010). Trade credit insurance aims to protect their accounts receivable from loss due to credit risks, such as protracted default, insolvency, and bankruptcy. Moreover, depending on the contract conditions, it can also cover losses as a result of political risk, such as currency inconvertibility, war, and civil disturbance.

The costs (called a 'premium') are usually charged monthly, and are calculated as a percentage of sales of the month or as a percentage of all outstanding receivables. It is important to stress that trade credit insurance ensures the payment risk of companies and not of individuals (Jones, 2010). Trade credit insurances were established in Western Europe between the first and the second world wars. During that time, several insurance companies were established across Europe targeting to manage the political risks associated with exports on behalf of their national states. Since then, trade credit insurance businesses have become multi-billion dollar businesses. In 2008, estimated Euro 5.3 billion of global credit insurance premiums covered about Euro 2.6 trillion of sales (Jones, 2010).

Trade credit insurance markets have grown over the last decades but simultaneously, the industry has consolidated. Presently, three companies, namely, Euler Hermes, Atradius, and Coface, account for more than 87 percent of the global credit insurance market. The 'big three' private trade credit insurers divided the global markets: Euler Hermes covers 36 percent of the world market; Atradius covers 31 percent; and Coface covers 20 percent (Van der Veer, 2015) (Figure 3.8).

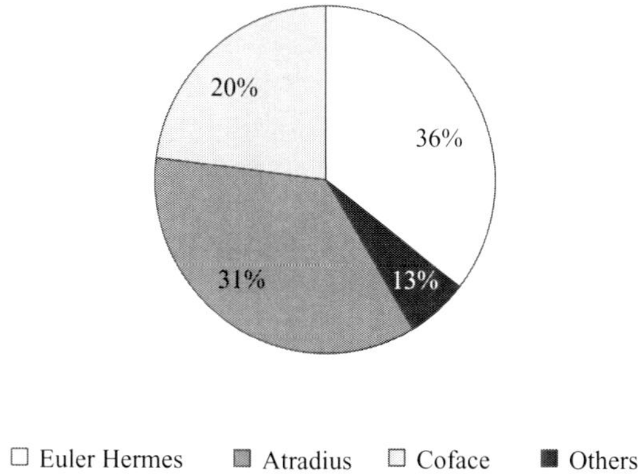

Figure 3.8 Globally leading credit insurance companies.
Source: *Author based on Van der Veer* (2015: 603).

Euler Hermes

Hermes Kreditversicherungs AG was founded in 1917 in Germany. In 1932, Hermes became the sole company in the sectors of goods insurance, installment payment insurance, and export credit insurance. In 1947, the German government started to provide export and investment credit guarantees via institutions, such as Hermes Kreditversicherungs AG. At the end of the 1980s, Hermes has grown and reached new domains in the European Union's domestic markets by supplying insurance products (Euler Hermes, 2016a).

In 2001, Allianz group and Assurances Générales de France (AGF) announced their intention to merge their respective credit insurance subsidiaries. The new company harmonized its branding and all subsidiaries and adopted the name Euler Hermes and became 'Euler Hermes.' In 2007, Euler Hermes established a partnership agreement with ICIC (Israeli Credit Insurance Company) and BOCI (subsidiary of Bank of China). In addition, Euler Hermes acquired UMA (USA) and R2C (Ireland), two debt collection specialists. In 2014, the company completed a global legal restructuring, merging French and German legal entities into Euler Hermes SA. In 2015, the company strengthened its Latin American presence through its joint venture named Solunion and launched operations in Panama, Peru, and Uruguay. Moreover, Euler Hermes reached other places overseas and opened offices in Bulgaria and South Africa. The company managed to establish distribution partnerships with five banks in Abu Dhabi, France, Ireland, Brazil, and Italy (Euler Hermes, 2016a).

In 2015, Euler Hermes has demonstrated strong profitability, the revenues amounted to EURO 2.6 billion, whereas the net income reached EURO 302.5 million (EulerHermes, 2016b). Euler Hermes' network of so-called 'risk offices' monitors the financial performance of its customers. The firm allocates each of the customers a grade, which reflects the health of their activity and the way they manage their business. By doing that, Euler Hermes aims that customers would pay their trade credit debts owed to the insured companies (Euler Hermes, 2016c).

Atradius

Atradius was founded in 1925 in The Netherlands as Nederlandsche Credietverzekering Maatschappij (NCM). At that time, the company was created to improve trade for companies in the Netherlands. In 1932, NCM established partnership with the Dutch government to provide export credit services to Dutch companies on behalf of the Dutch State (Atradius, 2016).

NCM and Gerling merged in 2001, establishing Gerling NCM. The German originated company, Gerling Credit was established in 1954 as the credit insurance business line of Gerling Group. Gerling Credit operated solely out of Germany until 1961 and was the first private credit insurer to offer export credit protection (Atradius, 2016). In 2004, Gerling NCM changed its name to Atradius. Presently, Atradius is considered to be one of the largest global credit insurance organizations in the word providing credit insurance and credit management products and services through 160 offices in 50 countries worldwide (Atradius, 2016).

In 2015, Atradius generated EURO 1.7 billion of total revenues, whereas the net investment (net income and share of income of associated companies) amounted to EURO 36 million (Atradius, 2015). In recent years, the company expanded its activities in Asia, Africa and Latin America and opened a new office for credit insurance in Russia and South Korea. Moreover, Atradius Collections entered new markets in Canada, China and India. The credit insurance business performs well with outstanding results in Spain, which is considered to be the largest credit insurance market of Atradius. The second largest insurance market of Atradius is Germany (Atradius, 2015).

Coface

The former state-owned French company Coface specializing in export credit insurance was established in 1946. In the early 1990s, the company expanded overseas and developed sales networks in countries such as Germany, Austria, the UK, and Italy. In 1994, Coface became privatized but continues to handle public guarantees on behalf of the French State. An important milestone occurred in 2006, when Coface became a wholly owned subsidiary of Natixis, the financial services arm of the BPCE Group, which is the second largest banking group in France.

Presently, Coface belongs to the three leading insurance companies worldwide. They have established strong presence in 67 countries and insurance guarantees are provided in nearly 200 countries (Coface, 2016a). In 2015, Coface generated a consolidated turnover of EURO 1.4 billion, while the net income amounted to EURO 126 million (Coface, 2016b). Coface provides credit insurance to protect companies against the risk of potential non-payments by their customers in almost 200 countries. Along with credit insurance, Coface offers factoring services, propriety business information, and a receivables collection service (Coface, 2016c).

International management and marketing

Perlmutter (1969) is one of the first scholars who categorized the characteristics of a multinational organization in a concept known as the ethnocentric-polycentric-regiocentric-geocentric scheme (EPRG model). Perlmutter (1969) was ahead of his time claiming that the multinational corporation is a new kind of institution, which, from his point of view, could make a valuable contribution to world order and conceivable exercise a constructive impact on the national states. When published in 1969, the EPRG model, due to its organizational-behavioral elements, was in fact novel and opposite to dominating main-stream 'rational thinking' approaches related to international business (Vernon, 1966). In terms of its international business activities, the management's attitude towards foreign people, ideas, and resources is crucial in assessing a firm's multinational competitive success. The value orientation and the firm's philosophies implemented by the management influence and shape, in large part, the firm's internationalization path (Perlmutter, 1969; Wind et al., 1973).

The EPRG model been further developed by Wind et al. (1973) concerning marketing strategies and by Bartlett and Goshal (1986, 1998) in light of increasingly globally shared value added activities (e.g. transnational strategy). The first element of EPRG the ethnocentric approach (home-country orientation) claims significant levels of control and standardized management procedures, implemented by top-down governance from the headquarters. The firm's international business concentrates on exports without significance in terms of the marketing mix (e.g. prices, products, and services that are similar to those at home). The ethnocentric concept has been defined by Barlett and Ghoshal (1990) as global strategy.

As each subsidiary is a distinct national entity, the headquarters of many multinational organizations have often lacked experience and knowledge of how things are done in the diverse environments and markets. Those organizations that have acknowledged the existence of national differences and the importance to consider these differences have pursued international expansion by adopting a polycentric approach (host-country oriented). Host-country oriented organizations tend to rely on locals' expertise and provide each subsidiary with a certain degree of autonomy to manage their operations, as it is best suitable in the given context (Perlmutter, 1986). According to Bartlett and Goshal (1990), the polycentric concept is described as international strategy.

A polycentric organization (region-oriented) consists of loosely connected quasi-independent subsidiaries where each subsidiary is usually comprised predominantly of local nationals, and the processes and practices are adapted to the local conditions and needs of the respective target market. Bottom-up decision-making has enabled organizations to capitalize on better-informed executives, better relationships with local authorities, and improved perceptions of the company among locals (Perlmutter, 1969; Lee et al., 2015). The regiocentric organized firm, termed by Bartlett and Goshal (1990) as multinational strategy, emphasizes the existence of diverse regional markets. Similarities, for example, between countries are summarized based on common characteristics when developing a regional strategy of the firm. Management decision authorities are mutually negotiated and agreed on within the regions, which are, to a certain degree, independent from other regions (Perlmutter, 1986).

In case of a geocentric approach, the firm emphasizes a mutual global exchange of resources between the entire organization's units. The firm sets universal standards to responsively react to local needs and the relationship between headquarters and its subsidiaries is characterized by collaboration. The aim is to utilize each country's markets and corresponding national resources that fits optimally and seems most suitable for increasing the profitability of the firm. Management norms, values, and styles are broadly interpreted and governance is mutually negotiated within the entire organization (Perlmutter and Heenan, 1974; Perlmutter, 1986).

Table 3.5 E.P.R.G. scheme, business focus, management policy, and business concept

E.P.R.G. Scheme	*Business Focus*	*Management Policy*	*Business Concepts*
Ethnocentric	Home market	Same management values and ethics like at home Top-down governance Placement of home country nationals	Focus on exports Standardized pricing Product and services similar to those at the home market
Polycentric	Target country	Emphasize local management expertise and autonomy Bottom-up decision-making Behavioral adaptation to target country circumstances Placement of host country nationals	International marketing (e.g. exports, licensing, franchising, joint ventures, and sales subsidiaries) Modification of the marketing mix according to local needs
Regiocentric	Geographic regions	Regional management expertise and autonomy Behavioral adaptation to target country circumstances Recruitment and placement of regional country managers	Region-specific sales and marketing concepts (e.g. exports, licensing, franchising, joint ventures, and sales subsidiaries)
Geocentric	Global demand and supply	Mutual resource exchange between subsidiaries and headquarters Collaboration between the organizations' units Management responsibilities and governance negotiated within the organization	Global marketing in response to local needs Markets served as opportunities come up

Source: Adapted from Wind et al. (1973).

In general, there is a permanent challenge for the firm's management in terms of the organization's centralization-decentralization degree and the uncertainty as to whether single country-based or region-oriented organizational structures fits best (Bartlett, 1986). The geocentric approach (transnational strategy) appears to be the ideal concept for multinational enterprises. Specific challenges concerning the geocentric approach are related to limited flexibility, opportunistic behavior, and local egoisms. The question is: Are all organizations' members always willing to voluntarily exchange knowledge when they compete as regional profit centers within the organization? In addition, the employees and managers, for example, with family-related responsibilities are naturally less agreeable to frequently move to any location worldwide where the firm wants to let them stay following global resource exchange necessities claimed by the geocentric model (Ahmadi et al., 2012).

Intercultural management

Intercultural relationships studies are often assigned to scientific disciplines like psychology, cultural, or societal and educational science. Within business disciplines, relationships are regularly used to explain social processes and evolutions among groups of people or different business units inside and outside an organization (Glowik and

Bruhs, 2014). Relevant to the term 'culture,' the literature distinguishes between 'organizational culture' and 'national culture.' Organizational culture is described as a system of assumptions, values, norms, and attitudes, displayed using symbols that the members of an organization have developed and adopted through mutual experience (Janićijevič, 2011).

According to Hofstede (2011), culture is the collective programming of the mind that distinguishes the members of one group or category of people from other groups. The term 'culture' is used to describe tribes or ethnic groups (in anthropology), nations (in political science and management), and organizations (in sociology and management). Differences in terms of behavior and work ethics that can be found in organizations may result from cultural national differences. There are various reasons regarding why it is important to develop a cultural sensitivity when performing international business activities such as:

- Customers differ in terms of their product performance, design tastes, and service expectations.
- There are different negotiation styles concerning the importance of 'the written versus the spoken word,' or 'the meaning of time,' expression of agreement and disagreements, confirmations, or critics.
- Cultural challenges between the partner firms usually emerge when managing international joint ventures or other cooperative agreements.
- Diversified political and legal national systems and religions influence business behavior.

Undoubtedly, cultural sensitivity supports global business success. The cultural phenomena resulted in the development of 'cultural models' as the most important approaches and, in parallel, provoked an intense discussion in the academic literature (Hatch and Schultz, 1997; Gouveia and Ros, 2000).

The cultural model of Hofstede

Hofstede (2001, 2010) developed a theoretical approach to classify values at the cultural level. His study is based on a survey at IBM conducted in 72 countries between 1968 and 1972. The results provided six main dimensions in which country differ according to cultural dimensions, as follows:

- **Power distance (PDI):** Degree to which societies handle human inequality. In other words, power distance refers to the way that members of organizations and institutions (like the family) accept and expect that power is distributed unequally. It suggests that a society's level of inequality is promoted by the followers as well as the leaders. In fact, power and inequality are fundamental concepts of any society and all societies can be considered as unequal but some are considered to be more unequal than others (Hofstede, 1994; Hofstede, 2001).
- **Individualism (IDV):** The second dimension named individualism is opposed to collectivism. It relates to the relationship between the individual and the collectivity in human society. In some cultures, the individualism is the most important concept; everyone is expected to think about himself as an individual. However, the collectivist concept can be expressed in societies in which people have the sense of collective identity and they would change their views together (Hofstede, 2001).
- **Masculinity (MAS):** The masculinity dimension versus its opposite pole femininity. The duality and the role of the genders are significant concepts that are

distinct between societies. The IBM study demonstrates that there are differences between men and women regarding the importance of work goals. Women feel that it is important to pursue social goals, e.g. maintain relationships and assist others, whereas men believe it is important to sustain ego goals, such as careers and money. Moreover, the IBM study reveals that feminine and masculine work goals varied across countries as well as across occupations (Hofstede, 2001). In light of modern times and gender roles, it is questionable whether woman and men differ in terms of their work goals. Gender differences are a result of the person's individual characteristics and the national cultural environment in which the person lives.

- **Uncertainty avoidance (UAI):** The degree to which members handle themselves in particular situations with uncertainty and ambiguity. It indicates to what extent a culture programs its members to feel uncomfortable or comfortable in unstructured situations. Unstructured situations refer to unknown, surprising, and different and unusual situations (Hofstede, 1994). The study found that different countries adapt to uncertainty in different ways. Mechanisms for coping with uncertainty belong to realms of technology, law, and religion (Hofstede, 2001). In contrast, uncertainty accepting cultures are considered to be more tolerant of different opinions and they try to enact as few rules as possible and allow many religions to flow side by side (Hofstede 1994).
- **Indulgence (IND):** indicates a society that allows relatively free gratification of basic and natural human drives related to enjoying life and having fun. Restraint stands for a society that suppresses gratification of needs and regulates it by means of strict social norms (Hofstede, 2010).
- **Long-term orientation (LTO):** LTO versus short-term orientation. The fifth dimension was found in the Chinese Value Survey (CVS) of 23 countries in 1985. LTO aspects relate to persistence and thrift to personal stability whereas short-term orientation aspects refer to respect for tradition and fulfilling social obligations (Hofstede, 2001). Important behavioral characteristics related to each cultural dimension are summarized below.

Table 3.6 Cultural dimensions as developed by Hofstede (2011)

Cultural Dimension		
Power Distance	*Small*	*Large*
	Hierarchy means inequality of the roles, established for convenience	Hierarchy means existential inequality
	Subordinates expect to be consulted	Subordinates expect to be told what to do
	Parents treat children as equals	Parents teach children obedience
	Use of power should be legitimate and is subject to criteria of good and evil	Power is a basic fact of society and its legitimacy is irrelevant
Individualism vs. Collectivism	*Individualism*	*Collectivism*
	Everyone is supposed to take care of herself/himself and immediate family and friends	People are born into extended families or clans, which protect them in exchange for loyalty

Individualism vs. Collectivism	*Individualism*	*Collectivism*
	Right of privacy	Stress of belonging
	Speaking one's mind is healthy	Harmony should always be maintained
	Personal opinion is expected	Opinions and votes predetermined by in-group and hierarchies
	Purpose of education is learning how to learn	Purpose of education is learning how to do
Masculinity vs. Femininity	*Masculinity*	*Femininity*
	Maximum emotional and social role differentiation between the genders	Minimum emotional and social role differentiation between the genders
	Men should be assertive and ambitious and women may be assertive and ambitious	Men and women should be modest and caring
	Work prevails over family	Balance between family and work
Uncertainty Avoidance	*Weak*	*Strong*
	The uncertainty inherent in life is accepted as taking every day as it comes	Uncertainty in life is felt as a continuous threat to be fought
	Tolerance of deviant persons and ideas	Intolerance of deviant persons and ideas
	What is different is curious	What is different is dangerous
	Low stress, self-control, low anxiety	High stress, emotionality, anxiety
	Changing jobs is not a problem	Staying in jobs even if disliked
Short-Term vs. Long-Term Orientation	*Short-Term*	*Long-Term*
	The most important events in life occurred in the past or take place now	Most important events in life will occur in the future
	Personal steadiness and stability	A good person adapts to the circumstances
	Traditions are sacrosanct	Traditions are adaptable to changed circumstances
Indulgence vs. restraint	*Indulgence*	*Restraint*
	Free expression of human feelings, enjoying life and having fun	Suppresses gratification of needs Strict social norms

According to these dimensions, Hofstede (2011) developed a country-specific scaling. For example, Scandinavian countries like Sweden and Norway indicate relatively high femininity (e.g. emphasis on education and social security) indices while, for example, Germany and Japan are categorized as masculine societies (e.g. materialistic status symbols are important). Countries located in the Far East, such as Japan, South Korea, and China, are characterized as collectivistic, high uncertainty avoidance, and long-term time oriented societies, in contrast to Anglo-Saxon countries, representing individualistic, low uncertainty avoidance, and short-term nationality-related cultures.

The cultural model of Schwartz

Schwartz (1999) developed an alternative theory to Hofstede's model. Schwartz compared 49 nations around the world and classified seven types of values in which cultures can be distinguished.

- **Conservatism:** Focus on maintenance of the status quo. Security, conformity, and tradition are priorities and it is important to avoid actions by individuals who challenge the social order (Gouveia and Ros, 2000).
- **Intellectual autonomy:** Values that emphasize the autonomy of individuals to pursue their own ideas and intellectual interests including curiosity, open mindedness, and creativity (Schwartz, 1999).
- **Affective autonomy:** Interest in achieving positive experiences (pleasure, exciting life, and varied life).
- **Hierarchy:** Cultural emphasis on the legitimacy of power, roles, and resources (social power, authority, humility, and wealth).
- **Egalitarianism:** Values that put off selfish interests in favor of engagement and commitment to promote values for the well-being of others, which consist of concepts such as equality, social justice, freedom, responsibility, and honesty.
- **Mastery:** An active management of goals and aims through self-assertion (ambition, success, daring, and competence). In contrast to accepting the world as it is, there is strong willingness to change the world.
- **Harmony:** Values that go hand in hand with protecting the environment and achieving unity in nature. These concepts are in contrast to an active role of challenging the world, which is addressed by mastery (Gouveia and Ros, 2000).

These seven categories are structured according to three dimensions: conservatism versus intellectual and affective autonomy; hierarchy versus egalitarianism; and mastery versus harmony. The first dimension distinguishes between the individual and the group, which can be associated with the individualism and collectivism dimension

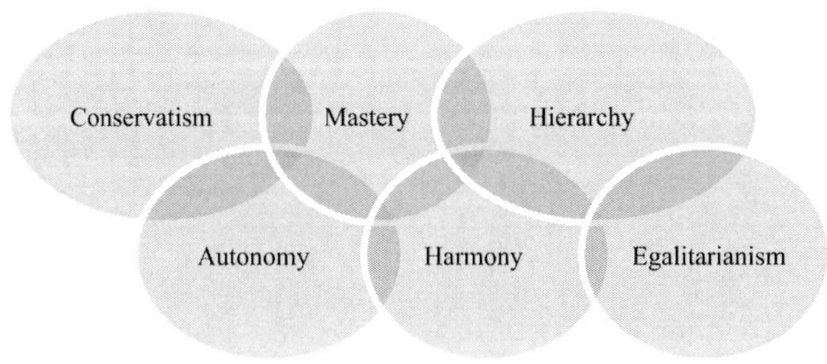

Figure 3.9 Cultural dimensions according to Schwartz (1999).

of Hofstede (2001). In this respect, the main question that refers to this dimension is: Whose interests should be considered—the individual's or the group's interests?

The second dimension implies that there is contradiction between unavoidable power relations relying on hierarchical systems, which mean that people are socialized and they are aware of the fact that they should follow the rules. The alternative concept consists of moral issues and the fact that people share basic ideas as human beings. The third dimension includes two contrasting concepts: Mastery aims to change the world and assert control, whereas harmony aims to adapt to the social environment and accept the world and try to fit in it.

According to the model of Schwartz, country-specific behavioral attitudes are summarized according to the above categories similar as in the case of Hofstede's cultural dimension model.

The GLOBE project

Critics related to Hofstede's (2001) model suggested that the number of cultural dimensions should be extended aiming to develop a more fine-grained perspective on behavioral attitudes. The GLOBE project amplified the five dimensions of Hofstede to nine dimensions. The GLOBE study was conducted in 1994 and involved 170 social scientists located in 62 countries. The study developed an integrated and cross-level approach of relationships containing cultural values, practices and leaderships, organizational, and societal effectiveness (House et al., 2004). The GLOBE study extended Hofstede's culture theory and proposed nine dimensions of cultures as follows:

- **Uncertainty avoidance:** The degree to which members of an organization or society try to avoid uncertainty by relying on established social norms and practices. People in high uncertainty avoidance cultures actively seek to reduce the probability to changeable future events that may influence the operation of organization and the society (House et al., 2004).
- **Power distance:** The degree to which members of an organization or society expect that power should be stratified and concentrated at higher levels of an organization or government.
- **Collectivism I:** The degree to which organizational and societal institutional practices encourage and reward collective distribution of resources and collective action.
- **Collectivism II:** The degree to which individuals in in-group collectivism express pride, loyalty, and cohesiveness.
- **Gender egalitarianism:** The degree to which an organization minimizes gender role differences and promotes gender equality.
- **Assertiveness:** The degree to which individuals in organizations are assertive, confrontational, and aggressive in social relationships.
- **Future orientation:** The degree to which individuals in organizations or societies engage in future-oriented behaviors, such as planning and investigating in the future.
- **Performance orientation:** The degree to which an organization or society encourages group members to achieve excellence and promote improvement.
- **Humane orientation:** The degree to which individuals in organizations encourage individuals to be fair, altruistic, friendly, and kind to others (House et al., 2004).

The GLOBE study has introduced several new cultural dimensions and has studied each dimension individually. The GLOBE study found that there are differences between cultural value scores and cultural practice scores for each dimension, which are larger at the societal level than at the organizational level. The study concluded that changing culture is likely to be easier at the organizational level rather than at the societal level (Bushardt et al., 2011). Distinguishing between national cultural and organizational dimensions makes the GLOBE model more applicable than Hofstede's and Schwartz's originally developed models purely focusing on national culture characteristics.

In general, related to all models describe above, critics come up because of the unified approach of cultural and organizational dimensions, which assumes that all people, regardless of their individual characteristics and personal life, fit into certain pre-defined 'behavioral boxes.' In addition, the intercultural management research is driven by Western scholars. Hofstede, for example, initiated his cultural dimension research project at the US-originated firm IBM. Thus, it is more than questionable whether the same research outcomes would have been delivered if the same project was launched, for example, at a Chinese firm.

As a 'home paradigm,' Western research is a product of centuries of Aristotelian binary logic of 'functionalism,' a way of seeing, an ideology or worldview, which consistently distinguishes between right and wrong, black and white, which is imposed to other cultures, such as Asian or African (Alon, 2003). In contradiction to the rationalist Western linear worldview, which consolidates 'either-or antinomies,' the Asian archetype is dialectic and emerges from an acceptance of simultaneous multiple realities of a non-linear worldview that sees contradiction and paradox as normal, experiential, and valuably coherent common sense. In Asian societies, nothing is 'black and white,' as everything is in the changing process from 'one shade of gray to another.' Fuzzy thinking emphasizes that structure is temporary and the process of change is immanent (Alon, 2003; Kosko, 1994). From an Asian manager's perspective, Western management styles are criticized because of its narrowed focus on individuality instead of collective responsibility. Individuality is expressed in a firm's-related business performance indicators, such as shareholder value and short-term oriented return on investment horizons. In Western societies, the manager's loyalty to the firm tends to be lower while manager's fluctuation is higher (continued looking for more profitable career opportunities) (Lessem and Palsule, 1997).

The Western attention on financial performance indicators is mirrored against the background of 'corporate governance'-related literature contributions, which tend to emphasize aspects such as debt and agency costs, return on investments, internal control, and transparency mechanisms for stakeholders (Gillan and Starks, 1998; Gillan and Starks, 2003; Zingales, 1995). Recent publications within the field of corporate governance, which, in addition to financial and shareholder transparency issues, outline the importance of corporate social responsibility within the framework of corporate governance (Wu, 2006; Gugler and Shi, 2009). The outcomes of the 2008 debt crisis as well as the accelerated ongoing change of climate hopefully further move the discussion towards the importance of business ethics and environmental and social responsibility (Glowik and Smyczek, 2011).

Despite methodological concerns of intercultural research, considering different cultural backgrounds (without narrowly overemphasizing them) is of vital importance for business success. Ethnocentric attitudes and behaviors of the management stemming from ignorance or from misguided beliefs, such as 'my way is the best', or 'what works at home will work here, too,' not only are inappropriate but usually cause international business failure (Dowling and Welch, 2004).

Structure (ideally) follows strategy

Changing environmental surroundings increases the complexity of information flows, communication, and organization efforts. Strategic reconfigurations usually require, sooner or later, the firm's structural reorganization. In the academic literature, it is theoretically said that the organization's structure follows the firm's strategy (Wheelen and Hunger, 2010; Mintzberg et al., 2003). In business reality, the opposite is often the case: The firm's strategy fails because it is built on an outdated organizational structure due to the fact that the management ignores changing environmental surroundings, which require organizational reconfigurations. Timely modifications of the organizational structure, for instance, changing the firm's environments and strategies, are important to achieve the firm's sustainable success.

A firm's organization groups individuals into teams that have hierarchically positioned departmental functions (Lee et al., 2015). An organization's structure includes formal and informal elements. The formal elements are hierarchical positions that illustrate decision-making processes-related functional responsibilities. The informal issues of an organization's structure reflect the company culture and corporate social expectations by the firm's stakeholders (Tolbert and Hall, 2015). In other words, an organization serves as a formal pattern of how a company groups its value added activities and functions (Gebauer and Kowalkowski, 2012). A well-developed organization enhances clarity and transparency of responsibilities. Formalization helps to fasten information flows and streamline decision-making processes and, as result, improves operational efficiency and speed (Naqshbandi and Kaur, 2013).

The organization is characterized by its degree of complexity, formalization, and centralization. Complexity refers to the differentiation of units, which are either based on specific task or decision-making processes. The term 'complexity' includes the industry and geographical-regional spread of the organization's businesses (Rao et al., 2015). Formalization is related to the degree to which organizational processes are standardized, whereas centralization refers to the degree to which decision-making authority is concentrated at particular nodes within the organization. The firm's organizations that are characterized by high levels of complexity, greater centralization, and standardization are perceived as hierarchical. Hierarchical organizations consist of lean top-down decision-making processes, relatively strict rules, and limited flexibility due to standardized policies and procedures observable by relevant stakeholders (Rao et al., 2015).

Contrary to hierarchical organizations, organic (informal) organizations are built on less strict policies and procedures targeting effective personal communication, rather than loose rules (Rao et al., 2015). An organic firm's organization targets communicative, consensual decision-making processes. Informal organizations, as they do not necessitate rigid formalities, are more loosely controlled than traditional, tightly controlled hierarchical organizations (Nayager and Van Vuuren, 2015). 'Organic' utilizes innovative knowledge resources of the employees and targets flexibility of individuals within the organization to facilitate the adaptability and quick responsiveness needed to meet changing environmental surroundings (Steiger et al., 2014).

As all start-up firms have experienced in the course of their growth, the larger its business, the higher is the complexity of work tasks and corresponding information flows. The necessity for specialization requires grouping certain job responsibilities into departmental functions (Burton et al., 2015). The functional structure indicates the simplest form (also in terms of hierarchical levels) of a firm's organization. As illustrated

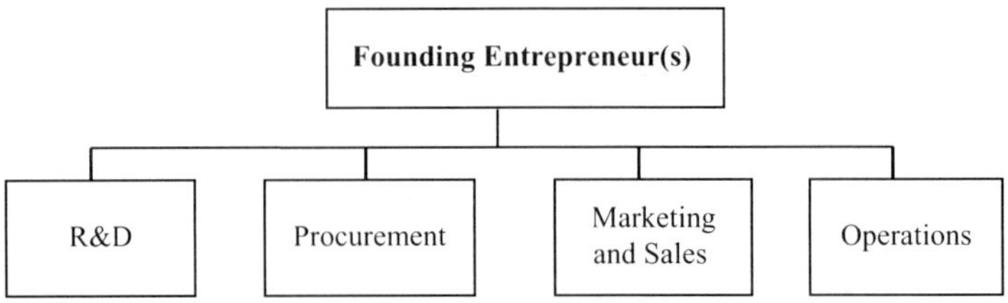

Figure 3.10 Functional structure (of a growing start-up firm).

in Figure 3.10, functional structures place particular emphasis on the skills, expertise, and professional knowledge of employees, allocating them to specific tasks or functions located in the firm's departments, such as research and development (R&D), procurement, marketing and sales, and operations (Lee et al., 2015).

In the course of further grow of the firm's business, complexity amplifies as well as the challenges of monitoring. The divisional structure provides more specific control because the firm's business is divided into different divisions. The division-related business expertise in terms of products, services, and markets belongs to the advantages of this structure type, as it also allows for minimizing the overall firm risk due to increased transparency and better monitoring (Steiger et al., 2014). On the one hand, fragmentation of business increases the organization's efficiency. On the other hand, as divisions operate independently, knowledge flows tend to be hindered and limited to the borders of each division, hence preventing valuable organizational learning (Steiger et al., 2014). The divisional structure, to a certain degree, duplicates management and staff activities and, thus, naturally leads to higher administrative costs (Lee et al., 2015).

As illustrated in Figure 3.11 in divisional-structured organizations, each division is left to coordinate its operations separately, which provides greater autonomy and closer

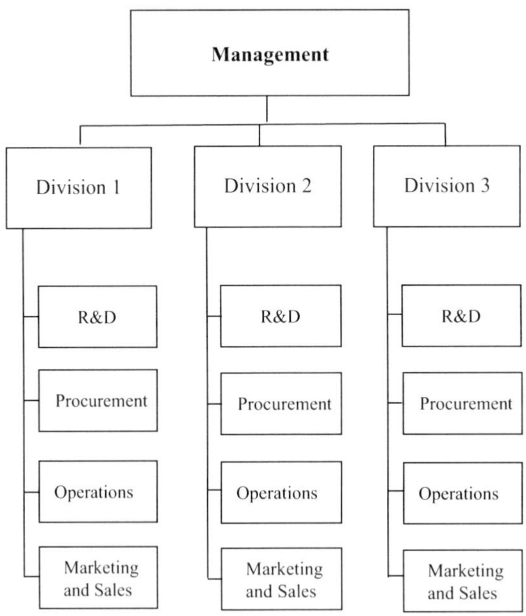

Figure 3.11 A layout example of an organization's divisional structure.

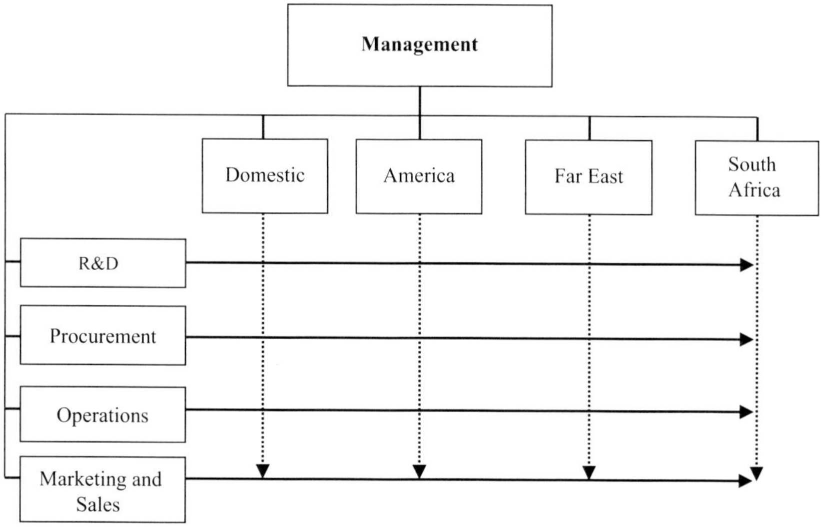

Figure 3.12 An example of a two-dimensional matrix structure (regions and functions).

focus on the respective markets. Consequently, each division can better concentrate on its respective customers, products and services, and geographical regions in which they operate and become more market-responsive, which is another main advantage of the divisional structure (Burton et al., 2015).

Large firms, such as MNEs, due to their size and business complexity usually operate as a matrix organization. In general, they are not standardized and flexibly developed according to the firm's requirements. Matrix organizations emphasize developing specific expertise, as, for example, related to the firm's sales areas. As shown in Figure 3.12, the organization's layout is usually aligned along the lines of authority, using functional and divisional chains of command simultaneously in the same part of the firm (dual reporting lines) (Lee et al., 2015). Therefore, it is suggested to encompass several different characteristics of the aforementioned models. As a result, matrix structures are more flexible and better able to adapt to the changing environments in which the firm operates its businesses. Matrix organizations focus on the potentials for knowledge transfer and, thus, support the overall organizational learning (Steiger et al., 2014).

When implemented properly, communication between functions facilitates which help to fasten decision-making processes and increases organizational flexibility and efficiency (Lee et al., 2015). The matrix structure is proposed as applicable to those firms, which require a combination of professional and operational skill sets and inter-organizational coordination efforts that enable the organization to optimally deliver products and services to meet diversified customer needs (Steiger et al., 2014). However, implementing matrix organizations in business practice is challenging because of its complexity, which naturally comes along with the firm size and degree of differentiating business activities.

Strategy Implementation and Control

Organizations do not change but people do: Individuals embedded in their organization usually undergo significant levels of change, learning, and adaptation to successfully execute a new strategy. Failure to recognize and act on these facts contributes to

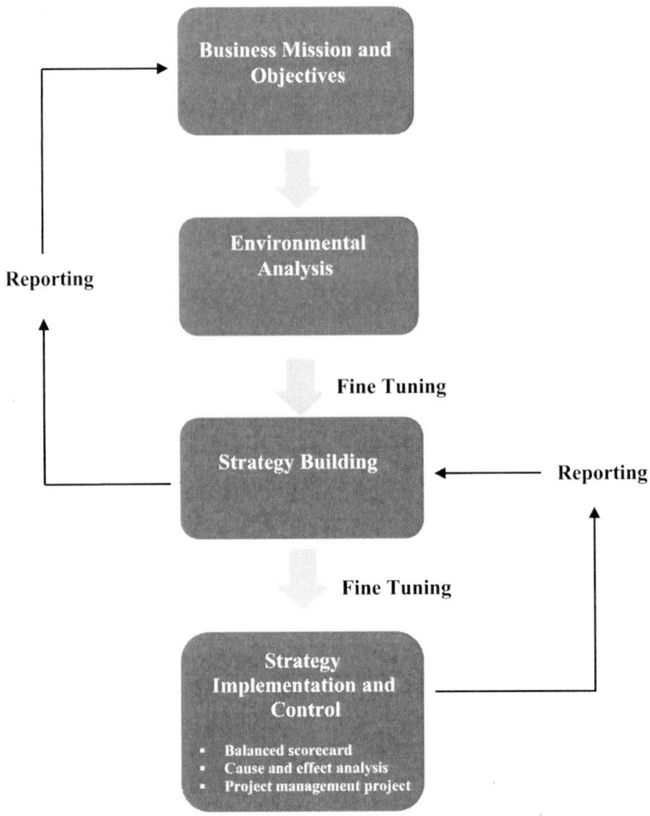

Figure 3.13 Process of strategy implementation and control stage.

consistently high strategy implementation failure rates. Recognizing changing realities and applying sound social-psychological principles to the process are likely to significantly help the management in their strategy implementation efforts (Carlopio and Harvey, 2012).

Actual strategy implementation (as opposed to strategy formulation) is not limited to the management. Strategy implementation is a complex and social-psychological process that occurs over periods of time and necessarily includes all relevant actors of the firm's relationship network. As shown in Figure 3.13, strategy implementation is consequently the final stage of the strategy process, which, at earlier stages, consists of the firm's mission and objectives formulation, followed by environmental analysis and strategy building. In business practice, the importance of implementation and control is often underestimated and therefore done insufficiently. Short-term (daily) operational business challenges are often perceived to be more important and, thus, overlap long-term strategy objectives. Efficient strategy implementation is usually limited when the communication between the top management and the operational management, as particularly witnessed in large organizations, is characterized by extended hierarchical levels. Consequently, the firm's mission and objectives formulated by the top management are not shared by all of employees, which naturally results in a firm's overall worsening business performance.

The strategic fit between the directional, competitive, and functional levels is of vital importance to ensure the firm's success. What does it mean? Assuming the management decides to launch a growth strategy in new international markets by launching innovative products combined with a profound customer driven service package, then differentiation strategy on the competitive level seems to be suitable and must be harmonized in accordance with strategy alternatives on the firm's functional (department) levels. For example, skimming and pull strategy implemented by the marketing department as well as technological leadership implemented by research and development fit best to promote growth through innovative and differentiated products and services. There is an obvious strategic misfit, when the firm's growth strategy, if we take the case of technologically innovative products and services, is combined with technological followership (suitable for rather standardized products positioned at later stages of the product life cycle) and penetration pricing (rather low prices targeting mass markets) and push strategy (large volume sales pushed through the distribution channels in order to realize scale effects).

Assuming another case that the firm's management decides to launch a retrenchment strategy on the directional level and consequently draws back its activities from the less promising markets, and instead concentrates on their core products, strategies on the competitive and functional levels should be adjusted accordingly. The environmental analysis plays an important role not only in terms of strategic decision processes but also in terms of strategic implementation processes. Due to the permanently changing environmental surroundings, the environmental analysis on the macro, industry, and micro levels must be frequently updated during strategy implementation.

The balanced scorecard indicates an important performance measuring system within the process of strategy implementation and control. A balanced scorecard combines conventional financial performance indicators, for example, turnover, product margins, and market shares, and non-financial performance indicators, such as customer satisfaction. Thus, balanced scorecard takes a long-term perspective (Zell, 2008; Kaplan and Norton, 1992). The definition of critical input determinants, which are important for realizing important strategic objectives, is called 'cause and effect analysis,' which can be illustrated in a 'fishbone diagram' (John et al., 2006). Figure 3.14 serves as an example of defined causes (X1–X8), which have major impacts on the firm's successful implementation of its growth strategy (Y = effect).

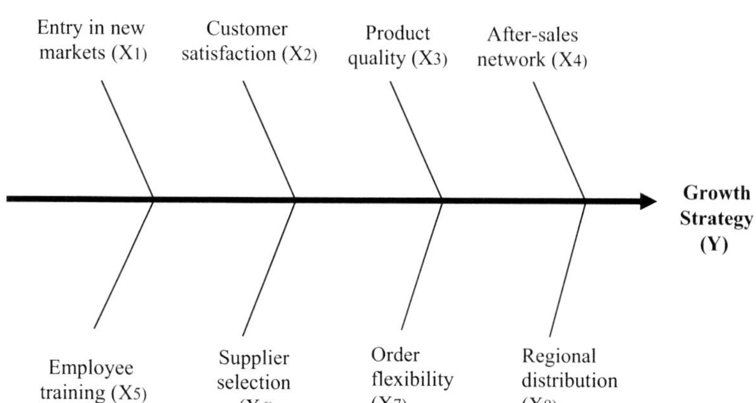

Figure 3.14 Critical success factors for a firm's growth strategy.

Large and complex tasks with corresponding strategic importance for the firm's business success often require project management for its successful implementation. A project consists of people who are brought together and become project team members. The more specified the firm's products and services, the more recommendable become the project management activities where internal and external specialists (e.g. engineers, marketing and sales staff, and information technology specialists) are brought together. The project team members are selected by the management, who ensures that the project rolls out according to the firm's major aims (Bordean et al., 2011).

Strategy implementation and control through project management are recommended for several reasons, as the following examples illustrate (Glowik and Bruhs, 2014):

- In terms of a firm's growth strategy, a new product development requires meetings with important suppliers to investigate each vendor's technological expertise and component supply reliability to ensure that the desired quality and technological performance are secured. Internal project members are typically from the research and development, marketing and sales, quality assurance, and procurement departments. The project leader should be a person with strong technological knowledge.
- A firm plans to outsource its transportation activities to an external logistics firm. Internal project members should be selected from the shipment, strategic controlling, sales, personnel, and quality assurance departments. The project leader should preferably be a person with logistic or controlling expertise and should be positioned at higher levels of the firm's management due to the relatively large impact that outsourcing logistics activities would have on the firm's future organization.
- The firm establishes an international joint venture with a current competitor. Each parent firm seeks to outsource a selected business segment to the joint venture in order to bundle its resources with the partner firm in the market. Internal project team members are preferably selected from those business units that are transferred to the joint venture. The project is usually led by the firm's top management due to the impact on the overall firm strategy.
- A firm seeks to get a quality safety certificate (e.g. TUV, ISO) from an external auditor. Internal project team members are appointed from the quality assurance, research and development, and procurement departments. The project leader should have the specific expertise necessary to realize and implement the certificate requirements provided by the auditors (Glowik and Bruhs, 2014).

The greater the project complexity and the greater the strategic dimension for the firm's management, the higher is the number of project stakeholders and the greater is the necessity for project management professionalism. Therefore, the project leader should have not only the professional qualifications to solve the emerging project tasks but also societal and leadership skills, which are vital for sustainable project success (Koester, 2010).

Bibliography

Ahmadi, SA, Salamzadeh, Y, Daraei, M & Akbari, J 2012, Relationship between organizational culture and strategy implementation: typologies and dimensions, *Global Business and Management Research: An International Journal*, vol. 4, pp. 286–299.

Albaum, G, Duerr, E & Strandskov, J 2008, *International marketing and export management*, Pearson Education Limited, Essex.

Alon, I 2003, *Chinese culture, organizational behavior, and international business management*, Praeger Publishers, Westport.

Atradius 2015. *Annual Report 2015 Atradius N.V.* [Online]. Available from: https://group.atradius.com/about-us/annual-reports.html. [August 24, 2016].

Atradius 2016. *History* [Online]. Available from: https://group.atradius.com/about-us/history.html. [August 24, 2016].

Azambuja, MM, Ponticelli, S & O'Brien, WJ 2014, Strategic procurement practices for the industrial supply chain, *ASCE Journal of Construction Engineering and Management*, vol. 140 (7), p. 4.

Backer, KD & Miroudot, S 2013, *Mapping global value chains* [Online]. OECD Publishing. Available from: http://purochioe.rrojasdatabank.info/OECDonGVC2013.pdf. [December 15, 2015].

Backhaus, K 2003, *Industriegütermarketing*, Verlag Franz Vahlen, München.

Baldwin, R & Lopez-Gonzalez, J 2015, Supply-chain trade: a portrait of global patterns and several testable hypotheses, *The World Economy*, vol. 38, pp. 1682–1721.

Bartlett, CA 1986, Building and managing the transnational: the new organizational challenge. *Competition in global industries: a conceptual framework*, Harvard Business School Press, Boston.

Bartlett, CA & Ghoshal, S 1990, *Internationale Unternehmensführung. Innovation, globale Effizienz, differenziertes Marketing*, Campus, Frankfurt.

Bartlett, CA & Ghoshal, S 1998, *Managing across borders: the transnational solution*, Harvard Press, Cambridge, MA.

Bertrand, O & Mol, MJ 2013, The antecedents and innovation effects of domestic and offshore R&D outsourcing: the contingent impact of cognitive distance and absorptive capacity, *Strategic Management Journal*, vol. 34, pp. 751–760.

Bordean, O, Borza, A & Maier, V 2011, The involvement of boards in strategy implementation, *Review of International Comparative Management*, vol. 12, pp. 986–993.

Brouthers, KD 2013, Institutional, cultural and transaction cost influences on entry mode choice and performance, *Journal of International Business Studies*, vol. 44, pp. 1–13.

Brouthers, KD & Hennart, J-F 2007, Boundaries of the firm: insights from international entry mode research, *Journal of Management*, vol. 33, pp. 395–425.

Burton, RM, Obel, B & Håkonsson, DD 2015, *Organizational design: a step-by-step approach*, Cambridge University Press, Cambridge.

Bushardt, SC, Glascoff, DW & Doty, DH 2011, Organizational culture, formal reward structure, and effective strategy implementation: a conceptual model, *Journal of Organizational Culture, Communications and Conflict*, vol. 15, pp. 57–71.

Carlopio, J & Harvey, M 2012, The development of a social psychological model of strategy implementation, *International Journal of Management*, vol. 29, pp. 75–85.

Carroll, AB 1991, The pyramid of corporate social responsibility: toward the moral management of organizational stakeholders. *Business Horizons*, vol. 34, pp. 39–48.

Caruth, DL, Pane Haden, SS & Caruth, GD 2012, Critical factors in human resource outsourcing. *Journal of Management Research*, vol. 13, pp. 187–195.

Cateora, PR, Gilly, MC & Graham, JL 2009, *International marketing*, McGraw-Hill Irwin, Boston.

Cattaneo, O, Gereffi, G, Miroudot, S & Taglioni, D 2013, Joining, upgrading and being competitive in global value chains: a strategic framework, *World Bank Policy Research Working Paper*, vol. 1, pp. 2–50.

Cavusgil, T. S., Knight, G. & Riesenberger, J. R. 2008. *International business. Strategy, management and the new realities*, Pearson Education, Harlow, UK, and New York.

Chandler, A. D. 1962. *Strategy and structure. Chapters in the history of industrial enterprise*, MIT Press, Cambridge, MA.

Charterina, J & Landeta, J 2013, Effects of knowledge-sharing routines and dyad-based investments on company innovation and performance: an empirical study of Spanish manufacturing companies. *International Journal of Management*, vol. 30, pp. 197–216.

Chen, I & Paulraj, A 2004, Towards a theory of supply chain management: the constructs and measurements, *Journal of Operations Management*, vol. 22, pp. 119–150.

Chopra, S & Meindl, P 2014, *Supply chain management*, Pearson, Harlow.

Christmann, P. 2000, Effects of 'best practices' of environmental management on cost advantage: the role of complementary assets, *Academy of Management Journal*, vol. 43, pp. 663–680.

Christopher, M 2011, *Logistics and supply chain management: creating value-added networks*, Pearson Education, Harlow, UK.

Ciliberti, F, Pontrandolfo, P & Scozzi, B 2008, Investigating corporate social responsibility in supply chains: a SME perspective, *Journal of Cleaner Production*, vol. 16, pp. 1579–1588.

Coface 2016a, *Our history* [Online]. Available from: www.coface.com/Group/Our-history. [August 24, 2016].

Coface 2016b, *Financial summary* [Online]. Available from: www.coface.com/Group/Financial-summary. [August 24, 2016].

Coface 2016c, *Our business* [Online]. Available from: www.coface.com/Our-business. [August 24, 2016].

Combs, JG, Michael, SC & Castrogiovanni GJ 2004, Franchising: a review and avenues to greater theoretical diversity, *Journal of Management*, vol. 30, pp. 907–931.

Coyle, J, Langley, C, Novack, R & Gibson, B 2012, *Supply chain management: a logistics perspective*, Cengage Learning, Hampshire.

Daniel, RM 2015, Revisiting the strategic management process through the levels of strategy analysis, *Asian Journal of Management Research*, vol. 6, pp. 29–34.

Danis, WM, Chiaburu, DS & Lyles, MA 2010, The impact of managerial networking intensity and market-based strategies on firm growth during institutional upheaval: a study of small and medium-sized enterprises in a transition economy, *Journal of International Business Studies*, vol. 41, pp. 287–307.

Das, T & Rahman, N 2010, Determinants of partner opportunism in strategic alliances: a conceptual framework, *Journal of Business & Psychology*, vol. 25, pp. 55–74.

De La Merced, MJ & Picker, L 2015, *Dow Chemical and DuPont set merger and plans to split* [Online]. Available from: www.nytimes.com/2015/12/12/business/dealbook/dow-chemical-and-dupont-merger.html?_r=1. [August 24, 2016].

Deutsche Telekom. 2015. *Press release: Deutsche Telekom and Orange sell their mobile Joint Venture EE to BT for GBP 12.5 billion* [Online]. Available from: www.telekom.com/media/company/265230. [August 21, 2016].

Dey, B, Sorour, K & Filieri, R 2016, *ICTS in developing countries*, Palgrave Macmillan, Hampshire.

Dowling, PJ & Welch, DE 2004, *International Human Resource Management. Managing people in a multinational context,* Thomson, London.

Du, S, Bhattacharya, CB & Sen, S 2010, Maximizing business returns to corporate social responsibility (CSR): the role of CSR communication, *International Journal of Management Reviews*, vol. 12, pp. 8–19.

Dunning, JH & Lundan, SM 2008, *Multinational enterprise and the global economy*, Edward Elgar, Cheltenham.

Dutta, S, Narasimhan, O & Rajiv, S 1999, Success in high-technology markets: is marketing capability critical? *Marketing Science*, vol. 18, pp. 547–568.

Euler Hermes 2016a, *100+ years of experience* [Online]. Available from: www.eulerhermes.com/group/who-we-are/pages/a-hundred-years-history.aspx. [August 24, 2016].

Euler Hermes 2016b, *Euler Hermes maintains strong 2015 profitability in a more difficult environment* [Online]. Available from: www.eulerhermes.com/mediacenter/news/Pages/press-release-full-year-2015-financial-results.aspx. [August 25, 2016].

Euler Hermes 2016c, *Credit insurance* [Online]. Available from: www.eulerhermes.com/products-solutions/credit-insurance/Pages/default.aspx. [August 24, 2016].

European Union 2016, *Green public procurement (GPP)* [Online]. Available from: http://ec.europa.eu/environment/gpp/what_en.htm. [August 17, 2016].

Freytag, PV & Clarke, AH 2001, Business to business market segmentation, *Industrial Marketing Management*, vol. 30, pp. 473–486.

Garaventa, E & Tellefsen, T 2001, Outsourcing: the hidden costs, *Review of Business*, vol. 22, pp. 28–31.

Gebauer, H & Kowalkowski, C 2012, Customer-focused and service-focused orientation in organizational structures, *Journal of Business and Industrial Marketing*, vol. 27, pp. 527–537.

Gereffi, G & Luo, X 2015, Risks and opportunities of participation in global value chains, *Journal of Banking and Financial Economics*, vol. 2, pp. 51–63.

Gillan, SL & Starks, LT 1998, A survey of shareholder activism: motivation and empirical evidence. *Contemporary Finance Digest*, vol. 2, no. 3, pp. 10–34.

Gillan, SL & Starks, LT 2003, Corporate governance, corporate ownership, and the role of institutional investors: a global perspective, *Journal of Applied Finance*, vol. 13, no. 2, pp. 4–22.

Glowik, M 2016, *Market entry strategies*, DeGruyter, Berlin and Boston.

Glowik, M & Bruhs, SM 2014, *Business-to-business. A global network perspective*, Routledge, Taylor and Francis Group, London and New York.

Glowik, M & Smyczek, S 2011, *International marketing management. Strategies, concepts and cases in Europe*, Verlag, München, Oldenbourg.

Goebal, P, Reuter, C, Pibernik, R & Sichtmann, C 2012, The influence of ethical culture on supplier selection in the context of sustainable sourcing, *International Journal of Production Economics*, vol. 140, pp. 7–17.

Gouveia, VV & Ros, M 2000, Hofstede and Schwartz's models for classifying individualism at the cultural level: their relation to macro-social and macro-economic variables, *Psicothema*, vol. 12, pp. 25–33.

Gov.UK 2016, *Incoterms (International Commercial Terms)* [Online]. Available from: www.gov.uk/incoterms-international-commercial-terms/overview. [September 16, 2016].

Gugler, P & Shi, JYJ 2009, Corporate social responsibility for developing country multinational corporations: lost war in pertaining global competitiveness? *Journal of Business Ethics*, vol. 87, pp. 3–24.

Halpern, P 1983, Corporate acquisitions: a theory of special cases? A review of event studies applied to acquisitions, *The Journal of Finance*, vol. 38, pp. 297–317.

Hatch, MJ & Schultz, M 1997, Relations between organizational culture, identity and image, *European Journal of Marketing*, vol. 31, pp. 356–365.

Hendrikse, G & Jiang, T 2007, Plural form of franchising: an incomplete contracting approach, in *Economics and Management of Networks*, eds G Cliquet, G Hendrikse, M Tuunanen & J Windsperger, Physica-Verlag, Heidelberg.

Hennart, J-F & Reddy, S 1997, The choice between mergers/acquisitions and joint ventures: the case of Japanese investors in the United States, *Strategic Management Journal*, vol. 18, pp. 1–12.

Hill, CWL 1990, Cooperation, opportunism, and the invisible hand: implications for transaction cost theory, *Academy of Management Review*, vol. 15, pp. 500–513.

Hill, CWL 2012, *International business: competing in the global marketplace*, McGraw-Hill/Irwin, Boston.

Hitt, MA, Li, D & Hu, K 2016, International strategy: from local to global and beyond, *Journal of World Business*, vol. 51, pp. 58–73.

Hofmann, E 2005, Supply chain finance—some conceptual insights, *Beiträge zu Beschaffung und Logistik*, pp. 203–214.

Hofstede, G 1994, The business of international business is culture, *International Business Review*, vol. 3, pp. 1–14.

Hofstede, G 2001, *Culture's consequences—comparing values, behaviours, institutions and organization across nations*, Sage Publications Inc., Thousand Oaks, London, and New Delhi.

Hofstede, G 2011, Dimensionalizing cultures: the Hofstede model in context, *Online Readings in Psychology and Culture*, vol. 2, pp. 1–26.

Hollensen, S 2010, *Global marketing: a decision-oriented approach*, Pearson, Harlow.

Hollensen, S 2014, *Global marketing. A decision-oriented approach*, Pearson Education Limited, Harlow.

Hollensen, S, Boyd, B & Ulrich, AMD 2011, Choice of foreign entry modes in a control perspective, *IUP Journal of Business Strategy*, vol. 8, pp. 7–31.

House, RJ, Hanges, PJ, Javidan, M, Dorfman, PW & Gupta, V 2004, *Culture, leadership, and organizations: The GLOBE study of 62 societies*, Sage Publications Inc., Thousand Oaks, London, and New Delhi.

Hung, RYY, Lien, BY-H, Yang, B, Wu, C-M & Kuo, Y-M 2011, Impact of TQM and organizational learning on innovation performance in the high-tech industry, *International Business Review*, vol. 20, pp. 213–225.

ICC 2010, *About the International Chamber of Commerce* [Online]. Available from: www.iccwbo.org/privacy/. [December 30, 2016].

IMAA Institute 2015, *Statistics* [Online]. Available from: https://imaa-institute.org/statistics/. [August 23, 2106].

Incoterms 2010, *Revised trade rules for an inter-connected world*, International Chambre of Commerce, Paris.

Janićijevič N 2011, Methodological approaches in the research of organizational culture, *Economic Annals*, vol. 56, no. 189, pp. 69–99.

Johanson, J & Vahlne, J-E 2009, The Uppsala internationalization process model revisited: from liability of foreignness to liability of outsidership, *Journal of International Business Studies*, vol. 40, pp. 1411–1431.

John, A, Meran, R, Roenpage, O & Staudter, C 2006, *Six sigma + ean toolset*, Springer, Berlin, Heidelberg, New York.

Johnson, G, Scholes, K & Whittington, R 2009, *Exploring corporate strategy*, Pearson, Harlow.

Jones, PM 2010, *Trade credit insurance* [Online]. The World Bank. Available from: www.smyyth.com/wp-content/uploads/2016/03/Trade-Credit-Insurance-Primer-The-World-Bank.pdf. [August 24, 2016].

Kalish, S, Mahajan, V & Muller, E 1995, Waterfall and sprinkler: new product strategies in competitive global markets, *International Journal of Research in Marketing*, vol. 12, pp. 105–119.

Kaplan, RS & Norton, DP 1992, The balanced scorecard—measures that drive performance, *Harvard Business Review*, vol. 1, pp. 71–79.

Koester, K 2010, *International project management*, Sage Publications, Singapore.

Kohli, AK & Jaworski, BJ 1990, Market orientation: the construct, research propositions, and managerial implications, *Journal of Marketing Management*, vol. 54, pp. 1–18.

Kosko, B 1994, *Fuzzy thinking*, Flamingo, London.

Kotabe, M & Helsen, K 2008, *Global marketing management*, John Wiley & Sons, Hoboken, NJ.

Kotler, P & Armstrong, G 2011, *Marketing: an introduction*, Prentice Hall, Harlow, Essex.

Kotler, P, Keller, KL, Brady, M, Goodman, M & Hansen, T 2009, *Marketing management*, Pearson Education Limited, Harlow, Essex.

Kumar, V & Subramanian, V 1997, A contingency framework for the mode of entry decision, *Journal of World Business*, vol. 32, pp. 53–72.

Lan, W & Hua, S 2013, Supply chain finance, in *Supply chain perspectives and issues in China. A literature review*, ed S Hua. Fung Global Institute, Hong Kong, pp. 117–126.

Larimo, J 2007, International joint venture performance: impact of performance measures and foreign parent, target country and investment specific variables on performance, in *Economics and management of networks*, eds G Cliquet, G Hendrikse, M Tuunanen & J Windsperger, Physica-Verlag, Heidelberg.

Lee, JY, Kozlenkova, IV & Palmatier, RW 2015, Structural marketing: using organizational structure to achieve marketing objectives, *Journal of the Academy of Marketing Science*, vol. 43, pp. 73–99.

Lessem, R & Palsule, S 1997, *Managing in four worlds: from competition to co-creation*, Blackwell Publishers, Oxford.

Li, M, Zhang, Y & Jing, R 2008, Does ownership and culture matter to joint venture success? *International Management Review*, vol. 4, pp. 90–103.

Lindgreen, A & Swaen, V 2010, Corporate social responsibility, *International Journal of Management Reviews*, vol. 12, pp. 1–7.

Lindgreen, A & Wynstra, F 2005, Value in business markets: what do we know? Where are we going? *Industrial Marketing Management*, vol. 34, pp. 732–748.

López-Duarte, C & Vidal-Suárez, MM 2010, External uncertainty and entry mode choice: cultural distance, political risk and language diversity, *International Business Review*, vol. 19, pp. 575–588.

Madrakhimova, F 2013, Evolution of the concept and definition of corporate social responsibility, *Global Conference on Business and Finance Proceedings*, vol. 8, 113–118.

Mahoney, J 1992, The choice of organizational form: vertical ownership versus other methods of vertical integration, *Strategic Management Journal*, vol. 13, 559–584.

Mathews, JA 2002, *Dragon multinational. A new model for global growth*, Oxford University Press, New York.

Mathews, JA 2006, Catch-up strategies and the latecomer effect in industrial development, *New Political Economy*, vol. 11, pp. 313–335.

Matzler, K, Stieger, D & Füller, J 2011, Consumer confusion in Internet-based mass customisation: testing a network of antecedents and consequences, *Journal of Consumer Policy*, vol. 34, pp. 231–247.

Mckinnon, A, Browne, M, Whiteing, A & Piecyk, M (eds) 2015, *Green logistics: improving the environmental sustainability of logistics*, Kogan Page Publishers, London.

Mintzberg, H, Lampel, J, Quinn, JB & Ghoshal, S 2003, *The strategy process. Concepts, contexts, cases*, Pearson Education Limited, Essex.

Müller-Stewens, G & Lechner, C 2011, *Strategisches Management. Wie strategische Initiativen zum Wandel führen*, Schäffer-Poeschel, Stuttgart.

Napier, NK 1989, Merger and acquisitions, human resource issues and outcomes: a review and suggested typology, *Journal of Management Studies*, vol. 26, pp. 271–289.

Naqshbandi, DMM & Kaur, S 2013, A study of organizational citizenship behaviours, organizational structures and open innovation, *International Journal of Business and Social Science*, vol. 2, pp. 182–193.

Nayager, T & Van Vuuren, JJ 2015, An analysis of an organisational strategy, structure and culture that supports corporate entrepreneurship in established organisations, *South African Journal of Economic and Management Sciences*, vol. 8, pp. 29–38.

Newbert, SL 2008, Value, rareness, competitive advantage, and performance: a conceptual-level empirical investigation of the resource-based view of the firm, *Strategic Management Journal*, vol. 29, pp. 745–768.

Nielsen, BB & Nielsen, S 2011, The role of top management team international orientation in international strategic decision-making: the choice of foreign entry mode, *Journal of World Business*, vol. 46, pp. 185–193.

North, DC 1990, *Institutions, institutional change and economic performance*, Cambridge University Press, Cambridge.

Park, J-Y & Harris, S 2014, Microfoundations for learning within international joint ventures, *International Business Review*, vol. 23, pp. 490–503.

Pedersen, T, Petersen, B & Benito, GRG 2002, Change of foreign operation method: Impetus and switching costs, *International Business Review*, vol. 11, pp. 325–345.

Penrose, E 1959, *The theory of the growth of the firm*, Oxford University Press, New York.

Penrose, E 1995, *The theory of the growth of the firm*, Oxford University Press, Oxford.

Perlmutter, HV 1969, The tortuous evolution of the multinational corporation, *Columbia Journal of World Business*, vol. 4, pp. 9–18.

Perlmutter, HV 1986, The tortuous evolution of the multinational corporation, *Columbia Journal of world business*, vol. 4, pp. 9–18.

Perlmutter, HV & Heenan, D 1974, How multinational should your top managers be? *Harvard Business Review*, vol. 52 (6), pp. 121–132.

Pezza, S 2011, Supply chain finance: gaining control in the face of uncertainty, in Group, A. (ed.). //Author: Please provide book title, name of editor, publisher, and publisher's city.//.

Pfohl, HC & Gomm, M 2009, Supply chain finance: optimizing financial flows in supply chains, *Logistics Research*, vol. 1, pp. 149–161.

Piller, FT 2005, Mass customisation: reflections on the state of the concept, *International Journal of Flexible Manufacturing Systems*, vol. 16, pp. 313–334.

Pisano, GP 1991, The governance of innovation: vertical integration and collaborative arrangements in the biotechnology industry, *Research Policy*, vol. 20, pp. 237–249.

Porter, ME 1980, *Competitive strategy*, Free Press, New York.

Porter, ME 1999, *Wettbewerbsstrategie. Methoden zur Analyse von Branchen und Konkurrenten*, Campus Verlag, Frankfurt/M. //Author: What does "M." stand for?//.

Porter, ME & Kramer, M 2011a, The big idea. Creating shared value. How to reinvent capitalism and unleash a wave of innovation and growth, *Harvard Business Review*, pp. 1–17. //Author: Provide vol. no., if possible.//.

Porter, ME & Kramer, M 2011b, Strategy and society. The link between competitive advantage and corporate social responsibility, *Harvard Business Review*, vol. 84, pp. 78–92.

Porter, ME & Kramer, M 2014, Contesting the value of creating shared value, *California Management Review*, vol. 56, pp. 130–153.

Potkány, M 2008, Personnel outsourcing processes, *Ekonomie a Management*, vol. 11, pp. 53–62.

Qui, LD & Wang, S 2011, FDI policy, greenfield investment and cross-border mergers. *Review of Financial Economics*, vol. 19, pp. 836–851.

Raduan, CR, Jegak, U, Haslinda, A & Alimin, II 2009, Management, strategic management theories and the linkage with organization competitive advantage from the resource based view, *European Journal of Social Sciences*, vol. 11, pp. 402–417.

Ram, S & Sheth, JN 1989, Consumer resistance to innovations: the marketing problem and its solutions, *The Journal of Consumer Marketing*, vol. 6, pp. 5–14.

Rao, PS, Mellam, AC & Manohar, P 2015, Contribution of organisational structures to leaders and followers: performances in business enterprises in Papua New Guinea, *Universal Journal of Management*, vol. 3, pp. 303–308.

Rent, R & Monczka, R 2003, Understanding integrated global sourcing, *International Journal of Physical Distribution and Logistics Management*, vol. 33, pp. 607–629.

Ren, H, Gray, B & Kim, K 2009, Performance of international joint ventures: what factors really make a difference and how? *Journal of Management*, vol. 1, pp. 1–27.

Rogers, EM 2003, *Diffusion of innovations*, Free Press, New York.

Rottig, D, Reus, TH & Tarba, SY 2014, The impact of culture on mergers and acquisitions: a third of a century of research, *Advances in Mergers and Acquisitions*, vol. 12, pp. 135–172.

Sanchez-Peinado, E, Pla-Barber, J & Hébert, L 2007, Strategic variables that influence entry mode choice in service firms, *Journal of International Marketing*, vol. 15, pp. 67–91.

Schwartz, SH 1999, A theory of cultural values and some implications for work, *Applied Psychology: An International Review*, vol. 48, pp. 23–47.

Shrader, RC 2001, Collaboration and performance in foreign markets: the case of young high-technology manufacturing firms, *Academy of Management Journal*, vol. 44, pp. 45–60.

Slamanig, M 2011, *Produktwechsel als Problem im Konzept der Mass Customization: Theoretische Überlegungen und empirische Befunde*, Gabler, Wiesbaden.

Slater, S & Robson, MJ 2012, Cultural interpretations of destructive acts and trust in Japanese supply channel relationships. *International Business Review*, vol. 21, pp. 357–368.

Slater, SF & Narver, JC 1994, Market orientation, customer value, and superior performance, *Business Horizon*, vol. 37 (2) (March/April), pp. 22–28.

Smith, C, Palazzo, G & Bhattacharya, CB 2010, Marketing's consequences: stakeholder marketing and supply chain corporate social responsibility issues, *Business Ethics Quarterly*, vol. 20, pp. 617–641.

Smith, R 2008, Harnessing competencies, capabilities and resources, *Research Technology Management*, vol. 51, pp. 47–53.

Song, Y, Su, Q, Liu, Q & Wang, T 2012, Impact of business relationship functions on relationship quality and buyer's performance, *Journal of Business & Industrial Marketing*, vol. 27, pp. 286–298.

Steiger, JS, Hammou, KA & Galib, MH 2014, An examination of the influence of organizational structure types and management levels on knowledge management practices in organizations, *International Journal of Business and Management*, vol. 9, pp. 43–57.

Tan, Q & Sousa, CMP 2013, International marketing standardization: a meta-analytic estimation of its antecedents and consequences, *Management International Review*, vol. 53, pp. 711–739.

Taylor, CR, Zou, S & Osland, GE 1998, A transaction cost perspective on foreign market entry strategies of US and Japanese firms, *Thunderbird International Business Review*, vol. 40, pp. 389–412.

Tolbert, P & Hall, R 2015, *Organizations: structures, processes and outcomes*, Routledge, Oxfordshire and New York.

Ulijn, JM, Duysters, G & Meijer, E 2010, *Strategic alliances, mergers and acquisitions: the influence of culture on successful cooperation*. Edward Elgar Publishing, Cheltenham and Northampton.

Van Der Veer, KJM 2015, The private export credit insurance effect on trade, *The Journal of Risk and Insurance*, vol. 82, 601–624.

Vernon, R. 1966, International investment and international trade in the product cycle. *Quarterly Journal of Economics*, 80, pp. 190–207.

Vernon, R 1972, International trade: the product life cycle approach, in *The product life cycle and international trade,* ed. LT Wells, Harvard University, Boston.

Waters, D & Rinsler, S 2014, *Global logistics: new directions in supply chain management*, Kogan Page Publishers, London.

Wheelen, TL & Hunger, JD 2010, *Strategic management and business policy. Achieving sustainability*, Pearson Education Ltd., Boston.

Williamson, OE 1975, *Markets and hierarchies—analysis and antitrust implications*, Free Press, New York.

Williamson, OE 1985, *The economic institutions of capitalism: firms, markets, relational contracting*, Free Press, New York.

Wind, Y, Douglas, SP & Perlmutter, HV 1973, Guidelines for developing international marketing strategies, *Journal of Marketing*, vol. 37, pp. 14–23.

Wu, CF 2006, The study of the relations among ethical considerations, family management and organizational performance in corporate governance, *Journal of Business Ethics*, vol. 68, pp. 165–179.

Yeniyurt, S, Henke, JW & Cavusgil, E 2013, Integrating global and local procurement for superior supplier working relations, *International Business Review*, vol. 22, pp. 351–362.

Zell, M 2008, *Kosten- und Performance Management. Grundlagen, Instrumente, Fallstudie*, Gabler Verlag, Wiesbaden.

Zingales, L 1995, What determines the value of corporate votes, *Quarterly Journal of Economics*, vol. 110, pp. 1047–1073.

4.1 Case study: Alibaba group

A successful Chinese and international digital business giant?

Mario Glowik

Case review questions

1. Today, in which businesses and industries does Alibaba operate as a result of its various acquisitions, alliances, and joint ventures? What makes the company different from others?
2. Where is currently the regional sales focus of Alibaba and what might be the next step in terms of Alibaba's internationalization strategy?
3. When you combine the various business activities of Alibaba Group, which opportunities and threats can you describe for Alibaba's stakeholders? What is the impact of the Alibaba Group on the society in China and other countries?
4. Would you invest in Alibaba? What is your opinion regarding the financial configuration of Alibaba from the perspective of a Chinese investor, as well as from the perspective of a foreign investor? Finally, what is your opinion concerning corporate ethical (tax paying) responsibilities of large multinational firms?

Company background and business segments

Alibaba Group has become one of the most powerful e-commerce business companies. The firm was established by an English teacher named Jack Ma in 1999 and is headquartered in Hangzhou, China. The aim was to launch a website that would help small Chinese exporters and entrepreneurs to sell their products.

An important millstone occurred in 2005, when Alibaba Group formed a strategic partnership with Yahoo. Alibaba.com, an online marketing technology platform, was launched in 2007, and after two years, Alibaba Cloud was established. Moreover, another landmark in this year was the acquisition of HiChina, China's leading Internet infrastructure service provider. In 2010, AliExpress site was launched and enabled exporters in China to reach consumers all over the world.

The largest online commerce company went public in 2014, when it launched its IPO. The Chinese company expanded overseas and founded offices abroad in Hong Kong, USA, UK, Taiwan, and India (Alibaba Group, 2016a; Alibaba Group, 2016d).

Today, the company and its segment businesses operate wholesale and retail online marketplaces in addition to Internet-based businesses, which offer advertising, electronic payment, cloud-based computing, network services, and others (Alibaba Group,

2016a). Its dominant operations run through three websites: Tmall, which offers online sales of branded products and focuses on China's middle class; Taobao, China's largest shopping site; and Alibaba.com, which connects Chinese exporters with other companies worldwide (Wright, 2015).

Alibaba became the world's largest online retailer, which operates the following marketplaces for consumers in China:

1 Taobao.com
   - It is an online shopping website in China.
   - Shoppers can choose from a wide range of products and services.
   - Consumers are able to contact other consumers and receive updates from merchants.
   - The site earns money by selling advertisements.
2 Tmall.com
   - It is China's largest 'third-party' platform for brands and retailers.
   - The firm provides a premium shopping experience for Chinese consumers.
   - Tmall charges its merchants yearly fees.
3 Juhuasuan.com
   - It is a sales and marketing platform.
   - The firm provides discounts and promotional events (Alibaba Group, 2016b; Zucchi, 2014).
4 1688.com
   - It is a leading online wholesale marketplace in China.
   - It is a wholesale channel for merchants to source products from domestic wholesalers (AlibabaGroup, 2016b).

In addition, Alibaba Group operates international marketplaces:

5 Alibaba.com
   - It is the first business established by Alibaba Group.
   - It is a leading English-language wholesale marketplace for global trade.
   - Millions of buyers and suppliers engage in the platform.
   - It provides a wide range of products, including consumer electronics, machinery, and apparel.
   - Alibaba.com charges money for listing transactions as well as subscription fees for maintaining storefronts in the marketplace (Alibaba.com, 2016; Zucchi, 2014).
6 AliExpress
   - It is a global retail marketplace targeting consumers worldwide.
   - Consumers are able to buy directly from manufacturers in China (Alibaba Group, 2016b; Zucchi, 2014).

Moreover, Alibaba's cloud computing segment offers cloud computing services to sellers in its marketplaces and to 'third-party' customers. The aim of Alibaba Group is to promote its cloud computing business in order to overtake Amazon from the US not only in cloud storage services but in all fields, where Amazon currently has competitive advantages and represents a powerful market presence (Forbes, 2016). The organization structure of Alibaba Group [status 2016] is illustrated in Figure 4.1.1.

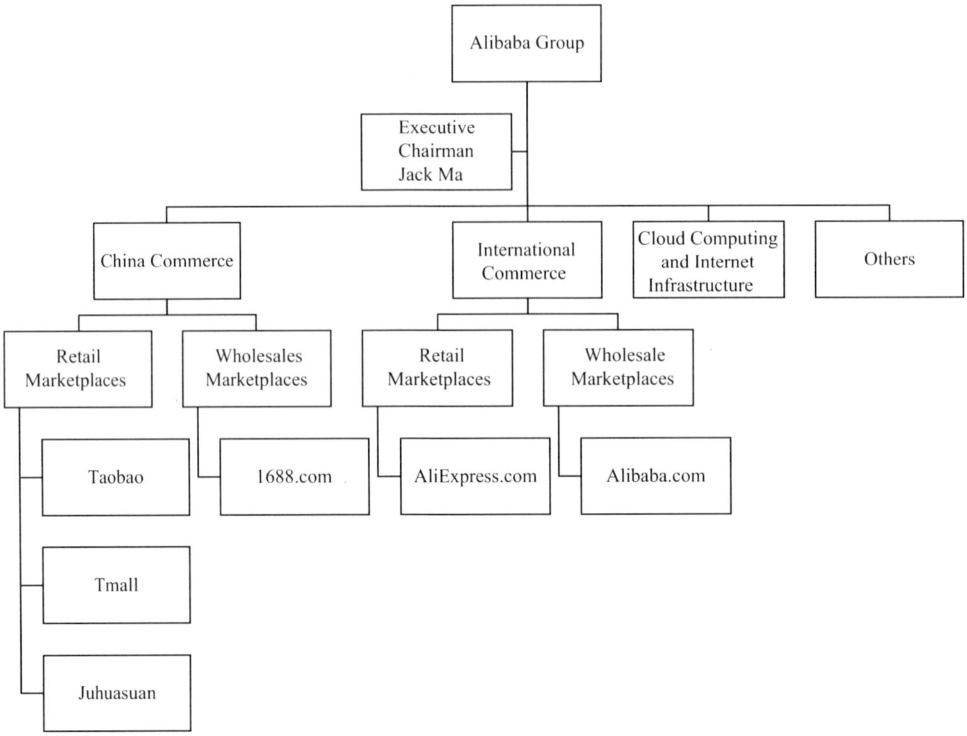

Figure 4.1.1 Organization of Alibaba Group.
Source: Author based on Alibaba's business segments (2016b, 2016c).

The financial results of Alibaba Group show its dominant position as the world's largest retailer with revenues of 101,143 million yuan (USD 15.3 billion), overtaking its competitor, Walmart (Lim, 2016). The net income of Alibaba Group in 2016 (Figure 4.1.2) amounted to 71,289 million yuan (USD 11.0 billion) (Alibaba Group, 2016c). In addition to Amazon, the Chinese company competes with eBay and PayPal (Zucchi, 2014). In other words, Alibaba is not only involved in digital business-to-business (B2B) transactions but also the Chinese firm launched its own e-payment systems, cloud computing, Internet infrastructure, and 'third party' e-commerce (similar to eBay) and digital business-to-consumer (B2C) platforms. The combination of B2B and B2C business platforms, together with e-payment which also includes financing instruments like loans, serves as an entirely new worldwide business concept, which differentiates Alibaba from its competitors.

Alibaba Group operates its primary businesses that are arranged in different regional marketplaces and related business segments. The domestic Chinese e-commerce market is the largest market for Alibaba and represents 82.6 percent of the total revenues in 2015. The international market generates 8.5 percent of total revenues. Cloud computing and Internet infrastructure constituted 1.7 percent of the total revenues. Finally, in 2015, other revenues, which consist of loans to sellers on Alibaba retail and wholesale marketplaces, represented 7.2 percent of the total revenues (Miglani, 2015) (Figure 4.1.3).

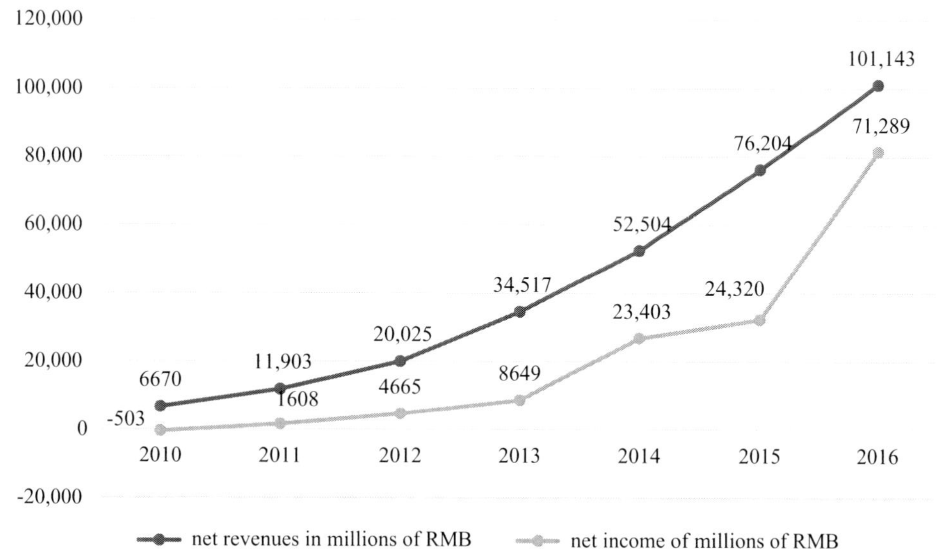

Figure 4.1.2 Alibaba Group: net sales versus net income (in millions of RMB) for the period of 2010–2016.

Source: Author based on annual report of Alibaba Group (2016c) and Statista (2016a; 2016b).

Note: 1 USD = 6.64 RMB (Bankenverband, 2016) as of August 16, 2016.

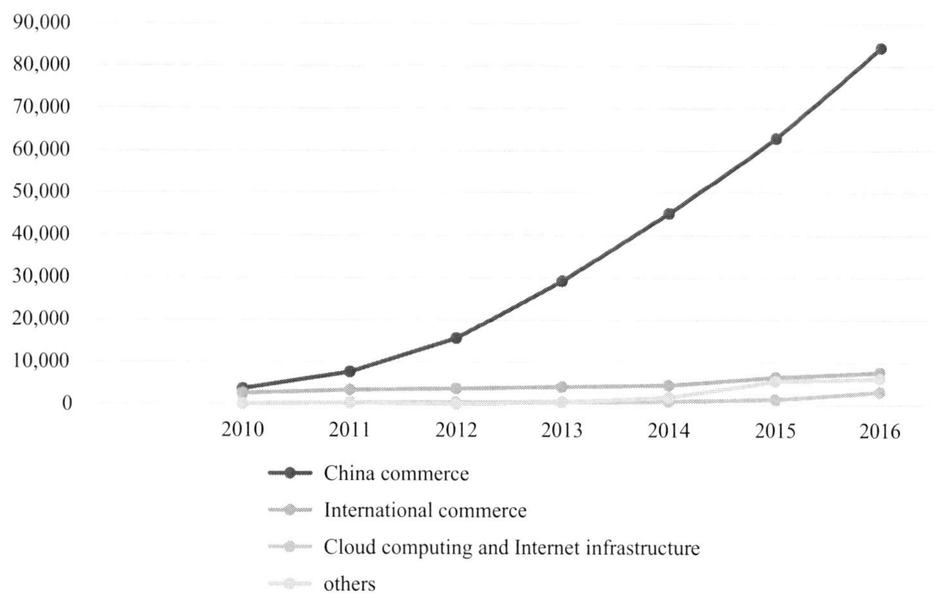

Figure 4.1.3 Alibaba Group: revenues by segment (in millions of RMB).

Source: Author based on annual reports of Alibaba Group (2016c) and Statista (2016c).

Note: 1 USD = 6.64 RMB (Bankenverband, 2016) as of August 16, 2016.

It is illegal for foreigners to invest in China's e-commerce, finance, and banking industries. Alibaba is a Chinese e-commerce company and, thus, cannot have foreigners as stockholders. Therefore, the organization structure of Alibaba is divided into two entities, one in China and one in the Cayman Islands. The China-based entity holds the essential permits and licenses, which are mandatory to conduct e-commerce, cloud, banking, and financing business in China. The second entity, the subsidiary, in the Cayman Islands serves as an offshore company (Nasdaq, 2014). Foreigners are allowed to buy Alibaba shares only of the Cayman Islands entity. Alibaba's subsidiary in the Cayman Islands is controlled by the holding company's top executives, first and foremost Jack Ma—it pays fees and royalties to the offshore company in the Cayman Islands, according to contracts between the two. Therefore, investors who bought shares of Alibaba on the New York Stock Exchange (where Alibaba is listed as well) actually purchased stocks of the holding company called Alibaba Group Holding Ltd. registered in the Cayman Islands with a claim on some of Alibaba's profits but no real ownership stake. This means that investors do not own shares of the actual Alibaba company and, therefore, have no voting rights in the company. Consequently, they also have no rights against any of its assets, including Taobao and Tmall. All the investors get is a share in Alibaba's profits (Nasdaq, 2014). The Cayman Islands is one of the most well-known 'tax havens' in the world. Unlike most countries, the Cayman Islands do not have a corporate tax, making it an ideal place for multinational corporations to base subsidiary entities to shield some or all of their incomes from taxation (Boyte-White, 2015).

The mission of Alibaba Group, as it is cited on its webpage, is 'to build the future infrastructure of commerce and be a company that lasts at least 102 years' (Alibaba Group, 2016e). Over the years, Alibaba Group has established strategic alliances and joint ventures to achieve business growth, and it has enhanced its international reach around the world. An abstract of the most important cooperative agreements in the history of Alibaba with other firms is presented below.

International strategic alliances (with and without mutual capital participation)

1 Alibaba.com and Yahoo
   - The partnership with Yahoo in 2005 is the one of the most significant agreements.
   - Yahoo invested USD 1 billion in cash to purchase Alibaba.com shares. As a result, Yahoo became one of the largest strategic investor in Alibaba.com.
   - The partnership enabled Alibaba.com to take advantage of Yahoo's global resources (Alibaba.com, 2005).
   - In 2012, Alibaba Group repurchased shares from Yahoo (AlibabaGroup, 2016a).

2 Alibaba.com and Infomedia
   - This alliance represents a collaboration with India's largest B2B media company in 2009.
   - Infomedia is the largest Yellow Pages and special interest publishing company in India.
   - The aim of the collaboration is to provide a business platform for small and medium-size enterprises (SMEs) in India.
   - The collaboration enabled Alibaba Group to improve its online B2B marketplace in India (Alibaba.com, 2009).

3 Alibaba Group and Sina Weibo
   - Alibaba Group acquired an 18 percent stake in Sina Weibo for $586 million in 2013.
   - Sina Weibo is a microblogging service provider similar to Twitter.
   - The alliance aimed to connect China's largest Twitter-like service and the largest e-commerce company.
   - Alibaba Group strengthened its presence in social networks and started to advertise on a Chinese social platform.
   - The partnership drives more web traffic to Alibaba's Taobao Marketplace (Mozur and Osawa, 2013; Ghosh and Ramakrishnan, 2013).

4 Alibaba Group and Suning Commerce
   - Suning Commerce is one of the largest consumer electronics retail chains in China.
   - Alibaba invested in 2015 approximately RMB 28.3 billion (USD 4.63 billion) for a 19.99 percent stake in Suning Commerce.
   - 'Alibaba and Suning have entered into a strategic collaboration agreement to build on synergies in e-commerce, logistics and incremental business through joint omni-channel initiatives' (Yahoo, 2015).

5 Alibaba Group and New Zealand Trade and Enterprise
   - In 2016, Alibaba Group and New Zealand Trade and Enterprise formed a partnership.
   - This strategic alliance aims to strengthen the trade between China and New Zealand and supports the communication of New Zealand brands in China (Businesswire, 2016).

Joint ventures

- In 2014, Alibaba Group and Intime established a joint venture to develop an online-to-offline (O2O) business in China. Alibaba invested USD 692 million in Intime, China's largest e-commerce operator integrating online and offline shopping.
- Alibaba as a major shareholder owns approximately 80 percent of the venture assets while Intime holds 20 percent (Barreto, 2014).
- Moreover, in 2015, Alibaba Group and Ant Financial Services Group formed a joint venture. Both parties invested USD 483.3 million and established 'New Company Koubei' that aimed at capturing offline consumption opportunities and focusing on the food and beverage segment. Koubei integrates aspects of mobile commerce and big data to transform and upgrade China's local services sector, including dining and shopping experiences (Alibaba Group, 2015).
- In May 2016, Alibaba Group and SoftBank established a joint venture, which aims to launch cloud computing services in Japan. SoftBank promotes Alibaba cloud business presence on the Japanese market (Alibaba Group, 2016f).

Acquisitions

In 2015, Alibaba Group invested approximately USD 15 billion in mergers and acquisitions (Abkowitz and Purnell, 2016; Salter-Robins, 2015). For example:

1 Acquisition of HiChina in 2009
   - HiChina Web Solutions provides domain name registration.
   - The aim of this purchase was to gain knowledge regarding web domain technology and management.

- The acquisition provided considerable benefits to Alibaba, such as a new, large customer base; newly developed value-added applications; advanced web site technology; and employee-management fund of expertise and skills in terms of web domain business.
- The total purchase volume amounted to RMB 539.98 million (USD 79.06 million) (Alibaba Group, 2009).

2 Acquisition of Vendio in 2010
- Alibaba.com acquired Vendio, a multi-channel e-commerce company.
- The company provides a one-stop solution for small business firms that sell across multiple channels.
- Alibaba.com gained access to small businesses in the US with potential sourcing needs from suppliers on Alibaba.com's sourcing platform and AliExpress.
- It was the first acquisition in the US-American market, which opens opportunities for new partnerships (Alibaba.com, 2010).

3 Acquisition of Shenzhen One-Touch Enterprise in 2010
- One-Touch is a provider of one-stop services for exporters in China.
- One-Touch is a leading provider of export-related services tailored to the needs of small businesses in China.
- Through the acquisition, Alibaba.com gained a wide range of export-related value-added services (Alibaba Group, 2010).

4 Acquisition of ChinaVision in 2014
- Alibaba Group bought a controlling stake in ChinaVision, a media firm that produces TV and movie contents.
- Alibaba Group paid USD 804 million, which gave the company access to ChinaVision's movie contents.
- The aim of this purchase was to attract more users to watch Ali TV (Reuters, 2014).

5 Acquisition of Youku Tudou in 2015
- Youku Tudou is considered to be China's 'YouTube.'
- Alibaba Group acquired the video site for a total equity purchase price of USD 4.8 billion.
- This acquisition enabled Alibaba to offer high quality US films and series to its consumers and strengthen its dominant position in Chinese e-commerce (Chen and Katz, 2015).

6 Acquisition of the South China Morning Post in 2015
- The acquisition of Hong Kong's leading English-language newspaper and other media assets of SCMP Group Ltd. raised the question regarding the editorial independence of the newspaper.
- Alibaba Group s purchased the newspaper for USD 266 million.
- In recent years, Alibaba has invested in a number of growing media outlets and content companies (Siu, 2015).

7 Acquisition of Lazada in 2016
- Alibaba Group acquired the Singapore e-commerce company Lazada Group.
- Lazada sells a variety of products ranging from rice cookers to smartphones and operates as an Amazon-like retail platform throughout Indonesia, Malaysia, Singapore, Thailand, Vietnam, and the Philippines.

- The acquisition enabled Alibaba Group to expand into e-commerce, logistics, and media in Southeast Asia.
- This is the largest overseas acquisition of Alibaba with a total purchase price of USD 1 billion (Abkowitz and Purnell, 2016).

Alibaba Group continues to develop its investment strategy and enhance its international expansion. For example, in 2015, Alibaba Group invested USD 200 million in the photo-messaging app Snapchat, (Wright, 2015). In addition, Alibaba invested USD 193.6 million into China Business News and has gained approximately 30 percent stake in the company. Alibaba invested in SingPost and became its second-largest single shareholder. SingPost offers mail, transportation, and e-commerce services in Singapore. Finally, Alibaba paid an unspecified amount of interest at Jet.com, a US-based e-commerce competitor of Amazon (Crouch, 2015).

The list of Alibaba's acquisitions is long and the success of the Chinese e-commerce firm is, in fact, amazing and impressive. Alibaba consequently makes use of a broad range of newly emerging digital business opportunities. However, some of the products offered at Alibaba platforms are of minor quality, indicating a low product lifetime and, thus, may hurt the environment. In addition, Alibaba is confronted with criticisms of harming intellectual property rights. Alibaba's founder and major owner Jack Ma commented in June 2016 to infuriate luxury goods makers who accuse the Chinese e-commerce group of profiting from the sale of knock-offs: 'We have to protect [intellectual property], we have to do everything to stop the fake products, but the problem is the fake products today are of better quality and better price than the real names' (Clover, 2016).

On the one hand, Alibaba benefits from the large Chinese home market, which provides them with a solid business ground supported by an e-commerce affinity of the Chinese population. On the other hand, it remains questionable how a previously unknown English teacher has been able to establish such a large conglomerate that, meanwhile, holds quasi-monopoly positions in various digital business markets in China. Excellent relations to relevant stakeholders in China obviously indicate another strong asset of Jack Ma.

Bibliography

Abkowitz, A & Purnell, N 2016, *Alibaba to invest $1 billion in e-commerce startup Lazada*. The Wall Street Journal. Available from: wsj.com/articles/alibaba-to-invest-1-billion-in-e-commerce-startup-lazada-1460445117. [June 18, 2016].

Alibaba.com 2005, *August 11, 2005: Yahoo! and Alibaba.com form strategic partnership in China*. Available from: http://resources.alibaba.com/article/352/August_11_2005_Yahoo_and_Alibaba_com_form_srategic_partnership_in_China.htm. [June 18, 2016].

Alibaba.com 2009, *Alibaba.com and Infomedia form strategic partnership in India*. Available from: http://news.alibaba.com/article/detail/alibaba/100096507-1-alibaba.com-infomedia-form-strategic-partnership.html. [June 18, 2016].

Alibaba.com 2010, *Alibaba.com acquires Vendio, continues to advance global E-Commerce platform*. Available from:http://news.alibaba.com/article/detail/alibaba/100340213-1-alibaba.com-acquires-vendio%252c-continues-advance.html. [June 18, 2016].

Alibaba.com 2016, *About Alibaba.com*. Available from: http://activities.alibaba.com/alibaba/following-about-alibaba.php?spm=a2700.7848340.a272z3.9.aTa9pH. [June 11, 2016].

Alibaba Group 2009, *Alibaba.com Completes acquisition of HiChina Web Solutions*. Available from: www.alibabagroup.com/en/news/press_pdf/p091228.pdf. [June 18, 2016].

Alibaba Group 2010, *Alibaba.com to acquire export service provider Shenzhen One-Touch*. Available from: www.alibabagroup.com/en/news/press_pdf/p101115.pdf. [June 18, 2016].

Alibaba Group 2015, Alibaba Group and Ant Financial Announce Local Services JV. Available from: www.alibabagroup.com/en/news/article?news=p150623. [June 18, 2016].

Alibaba Group 2016a, *History and milestones*. Available from: www.alibabagroup.com/en/about/history. [June 11, 2016].

Alibaba Group 2016b, *Our businesses*. Available from: hwww.alibabagroup.com/en/about/businesses. [June 11, 2016].

Alibaba Group 2016c, *Annual report 2016*. Available from: www.alibabagroup.com/en/ir/pdf/agm160524_ar.pdf. [October 30, 2016].

Alibaba Group 2016d, *Our offices*. Available from: www.alibabagroup.com/en/contact/offices. [June 17, 2016].

Alibaba Group 2016e, *Company overview*. Available from: www.alibabagroup.com/en/about/overview. [June 18, 2016].

Alibaba Group 2016f, Alibaba Group and SoftBank form joint venture to launch cloud computing services in Japan. Available from: www.alibabagroup.com/en/news/article?news=p160513. [June 18, 2016].

Bankenverband, D 2016, *Währungsrechner* [Online]. Available from: https://bankenverband.de/service/waehrungsrechner/. [August 16, 2016].

Barreto, E 2014, *Alibaba invests $692 million in Chinese department store operator*. Reuters. Available from: www.reuters.com/article/us-intime-alibaba-group-idUSBREA2U01K20140331. [June 18, 2016].

Boyte-White, C 2015, *Why is the Cayman Islands considered a tax haven?* [Online]. Available from: www.investopedia.com/ask/answers/100215/why-cayman-islands-considered-tax-haven.asp. [August 23, 2016].

Businesswire 2016, *Alibaba Group and New Zealand Government form strategic alliance to strengthen trade with China*. Available from: www.businesswire.com/news/home/20160417005102/en/Alibaba-Group-Zealand-Government-Form-Strategic-Alliance. [June 18, 2016].

Chen, L and Katz, L 2015, *Alibaba buys Youku in deal said to be valued at $4.8 billion*. Bloomberg. Available from: www.bloomberg.com/news/articles/2015-11-06/alibaba-agrees-to-buy-video-site-youku-tudou-for-27-60-a-share. [June 18, 2016].

Clover, C 2016, *Alibaba's Jack Ma says fakes are better than originals* [Online]. Available from: www.ft.com/cms/s/2/6700d5cc-3209-11e6-ad39-3fee5ffe5b5b.html#axzz4IAC1j6cv. [August 23, 2016].

Crouch, E 2015, *Alibaba's biggest investments of 2015*. Available from: www.techinasia.com/alibaba-biggest-investments-2015. [June 18, 2016].

Forbes 2016, *Can Alibaba's cloud business be its next driver of growth?* Available from: www.forbes.com/sites/greatspeculations/2016/05/09/can-alibabas-cloud-business-be-its-next-driver-of-growth/#49f82e7e20bc. [June 11, 2016].

Ghosh, S and Ramakrishnan, S 2013, *Alibaba pushes into social networking with Weibo investment*. Available from: www.reuters.com/article/net-us-sinaweibo-alibaba-stake-idUSBRE93S0DA20130429. [June 18, 2016].

Lim, J 2016, *Alibaba Group FY2016 revenue jumps 33%, EBITDA up 28%*. Forbes. Available from: www.forbes.com/sites/jlim/2016/05/05/alibaba-fy2016-revenue-jumps-33-ebitda-up-28/#2d32cf7c61a9. [June 18, 2016].

Miglani, J 2015, *How Alibaba makes money?* Available from: http://revenuesandprofits.com/how-alibaba-makes-money/. [June 17, 2016].

Mozur, P & Osawa, J 2013, *Chinese Web firms Alibaba, Sina form Alliance*. Available from: www.wsj.com/articles/SB10001424127887323982704578452611656117272. [June 18, 2016].

Nasdaq 2014, *Alibaba's business structure: Does it involve risks?—analyst log* [Online]. Available from: www.nasdaq.com/article/alibabas-business-structure-does-it-involve-risks-analyst-blog-cm397135. [August 23, 2016].

Reuters 2014, *Alibaba buys ChinaVision stake for $804 million; gains TV, movie content*. Available from: www.reuters.com/article/us-chinavision-alibaba-idUSBREA2B02C20140312. [June 18, 2016].

Salter-Robins, M 2015, *Chinese internet giant Alibaba could spend up to $38 billion on acquisitions in 2016*. Business Insider. Available from: www.businessinsider.de/alibaba-mergers-acquisitions-spend-2016-38-billion-2015-12?r=UK&IR=T. [June 18, 2016].

Siu, T 2015, *Alibaba agrees to $266 million acquisition deal with South China Morning Post*. Available from: www.reuters.com/article/us-scmp-group-alibaba-idUSKBN0TX01S20151214. [June 18, 2016].

Statista 2016a, *Annual revenue of Alibaba Group from 2010 to 2016 (in million yuan)*. Available from: www.statista.com/statistics/225614/net-revenue-of-alibaba/. [June 11, 2016].

Statista 2016b, *Annual net income of Alibaba from 2010 to 2016 (in million yuan)*. Available from: www.statista.com/statistics/298844/net-income-alibaba/. [June 11, 2016].

Statista 2016c, *Annual revenue of Alibaba from 2010 to 2016, by segment (in million yuan)*. Available from: www.statista.com/statistics/298839/revenue-of-alibabacom-segment/. [June 11, 2016].

Wright, C 2015, *Why is Alibaba investing in Snapchat?* Forbes. Available from: www.forbes.com/sites/chriswright/2015/03/12/why-is-alibaba-investing-in-snapchat/#1178453fba69. [June 11, 2016].

Yahoo! 2015, *Alibaba and Suning Commerce Enter Into Strategic Alliance*. Available from: http://finance.yahoo.com/news/alibaba-suning-commerce-enter-strategic-081700842.html. [June 18, 2016].

Zucchi, K 2014, *How does Alibaba make money? A simple guide*. Available from: www.investopedia.com/articles/investing/121714/how-does-alibaba-make-money-simple-guide.asp. [June 11, 2016].

4.2 Case study: Corporate Social Responsibility (CSR) taking the case of Facebook

Yael Kishon

Case review questions

1 How would you explain major drawbacks regarding Facebook users' privacy?
2 How would you describe the CSR program of Facebook?
3 In light of social responsibility, what is the personal responsibility to protect the online privacy of Facebook's users who constantly use the social network?
4 How would you discuss the challenges of Facebook for implementing CSR policy?
5 How would you describe similarities and differences between Facebook and other firms, which have a wide range of CSR programs and initiatives?

About the company

Facebook is a social networking service located in Menlo Park, California. Facebook was founded in 2004 by Mark Zuckerberg, who had the idea as a student to set up a social network service for Harvard students (Facebook, 2016a). The site has quickly expanded into other universities, and in 2006, the network extended its registration policy to allow anyone with a registered email address to join. The site features continued to develop in 2007, when the conventional Facebook platform, Facebook video and Facebook platform for mobile, were launched. In 2009, Facebook launched the Like button (Facebook, 2016a), which gave users the opportunity to express their thoughts about their friends' posts, status links, or any other information (Vincent, 2014).

In 2012, Facebook announced the acquisition of Instagram, the popular photo-sharing app. In 2013, the company acquired Atlas Advertiser Suite from Microsoft. Atlas is a leader in campaign management and measurement for marketers and agencies (Facebook Newsroom, 2013). Another important milestone occurred in 2014, when Facebook acquired WhatsApp, the rapidly growing mobile messaging app. In 2014, Facebook purchased Oculus, one of the leading companies in virtual reality technology (Facebook, 2016a; Facebook Newsroom, 2014).

In June 2016, Facebook had 1.71 billion monthly active users and has become the most popular social network worldwide (Facebook, 2016a). Facebook has achieved financial success with increased revenues and profits. The company generates most of its revenues from the sale of advertising space (MarketLine, 2012). In 2015, Facebook generated USD 17.9 billion of total revenues (Facebook, 2014; 2015) (Figure 4.2.1).

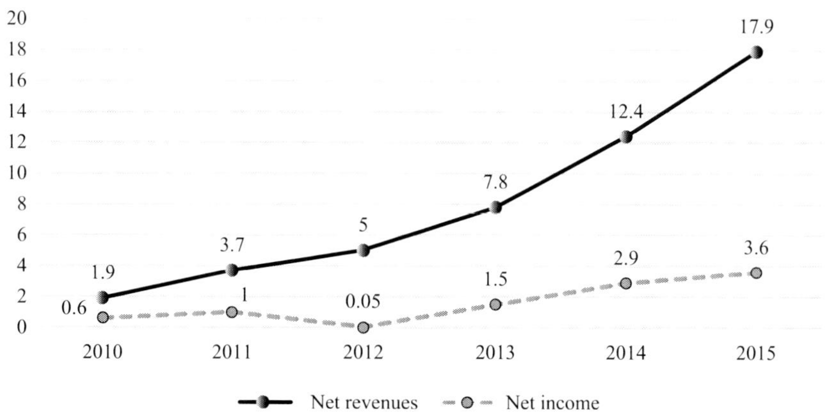

Figure 4.2.1 Facebook—net revenues versus net income 2010–2015 in billion US dollars.
Source: Author based on annual reports of Facebook (2014, 2015).

However, despite its tremendous success, it faces competition with other successful social networking sites such as Snapchat, Twitter, Google+, Instagram, and LinkedIn. Although Facebook owns Instagram, it is still competing with this social network for the users, who spend time on the social media platform (Investopedia, 2014).

In recent years, social network sites (SNS) have gained popularity and have become a useful platform for interaction between people who share their thoughts and opinions. In addition, these online spheres enable its users to be exposed to news and be informed about the activities of their 'friends' (Hull et al., 2010).

Facebook is considered to be the most popular social network. In June 2016, Facebook recorded 1.71 billion active monthly users (Facebook, 2016a). In comparison, Apple, the most valuable company worldwide (Forbes, 2016), announced in 2016 that the number of its active users has surpassed one billion (Apple, 2016). One can assume that Facebook belongs to the most powerful companies in the world. Facebook has changed the daily lives of millions of people.

In recent decades, corporate social responsibility (CSR) has been proposed as a framework to examine and monitor the relationship between the business and societies. CSR compromises the ethical, legal, social, economic, and philanthropic expectations of the society in terms of business organizations (Carroll, 2015). The mission of Facebook, as cited on its company website, is, 'to give people the power to share and make the world more open and connected' (Facebook, 2016a). However, it also functions as a corporation, which has gained its success through its abundant users and, therefore, has responsibility as any other corporation around the globe to address CSR practices. One of the main concerns that goes hand in hand with social network sites is the privacy issue. Therefore, the major aim of this case study is to provide light to the question: 'How does Facebook fulfill its social responsibility regarding users' privacy?'

In the next section, the conceptional framework of CSR in terms of social networking sites is introduced. In the second section, the issue of online privacy and the difficulties in terms of users' data protection are discussed. The final section of this Facebook case study examines relevant issues regarding the concept of users' privacy at Facebook, namely, privacy setting, selling information to third parties, and the role of Facebook (i.e. the recording of users' conversations through their microphones) (NBC4i.com, 2016).

Theoretical framework: CSR in social networking sites

Social networking sites have gained popularity in recent years and became significant tools and played an inherent part of daily life for many individuals, as well as for businesses involved in social networks either as services providers or as business participants (Chen, 2009). In general, a key assumption regarding the role of businesses is that greater power should come along with greater responsibility (Chen, 2009). In fact, social networks obviously became one of the most powerful platforms in terms of information gathering, information storage, and information transfer (Brezoiu, 2014). As these networks are used massively and, therefore, the commitment and responsibility towards society should be tightened.

Chen (2009) examined the corporate responsibilities of Internet-enabled networks. He provided the following two possible effects regarding network responsibilities: direct responsibilities resulting from the actions of the focal organization; and indirect responsibilities resulting from the actions of related parties over whom the focal organization has influential power.

Moreover, it is important to stress three important features concerning the relationship between social networks and its participants. The first feature compromises the relationship between actors in a social network. It is important to understand the power of relations, who holds the power and who is responsible for the activities of others (Chen, 2009). In this regard, one can assume that Facebook is responsible for ensuring the users' protection in different realms: data protection, privacy, safety and proper communication tools, and others.

The second aspect includes the direction of the relationships. There are different types of relationships: giver-receiver and supplier-customer, which may modify the responsibility to both sides. The last feature indicates the strength of ties. Strong ties are classified by emotional intensity, high frequency, and reciprocity, whereas weak ties are characterized by lower likelihood to be affected by the actions of each other. In addition, the relational and structural network properties are important determinants, which might influence the responsibility of a network (Chen, 2009).

Facebook, currently the most popular social network worldwide, consequently follows the logic of network dynamic configurations. Facebook's business activities have consequences for billions of users embedded in various societies around the world. As a result, Facebook gains an outstanding power. Therefore, it is noteworthy to examine how Facebook addresses its responsibility towards our global societies.

Online privacy within social networking sites

Privacy is described as a moral right of individuals to avoid intrusion into their personal affairs by third parties (Chaffey et al., 2006). Facebook and other social networking sites are naturally, due to their business mission, heavily involved in privacy concerns (Hull et al., 2010). Personal data, opinions, and preferences are considered main issues exchanged within the social network online sphere. However, the individual should have the right to control his/her personal data (van Dyke et al., 2007). As a result, the question arises regarding how individuals are able to protect their personal information and whether they are willing to do so, while, according to their business mission, social networking sites are designated to disclose information. Debatin et al. (2009) show that the wish of individuals to take part within social interaction via networking sites is enormous and actually obviously overruns privacy concerns.

There are various privacy risks that are associated with the use of social networking sites, such as documenting and gathering information, identity theft, damage of reputation, use of personal data by a non-authorized third party, and harassment and unwanted contacts (Debatin et al., 2009). In fact, there is inherent tension between the desire to participate in the online environment and the ability and willingness to safeguard and protect one's own privacy. The notion of social relationships established and maintained 'online' seems to be perceived differently from 'offline relationship' (Hull et al., 2010).

The category of 'friends' becomes ambiguous and widely interpreted. It may consist of friends who are considered to be a member of a 'close circle.' However, there are also casual acquaintances and online established relationships to even complete strangers, for example, individuals perceived as famous, such as actors or other known personalities who take part in the online environment (Debatin et al., 2009). Moreover, in the online sphere, it is common to have vast number of casual friends. The more friends registered, the higher is the perceived 'status' of the user within the online community (Hull et al., 2010). Therefore, concerns regarding privacy become even more visible, since hundreds of friends or more are able to witness and follow their 'friend's' activity. In other words, social networking sites, such as Facebook, make use of 'group dynamics' similar to those used in real life. Privacy issues on social networking sites are more demanding in terms of behaviors, privacy settings, monitoring and control, than they are in 'real life' (Hull et al., 2010).

Hull et al. (2010) provide three reasons for the privacy misfit between online and offline communication. First, in real life, everybody can decide to whom he or she would like to share information in a specific moment and place, which is not the case for online sites. The interaction on social network sites is conducted according to privacy settings that are defined a priori in the course of the user's registration. Through its settings, consciously or unconsciously, users determine the flow of information and agree or disagree who is allowed to connect within the online community and, thus, becomes able to have insights into privacy-related details at every time, at every place.

Second, there is a gap between how users estimate the audience who may have access to their personal data. Users are inclined to underestimate the scope of the potential audience for sharing their information (Hull et al., 2010). There is the illusion that the Facebook page and corresponding contents are the user's property. However, all posted information becomes the intellectual property of Facebook. Third, users do not take advantage of using privacy settings. The structure of social networking sites encourages a 'binarization' of social relations into 'friend' and 'non-friend.' This division actually smooths off any other habits of face-to-face interaction in everyday life (Hull et al., 2010).

CSR practices regarding privacy users and privacy settings

The privacy concerns raise several ethical questions concerning Facebook's business model. There are three relevant privacy problems that affect a large number of stakeholders. First, the problematic privacy setting of Facebook encourages ambiguity regarding data information protection (Hull et al., 2010). Second, personal data can be used by Facebook and other third parties (Debatin et al., 2009). Third, Facebook through its access to computer and smartphone microphones is able to listen to users' conversations even though the users have not specifically agreed to it (NBC4i.com, 2016).

To understand the privacy concern that is apparent within the Facebook business model, it is noteworthy to stress that Facebook's business mission—and the interest of its users to protect their privacy—are naturally contrasted. In fact, Facebook's concept 'to make the world more open and connected' (Facebook, 2016a) logically cannot be consistent with privacy protection. The lower are the privacy levels to exploit data information, the higher are the company's revenues through fine-grained (personalized) advertising (Busch, 2013).

The problem regarding privacy setting begins when users decide to open the Facebook page and sign up for the service. The length and the complex privacy policy and the licensing terms to which users should agree are frustrating most of the users, who in many cases are teenagers (Busch, 2013). The challenges in terms of misunderstanding the privacy policy are derived also from the design of the privacy setting menu, which leads to confusion. The user must navigate through multiple drop-down menus to change the settings. In fact, there is simply too much information that spreads over many pages that the user must consider to make a decision regarding his/her privacy settings (Stern and Kumar, 2014).

As a result of the procedure and the unawareness of limited privacy settings among the users, some of the users post information that could accidentally be shared with a wide range of people (Busch, 2013). Madejski et al. (2012) show in their study that 94 percent of the participants shared information that they would have preferred to hide due to misunderstanding of the privacy settings.

One can argue that it is the responsibility of the user to gain relevant information in advance before using the Facebook service in order to avoid accidentally sharing information. However, over the years, Facebook have promoted more open default privacy settings (Stern and Kumar, 2014). Moreover, the company has been criticized for making default privacy settings 'public,' which allowed everyone, not just Facebook users, but even all Internet users to view the users' content. As a result, in 2014, Facebook announced that the company would tighten default privacy settings. 'We recognize that it is much worse for someone to accidentally share with everyone when they actually meant to share just with friends, compared with the reverse,' the company declared (Nathan, 2014). This example displays the 'privacy paradox': Social networking sites encourage sharing personal data to the public; however, it is still necessary to protect the users' privacy issues (O'Brien and Torres, 2012).

Although Facebook has changed the default privacy settings, it is still perceived as problematic. In fact, Facebook privacy policy requires that some information be public, such as the user's name, age range, language, and country. As a result, other information will also be public, including the profile, cover photo, networks, gender, and user name (Facebook, 2016b). Moreover, the algorithm of Facebook enables one to identify information despite the fact that the user did not fill in any details. Facebook manages to recognize information, thanks to the user's friends on the network (Busch, 2013).

The problematic privacy settings and the mechanism that enables the company to have access to information through the users' friends disregard users' privacy, which emphasizes that privacy concerns regarding Facebook can be seen at many levels—not only between Facebook and its users but also among users themselves. Stern and Kumar (2014) claim that the individual user has to demonstrate a comprehensive understanding regarding Facebook's privacy settings. However, since the company defines its privacy policy and determines in which way users would be able to modify its settings, it holds the accountability and has responsibility with regard to privacy on its online platform (Busch, 2013).

From the business ethics perspective that aims to represent the moral duties and obligation that the company should fulfill (Carroll, 2015), one can deduce that privacy issues are not the main responsibility of Facebook.

There is no doubt that privacy concerns and the challenge of protecting users' information can be seen as a moral issue. In general, the question that arises is whether companies should address privacy issues as part of their CSR program. Pollach (2011) examined whether and how 95 information technology (IT) companies addressed privacy as a social responsibility. The results indicate that only a few companies addressed users' privacy and implemented concrete measures to protect privacy as part of their CSR program. Moreover, some of the companies aimed to fulfill legal responsibilities rather than ethical ones. Thus, Facebook is not a single case but one of the most powerful firms in terms of its global business volume and financial assets.

On the one hand, one can argue that privacy concerns should not be part of the CSR program. Moreover, privacy concerns can be considered as irrational and users will realize that there are positive results of sharing data (Busch, 2013). In 2010, Mark Zuckerberg argued that privacy was no longer a social norm when he explained that 'people have really gotten comfortable not only sharing more information and different kinds, but more openly and with more people' (Johnson, 2010). According to his view, if people would like to share data and have benefits that online social networking entails (Debatin et al., 2009), users' concerns regarding privacy are perhaps overemphasized.

On the other hand, companies should consider stakeholders' concerns in order to fulfill their responsibility as a business (Carroll, 2015). According to O'Brien and Torres's study (2012), most of the users claim that the company has a duty to provide control mechanism to protect their privacy. The majority of Facebook users do not believe that privacy is the main concern of Facebook (Busch, 2013).

Selling information to third parties

Facebook has become a powerful and pervasive company in recent years that has gained its market leader position through its users and utilization of their personalized data (Busch, 2013). The business model of Facebook encourages increasingly sharing information within the stakeholder network. Facebook wants to know more about its users to maintain its profitable model, which is mainly derived from selling data to advertisers (Marichal, 2012).

In this regard, the vision of Facebook is that its users never log out or leave its site. Therefore, the company offers a wide range of content and provides content directly to users' feed, including articles, photos, and videos that have been shared via their Facebook friends or commercial pages. This practice embedded in the Facebook business model compromises the distribution of users' data and advertisers' interests (Busch, 2013).

As a result, users are exposed to services that are provided by third party advertising, which stems from the users' personal preferences collected via Facebook. These services, which are provided by third party advertising firms like Google AdWords and AdChoices are finally retargeting the users and aiming to generate more business (Messineo, 2015). Certainly, Facebook collects an extremely large amount of users' personal information as well as behavioral data, which aim to customize services in order to display personalized services that perfectly fit to each user and thus increase their earnings from third-party advertisements (Busch, 2013).

Tucker's (2014) study reveals that in 2010 when Facebook claimed to enhance its control over privacy, users reacted more positively to personalized advertisements. In fact, advertisements that were targeted but did not use personalized text contents were not clicked. Logically, this situation indicates a business dilemma for Facebook when balancing fine-grained advertisements through individualized customer data against the customer's privacy standards.

José Marichal (2012) argues in his book *Facebook Democracy* that the strategy of Facebook as a profit-seeking enterprise leads to 'commodification of disclosure.' Facebook users distribute their data that are gathered and accumulated in larger marketing profiles, which means that finally the user is a commodity that is sold to advertisers. In 2015, advertising amounted to USD 17 billion, which indicates 95 percent of the total revenues (Facebook, 2015). The commodification of the disclosure expands beyond the practices of Facebook. The company relies on 'application programming interfaces (APIs) that allow for two or more sites to exchange data and for third parties to get or give data' (Marichal, 2012, p. 49).

The 'commodification' of users' activity on Facebook raises significant questions: Do users have the choice not to be treated as commodities? Does Facebook strategy go beyond its role as a business and social networking site and dictate to people what to think and how to act? In this regard, for instance, a concern that recently emerged is whether Facebook is able even to influence 2016 US presidential elections. The ability of Facebook to predict what people are likely interested in and its personalized news pages that are tailor-made to each user, eventually may influence the political opinion of a broader range of its users as a part of their societies (AES, 2016). Therefore, one can assume that the concerns regarding Facebook strategies of personalized advertising and selling data are going beyond changing consumers' behavior but also may impact social and political situations. According to Busch (2013), the personalization strategy of Facebook made the company a state-like regulator. The metaphor of Facebook as a virtual state requires that Facebook assumes its responsibility.

Consequently, Facebook is constantly under international scrutiny over privacy issues. In April 2016, the European Parliament approved new data protection regulation that aims to return to the citizens control of their personal data. The new rules include the right to 'be forgotten' and the right to transfer the data to another service, ensuring that the privacy policies are clearly explained, and other regulations (European Parliament, 2016).

In the case of Facebook, not only in terms of current social networking, it is difficult for users to figure out how to delete their data but also in terms of data profiles generated in the past and stored on Facebook servers over years and decades (Marichal, 2012). In this respect, the European Union tried to raise pressure on the privacy policy of Facebook. According to a new regulation, users can apply at Facebook to delete their account, and all of the data that are associated with their social networking activity should be erased (European Parliament, 2016).

Facebook's strategy is based on the notion of personalized services and personal data that are used by third parties as well. With regard to CSR, it is important to stress that Facebook is not the one and only company worldwide that applies the above-mentioned policy and practices (Tucker, 2014). Therefore, the question emerges: How does Facebook differ from other firms that collect users' personal data for commercial purposes? The answer lies in the power of Facebook and the business volume and the widespread consequences of collecting and selling data. Accordingly, Chen (2009) claims that social responsibilities of social network providers stem from its power. Thus, the activities and decisions taken by Facebook have a considerable impact on its users who are usually not aware of it. At the same time, the public awareness related to social networking activities has increased, too. Therefore, the company should take a more dynamic role in favor of its stakeholders in order to enhance the prevalence of ethical standards.

Kelli Burns, mass communication professor at the University of South Florida, has drawn attention to the likelihood that Facebook can employ the users' phone and track information for its own purposes. According to her experiment, the professor turned on the microphone feature and talked about her plan to go on a safari and which transportation method she was going to use there. One minute later, she noticed that a new post on her feed about a safari popped up. In addition, posts about rental car opportunities appeared on her page (NBC4i.com, 2016).

Facebook admitted that the company does listen to audio and collect information to identify what is happing 'around the phone.' However, gained data are not combined with other information and Facebook rejected to record conversations. 'Facebook does not use microphone audio to inform advertising or News Feed stories in any way. Businesses are able to serve relevant advertisements based on people's interests and other demographic information, but not through audio collection' (Griffin, 2016).

There is limited evidence that Facebook in particular listens to conversations to enhance its personalized services aimed to attract more 'clicks.' Facebook commented that the company has access to users' microphone but users should give their permission and they have to separately switch on the microphone feature (Chowdhry, 2016). Therefore, the claim that Facebook is permanently listening to you and therefore became titled as 'Big Brother' (NBC4i.com, 2016) seems hyperbolic.

However, this concern raised another question: Should Facebook be allowed to listen to their users' conversations and is this ethical? One can argue that the fact that Facebook is eavesdropping on the users' conversations 'outside the online territory' indicates a violation of privacy and, therefore, has a negative impact on consumer trust. Facebook emphasizes ethical and moral issues in terms of the individual's privacy from online platforms to audio recording devices.

Although Facebook is a very powerful company, the firm does not publish corporate social responsibility reports like various other companies. However, Facebook has tightened its privacy policy and offers users a 'privacy checkup,' which reminds users to update their current privacy settings (Nathan, 2014). Concerns that violate the users' privacy have implications for the future business of Facebook. The social acceptance and the popularity of Facebook may erode and challenge the firm's leading global position.

Bibliography

AES 2016, Could Facebook influence the outcome of the presidential election?, *Economist*, May 18. Available from: www.economist.com/blogs/economist-explains/2016/05/economist-explains-15. [July 23, 2016].

Apple 2016, 'Apple reports record first quarter results.' Available from: www.apple.com/pr/library/2016/01/26Apple-Reports-Record-First-Quarter-Results.html. [July 14, 2016].

Brezoiu, G-A 2014, 'How social media recruitment influences organizational social responsibility,' *Economia: Seria Management*, vol. 17, no. 1, pp. 172–180.

Busch, T 2013, 'Fair information technologies: the corporate responsibility of online social networks as public regulators,' PhD Dissertation, University of St. Gallen.

Carroll, AB 2015, 'Corporate social responsibility: the centerpiece of competing and complementary frameworks,' *Organizational Dynamics*, vol. 44, pp. 88–96.

Chaffey, D, Ellis-Chadwick, F, Johnston, K & Mayer, R 2006, *Internet marketing: strategy, implementation and practice*, third edition, Pearson Education Limited, Essex.

Chen, S 2009, 'Corporate responsibilities in internet enabled social networks,' *Journal of Business Ethics*, no. 90, pp. 523–536.

Chowdhry, A 2016, 'Facebook says it is not listening to your conversations for ads using microphone access.' Available from: www.forbes.com/sites/amitchowdhry/2016/06/07/facebook-audio-from-your-smartphone-microphone-is-not-being-used-for-ads/#7849bfd9cb4a. [July 24, 2016].

Debatin, B, Lovejoy, JP, Horn, A-K & Hughes, BN 2009, 'Facebook and online privacy: attitudes, behaviors, and unintended consequences,' *Journal of Computer-Mediated Communication*, no. 15, pp. 83–108.

European Parliament 2016, 'Data protection reform—Parliament approves new rules fit for the digital era.' Available from: www.europarl.europa.eu/news/en/news-room/20160407IPR21776/Data-protection-reform-Parliament-approves-new-rules-fit-for-the-digital-era. [July 23, 2016].

Facebook 2016a, 'Company info.' Available from: http://newsroom.fb.com/company-info/. [July 14, 2016].

Facebook 2016b, 'Help center: what is public information?' Available from: www.facebook.com/help/203805466323736. [July 22, 2016].

Facebook 2014, 'Annual report 2014.' Available from: https://s21.q4cdn.com/399680738/files/doc_financials/annual_reports/FB2014AR.pdf. [July 21, 2016].

Facebook 2015, 'Annual report 2015.' Available from: https://s21.q4cdn.com/399680738/files/doc_financials/annual_reports/2015-Annual-Report.pdf. [July 21, 2016].

Facebook Newsroom 2013, 'Facebook to acquire Atlas from Microsoft.' Available from: http://newsroom.fb.com/news/2013/02/facebook-to-acquire-atlas-from-microsoft//. [July 21, 2016].

Facebook Newsroom 2014, 'Facebook to acquire Oculus.' Available from: http://newsroom.fb.com/news/2014/03/facebook-to-acquire-oculus/. [July 21, 2016].

Forbes 2016, 'The world's most valuable brands.' Available from: www.forbes.com/powerful-brands/list/#tab:rank. [July 14, 2016].

Griffin, A 2016, 'Facebook is using smartphones to listen to what people say, professor suggests,' *Independent*. May 31. Available from: www.independent.co.uk/life-style/gadgets-and-tech/news/facebook-using-people-s-phones-to-listen-in-on-what-they-re-saying-claims-professor-a7057526.html. [July 24, 2016].

Hull, G, Lipford, HR & Latulipa, C 2010, 'Contextual gaps: privacy issues on Facebook,' *Ethics Inf Technol*, vol. 13, pp. 289–302.

Investopedia 2014, 'Who are Facebook's (FB) main competitors?' Available from: www.investopedia.com/ask/answers/120314/who-are-facebooks-fb-main-competitors.asp. [July 21, 2016].

Johnson, B 2010, 'Privacy no longer a social norm, says Facebook founder,' *The Guardian*, January 11. Available from: www.theguardian.com/technology/2010/jan/11/facebook-privacy. [July 22, 2016].

Johnson, M, Bellovin, SM, & Madejski, M 2012, 'A study of privacy settings errors in an online social network,' *Pervasive Computing and Communications Workshops*, IEEE International Conference, Lugano, Switzerland, pp. 340–345.

Marichal, J 2012, *Facebook democracy: the architecture of disclosure and the threat to public life*, Ashgate Publishing Group, Farnham.

MarketLine 2012, 'Facebook Inc: how a social network became a multi-billion dollar business,' July 21, 2016.

Messineo, M 2015, 'Induction ceremony keynote speech: what Facebook knows about you that you don't know they Know,' vol. 91, no. 2, pp. 1–22.

Nathan, G 2014, 'Facebook changes default share setting to private,' *Time*, May 22. Available from: http://time.com/108957/facebook-default-setting-private/. [July 22, 2016].

NBC4i.com 2016, 'Spying secrets: is Facebook eavesdropping on your phone conversations?' Available from: http://nbc4i.com/2016/05/24/spying-secrets-is-facebook-eavesdropping-on-your-phone-conversations/. [July 14, 2016].

O'Brien, D & Torres, AM 2012, 'Social networkings and online privacy: Facebook users' perceptions,' *Irish Journal of Management*, vol. 31, no. 2, pp. 63–96.

Stern, T & Kumar, N 2014, 'Improving privacy settings control in online social networks with a wheel interface,' *Journal of the association for information science and technology*, vol. 63, no. 3, pp. 524–538.

Tucker, CE 2014, 'Social networks, personalized advertising, and privacy controls,' *Journal of Marketing Research*, vol. 51, no. 5, pp. 546–562.

van Dyke, T, Midha, V &Nemati, H 2007, 'The effect of consumer privacy empowerment on trust and privacy concerns in e-commerce,' *Electronic Markets*, vol. 17, no. 1, pp. 68–81.

Vincent, J 2014, 'The inventor of the Facebook "like" button says he never made a "dislike" button because he feared the 'unfortunate consequences,' *Independent*, October 20. Available from: www.independent.co.uk/life-style/gadgets-and-tech/the-inventor-of-the-facebook-like-button-says-he-never-made-a-dislike-button-because-he-feared-the-9806435.html. [July 21, 2016].

4.3 Case study: Environmental analysis for Russia in light of economic sanctions

Corinna Hlozek and Mario Glowik

Case review questions

1. Based on the data and information provided in the case study, how would you develop an S.E.E.L.E analysis for Russia?
2. Reviewing the history and current macro-economic challenges, how would you develop scenarios for the future business development of Philips and Huawei in Russia?

Although Russia's economy already passed better times, the current trend can also be considered as a chance to change the country's energy industry-dominated focus. In light of economic sanctions and declining fossils prices, Russia needs to reconfigure its industry structure targeting to reduce its dependencies on Western commodity product imports and strong dependency (without alternatives) on its raw materials. Obviously, it will be challenging but it will provide an opportunity to enter new industries, which are important for the Russian economy.

In this case study, economic data of the macro-analysis of Russia are introduced. Foreign direct investment activities of the Chinese Huawei Technologies and Philips from the Netherlands in Russia are compared. Philips and Huawei have been selected because of their diverse regional background (Western versus China) in light of reconfiguring economic ties due to current sanctions and due to both firms' market importance for Russia.

Russia's macro economics

Gross domestic product (GDP)

In March 2014, the United States, the European Union, Japan, Switzerland, and other countries, imposed travel, financial, and economic sanctions against selected Ukrainian and Russian individuals and entities in response to Russia's interventions in Crimea and to developments in Eastern Ukraine. These sanctions argeted financial services, a limited access to capital markets and Russia's energy sector, among other areas. Several months later, in August 2014, Russia imposed counter sanctions on agricultural and food imports. Similar to a ping-pong game, sanctions and counter sanctions were subsequently extended by the European Union and the Russian Federation, which certainly disfavor the economic development of the involved parties (IMF[1], 2015a: 5).

In addition to geopolitical tensions, the Russian government has been facing economic challenges. Factors for the downward pressure on Russia's gross domestic product (GDP[2]) are, among others, the depreciation of the oil price, the inflationary trend of the Russian ruble, low investments in newly emerging industries (e.g. e-commerce), which are necessary to overcome the dependency on raw materials exports, and the country's restricted access to international capital markets (IMF, 2015b).

Although Russia's government is still promising a turnaround to growth in 2016, the World Bank forecasts a less optimistic economic outlook for the next year. Hit by a decline in oil prices, along with Western sanctions, the country's economy has been experiencing a persistent recession since 2014. According to the World Bank, Russia's GDP shrunk by 3.8 percent in 2015 and by an additional 0.6 percent in 2016 (Figure 4.3.1). It is the largest decrease since the financial crisis in 2009 (Ostroukh, 2015). Industrial production (-0.4 percent), completed construction projects (-4.7 percent), and retailing (-6.7 percent) declined between 2014 and 2015. The domestic agricultural sector serves as an exceptional case, which benefits by import restrictions. Agriculture grew by 3.5 percent between 2014 and 2015 and, thus, indicates a rare sector, which positively contributed to Russia's GDP (GTAI[3], 2015).

For years, critics have tried to make Russian authorities aware of structural weaknesses in the domestic economy. On the one hand, the lack of diversification in Russia's economy has caused a disproportional dependence on the sales of oil and gas, and a permanent promotion of Russia's resource sector had led to low investments in other industries in the past. Consequently, export losses in the energy sector could not be compensated by alternative industries in times of declining oil prices. On the other hand, even if the Russian government has identified this problem, the transformation process for a comprehensive modernization is still too slow to make other sectors competitive (GIZ[4], 2015). For several years, GDP growth has been inhibited by those weaknesses;

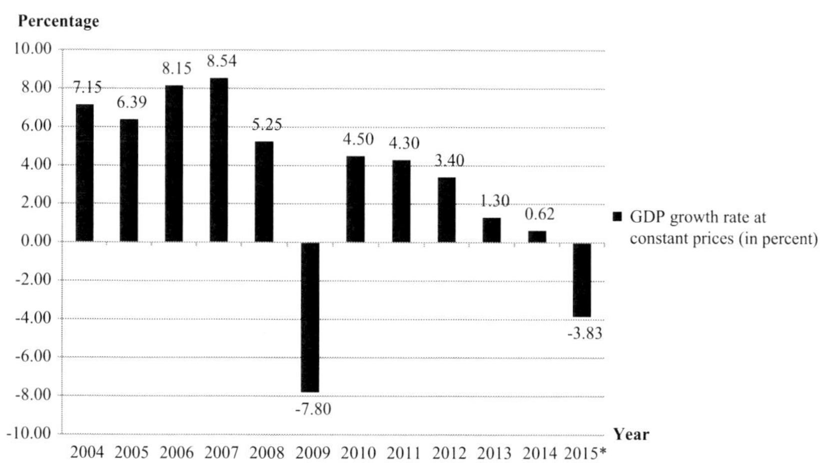

Figure 4.3.1 Growth of real GDP in the Russian Federation (2004–2015).
*Estimated.
Source: IMF, 2015c.

however, in 2014, additional external factors were added by the imposition of financial sanctions and the declining oil prices (GTAI, 2015) (Figure 4.3.2).

Inflation

In the course of declining oil prices and the sanctions policy, the Russian ruble depreciation against the US dollar amounted to approximately 123 percent between 2013 and 2015 (Table 4.3.1). This goes hand in hand with raising prices for consumers and corporations as well as a growing inflation rate (GIZ, 2015).

Within two years, the average inflation rate increased from 6.76 percent (2013) to 15.79 percent (2015), which, in turn, had a massive impact on private households (IMF, 2015d) (Figure 4.3.3). Through the erosion of real wages and incomes and growing poverty, the Russian population partially lost its confidence in political decisions, the currency, and its domestic economy. The demand in Russia decreased since households held back consumption and firms reduced investment activities and capacity expenditures. Finally, low investment and consumption resulted in a shrinking GDP (Khlebnikov, 2015). The World Bank also praised monetary and fiscal authorities for addressing the crisis and stabilizing the economy. By cutting interest rates during the last year, the Russian government tried to ease monetary activities and revive the economy (Ostroukh, 2015).

Moreover, the currency devaluation and bilateral sanctions also affect the country's exports and imports. The weak Russian ruble raises the prices of imports for companies and consumers. In September 2015, the value of imports decreased by 39 percent

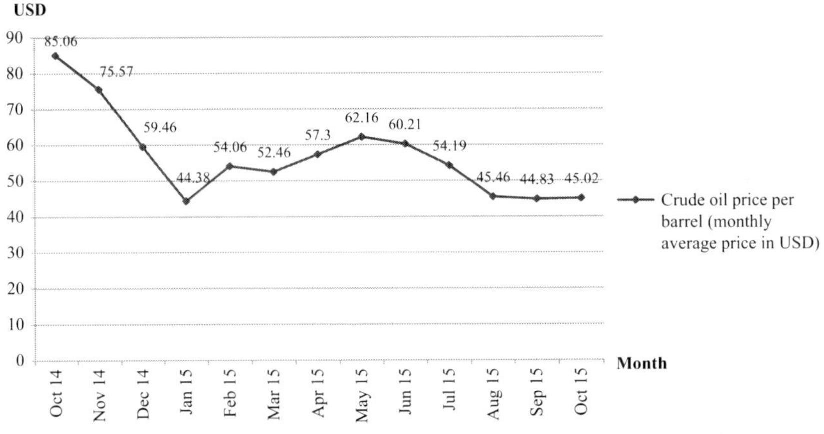

Figure 4.3.2 Price of selected OPEC crude oils (Oct. 2014–Oct. 2015).
Source: OPEC, 2015.

Table 4.3.1 Exchange rate between the US dollar and the Russian ruble

	US Dollar	*Russian Ruble*	*Depreciation*
31.12.2013	1.00	32.82	——
31.12.2014	1.00	59.25	-80.53 percent
31.12.2015	1.00	73.29	-23.70 percent

Source: Bankenverband, 2015.

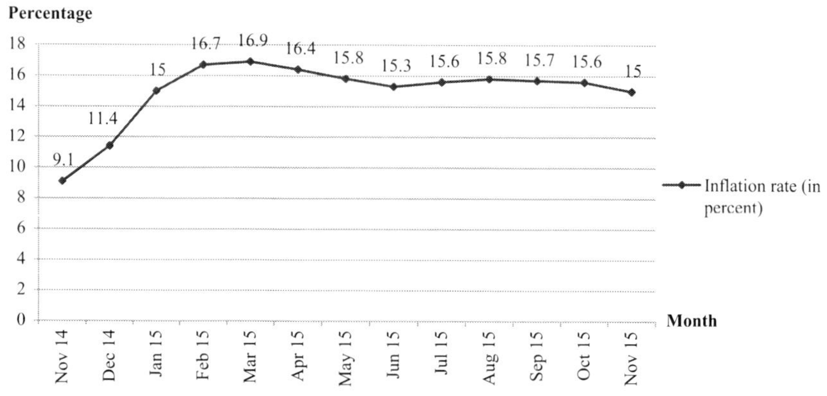

Figure 4.3.3 Change of inflation rate in Russia (compared to months in the previous year).
Source: Rosstat, 2015.

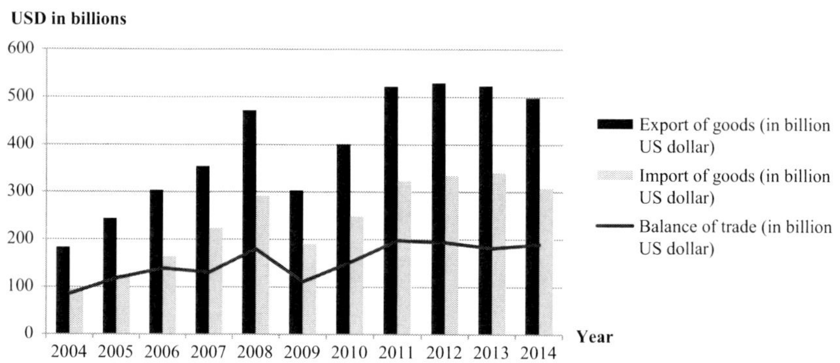

Figure 4.3.4 Balance of trade[5] in the Russian Federation (2004–2014).
Source: WTO, 2015a/2015b/2015c.

compared to the same period in 2014. Among other things, this applies to imports of food, chemicals, industrial equipment, and machinery (Hobson, 2015). Interestingly, Russia's trade surplus has remained relatively constant due to increased volumes compensating for lower unit prices (Figure 4.3.4). Due to its wealth of natural resources, the Russian Federation remains a leading exporter of oil, gas, metals, or gems. Despite political tensions, the EU is not able to waive Russian oil and gas Russian exports.

Foreign direct investment (FDI)

FDI initiatives serve as tools to attract foreign capital into a country. Overcoming the economic recession in 2009, the Russian government implemented the Russian Direct Investment Fund valued at USD 10 billion in order to make equity investments and establish international partnerships with locals to develop the Russian economy. According to the United Nations Conference on Trade and Development (UNCTAD), FDI increased by 83 percent between 2012 and 2013 to reach a record level of USD 94 billion, making the country the third largest global recipient of FDI (RDIF, 2014) (Figure 4.3.5).

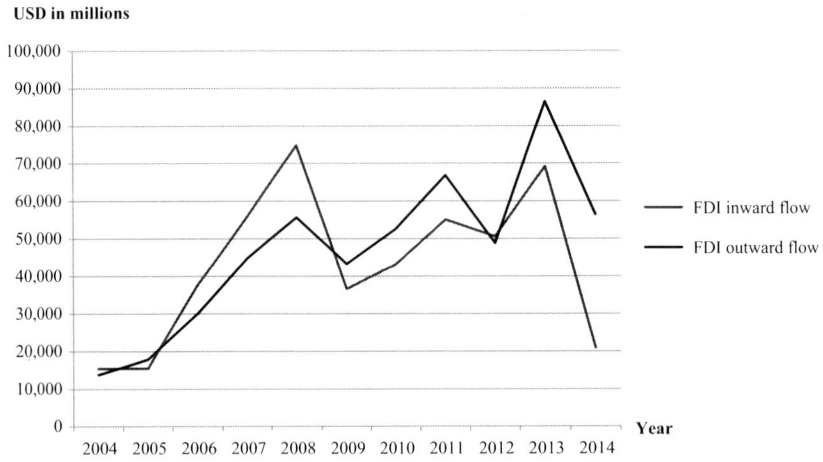

Figure 4.3.5 Development of FDI flows in the Russian Federation (2004–2014).
Source: UNCTAD, 2015a.

Table 4.3.2 Foreign Direct Investment in Russia

Foreign Direct Investment	*2012*	*2013*	*2014*
FDI Inward Flow *(million USD)*	50,588	69,219	20,958
FDI Stock *(million USD)*	514,926	565,654	378,543
Number of Greenfield Investments	328	283	178
FDI Inwards *(in % of GFCF)*	11.4	15.2	5.3
FDI Stock *(in % of GDP)*	25.6	27.2	20.4

Source: Santander, 2014.

However, the crisis in the Ukraine clearly reveals the intense dependence between political stability and economic development. The damaged economic relations to the EU and the US also weakened Russia's ability to attract foreign direct investments from these countries. Several European and US-American companies froze their investments or withdrew from the Russian market. As result of mutual sanctions, geopolitical tensions, and a weakened Russian ruble, the economy faced a tremendous change in FDI activities (Kuchma, 2014). Between 2013 and 2014, FDI inflow dropped by 70 percent from approximately USD 69 billion to 21 billion USD (Table 4.3.2). FDI outflow fell by 35 percent to USD 56.4 billion during the same period (UNCTAD, 2015). According to the World Investment Report published by UNCTAD, Russian future FDI—inflows and outflows—mainly depends on the future of economic sanctions.

Greenfield projects—great potential for Chinese investors

Chinese investors seem to be less concerned about the political and economic instability of the country: While Western companies exit the Russian market, Chinese firms take the chance of entering Russia, thus increasing their presence in leading industries and differentiating from competing nations (Fingar, 2015).

Table 4.3.3 The five largest greenfield FDI projects announced in the Russian Federation, 2014 (millions of US dollars)

Name of Investing Company	*Source Country*	*Sector*	*Value*
China Triumph International Engineering	China	Industrial machinery	3,000
Hawtai Motor Group	China	Automotive	1,100
Great Wall Motors (GWM)	China	Automotive	520
New Hope Group	China	Food and tobacco	500
Dongfeng Motor	China	Automotive	500

Source: UNCTAD, 2015.

In 2014, China became the fifth largest FDI investor in Russia and the most important investor in terms of greenfield projects (UNCTAD, 2015). Although greenfield investments decreased by 39 percent in absolute numbers of 134 projects, China has increased its relative share in the Russian market (Fingar, 2015). Among Russia's five largest greenfield investors, all of them are originated in China and they contributed in total more than USD 5 billion (Table 4.3.3) (UNCTAD, 2015). In particular, Chinese companies expanded their investments in the automotive, engineering and energy sector. For example, Hawtai Motor Group planned to invest USD 1.1 billion in the construction of a car plant (Fingar, 2015) or Great Wall Motors started to build a plant in the Tula region (UNCTAD, 2015).

Furthermore, it can be mentioned that China also discovered the high potential of greenfield investments in other sectors than the automobile or energy industry. In April 2016, Haier opened a new manufacturing plant to produce refrigeration equipment in the region of Tatarstan in response to increasing demand from the European market. This is the first joint Russian-Chinese business project in the non-primary industry. Dedicated to the production of refrigeration machinery, it is Haier's first step to localize in Russia an additional asset to pursue its growth plans throughout Europe. This endeavor should generate 500 new jobs at the factory and another 1,500 jobs among suppliers and service providers, such as logistics (Invest in Russia, 2015).

In the following section, two foreign multinational companies and their FDI projects in Russia are introduced: On the one hand, Huawei Technologies, a growing Chinese firm, and, on the other hand, Royal Philips, a Western company. We aim to describe how their market entry and penetration activities may have changed in recent challenging times.

First case: Huawei Technologies (China)

In 1987, Huawei Technologies Co. Ltd. was founded by Ren Zhengfei headquartered in Shenzhen, Guangdong. The Chinese firm provides customized network equipment for telecom carriers, information technology (IT) products and solutions in 170 countries worldwide (Huawei, 2015a). Huawei's company mission is described as the 'commitment to enrich life through communications and to address the issue of information security' (Huawei, 2012). The private equity-owned company reached sales revenues of USD 46.5 billion and a net profit of USD 4.5 billion in 2014 (Huawei, 2015b).

Research and technological development are considered by the company as one of the most essential core businesses (Ahrens, 2013). According to its corporate information, they steadily allocate 10 percent of its revenue into R&D. Approximately 70,000 people are employed in this sector that equals to 45 percent of the firm's total workforce. Based on statistics by the World Intellectual Property Organization, Huawei Technologies has recorded the highest number of international patent applications (3,442) in 2014. The Chinese company runs R&D centers in China, Germany, Sweden, the USA, France, Italy, Russia, India, and Russia (Huawei, 2015c). Huawei's foreign business activities indicate a high degree of internationalization. By first entering the Russian market in 1996, the company started its internationalization process and developed its sales, among others, in the fields of next generation network (NGN), optic network, and data communications (Dawei, 2008).

Business activities of Huawei Technologies in Russia in light of 2014 economic sanctions

In 1996, the firm started its business in Russia by forming an international joint venture with the Russian Beto Corporation/Telecom to manufacture and assemble communication switching equipment. In 1999, the first R&D center in Moscow was established to focus on wireless algorithm, applications, and software (Gong, 2013). Nevertheless, Huawei had to wait some time for its success on the Russian market. The firm's first sales volume amounted USD 12 million in 1999. However, by 2001, revenue rose to USD 100 million. In the following years, business prospered and Huawei was able to push its investments ahead (Fu, 2015).

Russia was one of Huawei's first international markets, and to the present day, the Chinese company remains confident regarding Russia's growth potential and development in the information and communication industry. For this reason, CEO Ren Zhengfei announced at the 16th St. Petersburg International Economic Forum in 2012 plans to expand investments and also develop its domestic electronics information industry in order to meet the demands of Russia. According to Huawei, investing in Russia means to invest in the development of a leading telecom industry. Only the creation of a comprehensive network of data pipes enables a smooth and fast data transmission and communication (Huawei, 2015).

Huawei is one of those companies that do not withdraw their business from Russia and instead has further expanded their engagement. The management rather emphasizes the attractiveness of the Russian market and the opportunity to differentiate from its Western competitors. In times of economic sanctions between Western countries and Russia, Huawei started to strengthen ties with Russian corporations as proven by various examples.

Huawei recently established a partnership with Russian Railways in Sochi regarding the expansion of wireless GSM-R networks and LTE networks and the modernization of data transmission data networks, broadband radio communications, and audio/video conference systems (Huawei, 2014a). In June 2014, Huawei expanded technology services for the Russian energy giant OAO Gazprom. Within this collaboration, Huawei tech systems were installed to manage pipelines and offshore fields in a proper way. Furthermore, the company provides data processing systems to Russia's largest financial institution OAO Sberbank (Wong, 2014).

Another important Russian partner of Huawei is Megafon, one of the leading mobile telecom services in Russia. After signing a deal amounting to USD 600 million to provide equipment and maintenance services in June 2014, Huawei Technologies also formed another research joint venture with Megafon at the end of the same year

Table 4.3.4 Huawei Technologies in Russia

	Joint Venture partner
1996	Beto Corporation
2014	Russian Railways
2014	OAO Gazprom
2014	OAO Sberbank
2014	Megafon

(Thomas, 2014). The agreement includes the installation and testing of 5G networks serving large-scale users and M2M devices with a view to the FIFA World Cup 2018 (Huawei, 2014b).

A final example is Huawei's first Russian turnkey[6] commercial data center established in Moscow for the company Comcor, which is part of the Akado Group. Apart from the supply of Huawei's hardware and technologies, such as server cabinets, power supply systems, cooling systems, or monitoring systems, the turnkey contract also involves a two-year support and consulting services. Finally, Huawei is responsible for the entire construction of the data center—from designing to producing equipment. The data center was launched in 2016 (Vedomosti, 2015).

Second case: Royal Philips (The Netherlands)

In general, Dutch investments reached USD 6.5 billion corresponding to 12 percent of total FDI in 2011 in Russia. The Netherlands has substantial direct investments in Russia with competitive positioned companies, such as Royal Dutch Shell, Unilever, or Royal Philips, which are doing business in technology, media, and telecom (TMT), healthcare, infrastructure, agriculture, and natural resources. Sales offices and production centers of the Dutch firms are, for most part, located in Moscow or St. Petersburg and its surroundings (KPMG, 2013).

Among the cluster of Dutch firms, Royal Philips, established in 1891, provides products and solutions in the sectors of healthcare, consumer lifestyle, and lighting. In particular, the firm is engaged in cardiac care, acute care, home healthcare, and energy-efficient lighting solutions where Philips holds a market leading position worldwide (Philips, 2015b). Headquartered in Amsterdam, Philips generated sales of Euro 21.4 billion in 2014 and employs approximately 108,000 people in more than 100 countries (Philips, 2015c). In 2015, Philips announced the company's reorganization by splitting off the lighting business to establish two independent companies, so-called Lighting Solutions and HealthTech, combining healthcare and consumer lifestyle (van Tartwijk, 2014).

Business activities of Royal Philips in Russia in light of 2014 economic sanctions

Economic ties between Russia and Royal Philips date back to the end of 19th century. Already in 1898, Anton Philips traveled to Russia to convince the Russian Tsar to light the Winter Palace in St. Petersburg. Anton Philips successfully returned to the Netherlands with its first international contract concerning the production and supply of 50,000 bulbs corresponding to approximately 50 percent of Philip's total sales in 1898. During its rapid expansion in Russia, Philips opened its first office in St. Petersburg in 1914. Since 1983, the Russian headquarter has been located in Moscow—followed by 23 offices that are spread across the country (Philips, 2008).

Especially, in the area of lighting and healthcare, Philips showed an extensive commitment in Russia. For example, 'Ivan the Great Bell Tower'—the tallest tower in the Moscow Kremlin—or buildings of 'Senate and Synode' in St. Petersburg were lit by Royal Philips. Moreover, the company participated in several road lighting modernization projects through energy-efficient lighting solutions (Philips, 2008). In healthcare, Philips set up a strategic cooperation with MEDSI, the leading private healthcare provider in Russia. In terms of this partnership, the Dutch firm has equipped Russia's largest network of private clinics with innovative medical solutions and provides consulting services to optimize hospital management and quality (Philips, 2014).

Philip's firm strategy aimed to establish strategic alliances with leading Russian companies in order to create business localization and expand the company's impact in the healthcare and lighting industries. The healthcare sector, according to Russia's former CEO Arjan de Jongste, is especially considered to be one of the most attractive business areas for Philips because the Russian healthcare modernization depends on the supply of state-of-the-art healthcare technologies (Jongste, 2011).

Electron, a leading Russian manufacturer for medical equipment, and the Russian State Atomic Energy Corporation (ROSATOM) belong to important strategic partners for Philips between 2010 and 2011. The Philips-Electron cooperation with an investment valued at approximately USD 20 million intended to develop innovative computer tomography (CT) products. The joint venture also targeted the reduction of Russia's dependence on medical devices import through local manufacturing (Philips 2010a). Several months after the joint venture establishment, the first jointly developed CT scanner was installed at the hospital of war veterans in St. Petersburg (Philips 2010b). Another joint venture agreement with ROSATOM was signed to develop a nuclear medicine industry in Russia. As part of the collaboration, both contractual partners aimed to produce essential imaging technologies in nuclear medicine and joint research. Philips licensed its know-how for the production and maintenance of medical devices; ROSATOM provided infrastructure and production facilities (ROSATOM, 2011). Moreover, Philips set up joint research initiatives with three leading Russian research institutes for medical imaging technology, such as with the St. Petersburg State Polytechnical University, the Vavilov State Optical Institute, and the Ioffe Physical Technical Institute. With the investment of Euro 2.5 million, the research project focused on the development of scintillation materials research to optimize the sensitivity of detectors used in computed tomography, positron emission tomography, and single photon emission computed tomography (Philips, 2012a).

Furthermore, Philips identified high growth potential of the Russian road lighting market and the related LED business in 2012. The market was expected to double to Euro 100 million by the end of 2015. As a consequence, Philips and Optogan, an important Russian manufacturer of LED bulbs, formed an international joint venture to meet the growing LED road lighting market. The Philips-Optogan JV is 51 percent owned by Philips and 49 percent owned by Optogan (Philips, 2012b). Only one year later, manufacturing was started at a production site in St. Petersburg.

Table 4.3.5 Royal Philips in Russia

	Joint Venture Partner
2010	Electron
2011	ROSATOM
2012	Optogan
2012	Vavilov State Optical Institute
2012	St. Petersburg State Polytechnical University
2012	Ioffe Physical Technical Institute
2014	MEDSI

As result of the conflict in the Ukraine, Philips's investment activities seemed to slow down since 2014. Because of unfavorable exchange rates and a low demand in Russia and China, Royal Philips had to post a net loss of USD 103 million for the third quarter of 2014, compared with a net profit of USD 281 million only a year before. After these insufficient results, Frans van Houten expressed his concerns about the global economic situation as follows: 'In Russia, the tensions are high,' [...] 'It's a market that will require a lot of investments in healthcare, in technology, in lighting, but for now, we see big headwinds in that space' (van Groningen, 2014). It reveals that Philips is afraid of doing business in a country with a risky economic and political environment. Nevertheless, current joint ventures were maintained during the last two years but additional comprehensive investment expansions have not been made.

The review of above firm case study discussions concerning Huawei and Philips and their current business ambitions in Russia illustrates the diversifying impact on Western versus Chinese firms in course of the recent crisis. Philips, which has been doing business for more than one century currently avoids further investments in the Russian market. In contrast, as the case of Huawei indicates, Chinese companies do not hesitate to conduct and even accelerate their business ambitions in Russia. Despite economic crisis, high inflation and a slow progress of Russia's domestic electronics industry Huawei have strengthened its investment activities since 2014. Chinese companies consider the Russian Federation as a market with significant growth prospects and corresponding investment opportunities. They want to increase their leading position against competitors from Western countries.

Another possibility for changing the economic focus is to concentrate more investments in Russia's resource rich Far Eastern region. At the Eastern Economic Forum in Vladivostok, Vladimir Putin announced intentions to create best conditions for domestic and foreign investors to conduct business—so that in performance and return on capital, the Russian Far East can successfully compete with leading business centers (Hodge, 2015), such as Moscow or St. Petersburg. That means, in turn, that the orientation to Russia's Far East also improves the ties to China (Hodge, 2015).

All in all, Russia would benefit from a structural transformation in the form of deep and sustained reforms. Modernizing and diversifying the domestic industries would not only reduce dependencies on Western imports and oil prices but also raise the attractiveness of the Russian market for foreign investors, apart from China (World Bank, 2015). The government should communicate a clear idea of their policy for the next years because Russia's population needs a political and economic signal regarding what they can expect in the future (Khlebnikov, 2015).

Notes

1 International Monetary Fund.
2 **Gross domestic product (GDP)** at constant prices refers to the volume level of GDP. Constant price estimates of GDP are obtained by expressing values in terms of a base period. In theory, the price and quantity components of a value are identified and the price in the base period is substituted for that in the current period. Two main methods are adopted in practice. The first, referred to as 'quantity revaluation,' is based on a methodology consistent with the above theory (i.e. by multiplying the current period quantity by the base period price). The second, commonly referred to as 'price deflation,' involves dividing price indexes into the observed values to obtain the volume estimate. The price indexes used are built up from the prices of the major items contributing to each value (OECD, 2003).
3 GTAI = Germany Trade and Invest.
4 Deutsche Gesellschaft für Internationale Zusammenarbeit.
5 '**Trade balance** is the difference between exports and imports of goods and services' (OECD, 2005).
6 'Turnkey operation: refers to a practice in which a company designs, constructs, and start-ups a project in a foreign country [...], qualifies local personnel, and then "turns the key over" to the local government in return for an agreed upon payment use fee' (Glowik, 2009: 84).

Bibliography

ACRNews 2016, Haier opens new factory in Russia. Available from: www.acr-news.com/haier-opens-new-factory-in-russia. [January 3, 2017].

Ahrens, N 2013, *China's competitiveness. Myth, reality, and lessons for the United States and Japan. Case study: Huawei*, Center for Strategic and International Studies, Washington, DC.

Bankenverband 2015, Währungsrechner. Available from: https://bankenverband.de/service/waehrungsrechner/?amount=1&from_=USD&to=RUB&date=31.12.2014&interbank=0. [December 31, 2015].

Dawei, G 2008, *Internationalization and entry strategy of enterprises: a case study of Chinese firm Huawei*. Available from: http://hh.diva-portal.org/smash/get/diva2:238972/FULLTEXT01.pdf. [September 22, 2015].

De Jongste, A 2011, *Philips: exploring Russia*. Available from: www.rt.com/business/phillips-russia-investment-expansion-509/. [October 29, 2015].

Fingar, C 2015, FDI to Russia slumps but Chinese investors step in as others pull back. Available from: www.ft.com/intl/cms/s/0/99ff3bc8-f338-11e4-8141-00144feab7de.html#axzz3qSpO20y1. [August 2, 2015].

Fu, X 2015, *China's path to innovation*, Cambridge University Press, Cambridge/UK.

GIZ 2015, Russland. Wirtschaft. Available from: http://liportal.giz.de/russland/wirtschaft-entwicklung/. [December 3, 2015].

Glowik, M 2009, *Market entry strategies. internationalization theories, network concepts and cases of Asian firms: LG Electronics, Panasonic, Samsung, Sharp, Sony and TCL China*, Oldenbourg Wissenschaftsverlag, München.

Gong, Y 2013, *Global operations strategy: fundamentals and practice*, Springer-Verlag, Berlin/Heidelberg.

GTAI (Germany Trade & Invest) 2014, Russland will Elektronikindustrie ausbauen. Available from: www.gtai.de/GTAI/Navigation/DE/Trade/Maerkte/suche,t=russland-will-elektronikindustrie-ausbauen,did=999172.html. [December 15, 2015].

GTAI 2015, *Wirtschaftstrends Jahresmitte 2015—Russland*. Available from: www.gtai.de/GTAI/Navigation/DE/Trade/Maerkte/Wirtschaftsklima/wirtschaftstrends,t=wirtschaftstrends-jahresmitte-2015--russland,did=1259090.html. [December 15, 2015].

Haier 2014, *Haier Group Profile*. Available from: www.haier.net/en/haier_industries/201110/t20111018_81797.shtml. [December 10, 2015].

Hobson, P 2015, *Russian imports plunge 39 percent as recession takes hold*. Available from: www.themoscowtimes.com/business/article/russian-imports-plunge-39-percent-as-recession-takes-hold/532468.html. [December 5, 2015].

Hodge, N 2015, *Putin pitches for foreign investment in Russia's Far East*. Available from: www.wsj.com/articles/putin-pitches-for-foreign-investment-in-russias-far-east-1441354851. [December 3, 2015].

Huawei 2012, *Huawei increases investment in Russia. Optimistic about growth prospects*. Available from: http://m.huawei.com/enmobile/industry/huawei-voices/hw-187392.htm. [August 17, 2015].

Huawei 2014a, *Huawei Delivers GSM-R Solution for Russia's Railway in Sochi*. Available from: www.huawei.com/enapp/1237/hw-336731.htm. [November 1, 2015].

Huawei 2014b, *Huawei and MegaFon announce 5G network plans for Russia*. Available from: http://pr.huawei.com/en/news/hw-397407-5g.htm#.VjktHIddG9Y. [November 1, 2015].

Huawei 2015a, *Corporate information*. Available from: http://m.huawei.com/en/about-huawei/corporate-info/index.htm. [September 24, 2015].

Huawei 2015b, *Financial highlights*. Available from: http://m.huawei.com/en/about-huawei/corporate-info/financial/index.htm. [September 24, 2015].

Huawei 2015c, *Research and development*. Available from: http://m.huawei.com/en/about-huawei/corporate-info/research-development/index.htm. [September 22, 2015].

IMF 2015a, *IMF Country Report No. 15/21. Russian Federation 2015. Article IV consultation—press release; and staff report*, Washington DC.

IMF 2015b, *Cheaper oil and sanctions weigh on Russia's growth outlook*. Available from: www.imf.org/external/pubs/ft/survey/so/2015/CAR080315B.htm. [October 30, 2015].

IMF 2015c, *World Economic Database*. Available from: www.imf.org/external/pubs/ft/weo/2015/01/weodata/weorept.aspx?sy=2004&ey=2015&scsm=1&ssd=1&sort=country&ds=.&br=1&c=922&s=NGDP_RPCH%2CNGDPD&grp=0&a=&pr.x=63&pr.y=8. [December 3, 2015].

IMF 2015d, *Russland: Inflationsrate von 2005 bis 2015 (gegenüber dem Vorjahr)*. Available from: http://de.statista.com/statistik/daten/studie/171867/umfrage/inflationsrate-in-russland/. [December 3, 2015].

Invest in Russia 2015, *Haier to construct a plant for the manufacturing of refrigeration equipment in Tatrstan*. Available from: http://investinrussia.ru/news/2702-haier-to-construct-a-plant-for. [July 31, 2015].

KPMG 2013, *Investing in Russia. An overview of the current investment climate in Russia*. Available from: https://ww:.google.de/?gws_rd=ssl#q=invest+in+russia+fdi+philips+kpmg. [October 28, 2015].

Khlebnikov, A 2015, *World Bank: Uncertainty is the main challenge facing the Russian economy*. Available from: www.russia-direct.org/qa/world-bank-uncertainty-main-challenge-facing-russian-economy. [December 3, 2015].

Kuchma, A 2014, Russia is facing record capital and investment outflow. Available from: http://rbth.com/business/2015/01/29/russia_is_facing_record_capital_and_investment_outflow_43261.html. [September 19, 2015].

Lee, C-F & Lee, AC 2013, *Encyclopedia of finance*, Springer, New York.

OECD 2003, *Glossary of statistical terms. Gross domestic product (GDP)—constant prices*.

Available from: https://stats.oecd.org/glossary/detail.asp?ID=1164. [December 22, 2015].

OECD 2005, *Glossary of statistical terms. Trade balance*. Available from: https://stats.oecd.org/glossary/detail.asp?ID=2739. [December 4, 2015].

OECD 2015, *Domestic product*. Available from: https://data.oecd.org/gdp/nominal-gdp-forecast.htm#indicator-chart. [December 3, 2015].

OPEC 2015, *Preisentwicklung ausgewählter OPEC-Rohöle von Oktober 2014 bis Oktober 2015 (Monatsdurchschnittswerte in US-Dollar je Barrel)*. Available from: http://de.statista.com/statistik/daten/studie/218658/umfrage/preisentwicklung-ausgewaehlter-opec-rohoele-monatsdurchschnittswerte/. [December 3, 2015].

Ostroukh, A 2015, *World bank downgrades Russia's economic outlook. But Moscow remains optimistic about growth in 2016*. Available from: www.wsj.com/articles/world-bank-downgrades-russias-economic-outlook-1443609118. [December 15, 2015].

Philips 2008, *Philips in Russia—background information*. Available from: www.newscenter.philips.com/main/standard/about/news/press/20081015_simplicity_event_philips_in_russia.wpd. [October 12, 2015].

Philips 2010a, *Philips and Electron announce partnership for development and production of Healthcare products in Russia*. Available from: www.newscenter.philips.com/main/standard/news/press/2010/20100517_electron_partnership.wpd#.VjY7G4ddGGc. [October 27, 2015].

Philips 2010b, *Philips and Electron complete first installation of a Russian-made CT scanner for the Russian market*. Available from: www.newscenter.philips.com/main/standard/news/press/2010/20101029_electron_ct_scanner.wpd#.VjY6W4ddGGc. [October 28, 2015].

Philips 2012a, *Philips teams up with three leading Russian research institutes for medical imaging technology research and development*. Available from: www.newscenter.philips.com/main/standard/news/press/2010/20100517_electron_partnership.wpd#.VjY3o4ddGGchttp://www.newscenter.philips.com/main/standard/news/press/2012/20120622-r-and-d-joint-venture-imaging-technologies.wpd#.VjYnUIddHzM. [October 30, 2015].

Philips 2012b, *Philips and Optogan sign up to cooperate in LED road lighting solutions in Russia*. Available from: www.newscenter.philips.com/main/standard/news/press/2012/20120410-philips-and-optogan-sign-up-to-cooperate-in-led-road-lighting-solutions-in-russia.wpd#.VjZKK4ddGGc. [October 24, 2015].

Philips 2014, Philips and MEDSI to enter new healthcare technology partnership in Russia. Available from: www.newscenter.philips.com/main/standard/news/press/2014/20140124-philips-and-medsi-to-enter-new-healthcare-technology-partnership-in-russia.wpd#.Vi-_OIddGGc. [October 27, 2015].

Philips 2015a, *History*. Available from: www.philips.com/about/company/history/index.page. [October 11, 2015].

Philips 2015b, *Company Profile*. Available from: www.philips.com/about/company/companyprofile.page. [October 11, 2015].

Philips 2015c, *Financial results*. Available from: www.philips.com/about/investor/financialresults/index.page. [October 11, 2015].

RDIF 2014, *FDI into Russia increased by 83% in 2013, Russia rises to 3rd in global rankings for the first time—UNCAD*. Available from: www.rdif.ru/Eng_fullNews/818/. [November 2, 2015].

ROSATOM 2011, *Philips and ROSATOM intend to develop nuclear medicine in Russia*. Available from: www.rosatom.ru/en/presscentre/news/c9aaad00474c46628b099b86442d90bd. [October 26, 2015].

Rosstat 2015, *Russland: Inflationsrate von November 2014 bis November 2015 (gegenüber dem Vorjahresmonat)*. Available from: http://de.statista.com/statistik/daten/studie/203901/umfrage/monatliche-inflationsrate-in-russland/. [December 3, 2015].

Thomas, D 2014, *Megafon signs equipment deal with Huawei*. Available from: www.ft.com/intl/cms/s/0/dec0fd40-efca-11e3-bee7-00144feabdc0.html#axzz3qSpO20y1. [October 31, 2015].

Santander 2014, *Foreign investment in Russia*. Available from: https://en.santandertrade.com/establish-overseas/russia/foreign-investment. [November 2, 2015].

UNCTAD 2015, *World Investment Report 2015*, New York.

UNCTAD 2015a, *Foreign direct investment: Inward and outward flows and stock, annual, 1980–2014*. Available from: http://unctadstat.unctad.org/wds/TableViewer/tableView.aspx. [December 5, 2015].

Van Groningen, E2014, *Philips profit misses estimates on woes in China, Russia*. Available from: www.bloomberg.com/news/articles/2014-10-20/philips-profit-misses-analyst-estimates-on-woes-in-china-russia. [September 1, 2015].

Van Tartwijk, M2014, *Philips plans to split into two companies*. Available from: www.wsj.com/articles/philips-to-split-operations-1411454665. [October 4, 2015].

Vedomosti 2015, *Huawei to build data center for Akado.* Available from: www.investinrussia.ru/news/4165-huawei-to-build-data-center-for. [August 17, 2015].

WIPO 2014, *Who filed the most PCT patent applications in 2014?* Available from: www.wipo.int/export/sites/www/ipstats/en/docs/infographics_pct_2014.pdf. [October 4, 2015].

Wong, K 2014, *Huawei expands in Russian tech services after Putin's China deal.* Available from: www.bloomberg.com/news/articles/2014-06-18/huawei-expands-in-russian-tech-services-after-putin-s-china-dea. [September 24, 2015].

WTO 2015a, *Russland: Handelsbilanzsaldo von 2004 bis 2014 (in Milliarden US-Dollar).* Available from: http://de.statista.com/statistik/daten/studie/15645/umfrage/handelsbilanz-von-russland/. [December 5, 2015].

WTO 2015b, *Russland: Export von Gütern von 2004 bis 2014 (in Milliarden US-Dollar).* Available from: http://de.statista.com/statistik/daten/studie/15729/umfrage/export-von-guetern-aus-russland/. [December 5, 2015].

WTO 2015c, *Russland: Import von Gütern von 2004 bis 2014 (in Milliarden US-Dollar).* Available from: http://de.statista.com/statistik/daten/studie/15687/umfrage/import-von-guetern-nach-russland/. [December 5, 2015].

4.4 Case study: Healthcare industry in Japan

Constantin Wendlandt and Mario Glowik

Case review questions

1 How would you summarize the major findings of an environmental analysis (at the macro and industry levels) for Japan from the perspective of a diagnostic imaging products (DIP) manufacturer?
2 How would you develop a SWOT analysis for Siemens Healthcare for the Japanese market?

Macro environmental analysis

Society

The Asian healthcare market is the fastest growing healthcare market in the world. During the last decade, spending on healthcare has more than doubled in the region (Perkowski, 2014; WHO, 2014). With increasing wealth, demand for more sophisticated treatments increases. Thus, treatment costs gradually increase too, which puts pressure on the countries' health insurance systems. However, huge disparities exist when looking at the development level of the healthcare sector in Asia divided by countries: Laos and Cambodia are at an early stage of their development; China is located in the middle indicating significant regional disparities, whereas countries such as Singapore, Thailand, Malaysia and Japan are highly developed (Duscha et al. 2014).

There are three major societal peculiarities that have an impact on Japan's medical device sector: First, there is the aging of its society, which increases the demand for therapeutic devices. In 2013, 25.1 percent of the Japanese were older than 65 years and until 2060 their share is expected to increase to almost 40 percent (Sauermost, 2014). Second, the high frequency of doctor visits in Japan (Walsh, 2012) which is possible due to Japan's comprehensive social insurance program. Every Japanese citizen is obligated to have health insurance (Orlanes, 2014). Finally, personal relationships are of particular importance, especially when it comes to sales and distribution on the Japanese medical device market (Gross, 2015).

Ecology

Japan is highly dependent on the import of natural resources as domestic resources are scarce. In order to limit the dependence on other countries, Japan had been increasingly relying on nuclear energy. The public opinion towards nuclear energy worsened after the Fukushima nuclear incident of 2011 (Goto, 2013). The catastrophe also had a negative effect on Japan's healthcare market (Anzai, 2012). Boehringer Ingelheim, for example, shut down a production facility close to the affected area as a result of the nuclear incident (Wirtschaftswoche, 2011). The incident was a direct result of the Tōhoku earthquake and the following tsunami, which resulted in the death of more than fifteen thousand people (NPA, 2015). Major earthquakes, like this, occur about once in 70 years. As a result, 11 cities out of the '100 cities with the greatest exposure to natural hazards' worldwide are located in Japan (Verisk Maplecroft, 2015).

Critical opinion on nuclear technology is wide spread throughout Japanese society, as a result of the drop of the atomic bombs in 1945. After the Fukushima Daiichi incident in 2011, Japanese patients became even more concerned about negative effects of radiation exposure. Consequently, low dosage imaging procedures are increasingly requested by the patients (Gross, 2013a).

Economy

Japan belongs to the most indebted countries in the world. Japanese health expenditures in 2012 accounted for 10.3 percent of its GDP, which is one percent above OECD average. The consulting company McKinsey has predicted, that the share might increase to 13.5 percent by 2035 (Sauermost, 2014), which will put even more pressure on the national debt and Japan's budget deficit. However, due to the rapid aging of society, there will be no alternative (Wada, 2015). Given this situation the current Japanese administration wants to increase Japan's international competitiveness in the medical technology segment. In June 2013, it passed the 'Healthcare and Medical Strategy' to strengthen the technological development of pharmaceutical products and medical devices, as well as of care robots. In order to create the right framework for the restructuring program, the government has announced further deregulations as well as the creation of five special economic zones providing incentives for investors (Sauermost, 2014).

Law

The regulatory environment of Japan has a huge effect on the competitiveness of the Japanese medical device industry. In Japan regulation of medical devices always fell under the Pharmaceutical Affairs Law (PAL). The law was originally designed to regulate pharmaceuticals, which caused major problems as it included numerable restrictions unnecessary for medical devices. These overly strict regulations negatively affected the speed and amplitude of medical device research and development activities in Japan. Subsequently, developers in the United States and Europe gained a competitive advantage over Japanese manufacturers, as they operated in a more deregulated environment. The Japanese regulatory environment led to a risk aversion amongst Japanese manufacturers, which hindered them from developing innovative diagnostic devices (Anzai, 2010). The strict regulations have sometimes even scared off investors in the past

(Sauermost, 2014). Extremely long approval times for new medical devices, so called 'device lag' and 'device gap,' are a well-known challenge for medical device manufacturers, targeting the Japanese market (Japanmarkt, 2014).

Expertise

Despite the negative impact of PAL, Japan remains the country indicating the highest number of medical device patents granted by the U.S. Patent and Trademark Office (USPTO). In comparison, China is currently ranked 20th (USPTO, 2014). Japanese hospitals are often equipped with the newest diagnostic technology. In 2011, for example, the OECD has found out, that there were 46.9 magnetic resonance imaging systems per 1 million inhabitants, the OECD average was just 13.3 (Sauermost, 2014). However, the high number could also be regarded as a sign of inefficiency of Japan's healthcare system, as many small clinics and physicians try to have a full portfolio of state of the art products, instead of leaving it to the respective specialists (Japanmarkt, 2013). The high number of qualified staff in the healthcare sector is one of the strength of Japan's medical device market (AMDD, 2011).

An analysis of the diagnostic imaging industry in Japan

The World Health Organisation (WHO) defines medical devices as means of any instrument, apparatus, implement, machine, appliance, implant, and reagent for in vitro use, software, material or other similar or related article, intended by the manufacturer to be used, alone or in combination, for human beings, for one or more of the specific medical purpose(s) of:

- diagnosis, prevention, monitoring, treatment or alleviation of disease,
- diagnosis, monitoring, treatment, alleviation of or compensation for an injury,
- investigation, replacement, modification, or support of the anatomy or of a physiological process,
- supporting or sustaining life,
- control of conception,
- disinfection of medical devices, and
- providing information by means of in vitro examination of specimens derived from the human body; and does not achieve its primary intended action by pharmacological, immunological or metabolic means, in or on the human body, but which may be assisted in its intended function by such means (WHO, 2015).

In order to guarantee safety, the WHO and the Global Harmonisation Task Force (GHTF), have recommended certain technical standards for medical devices to be fulfilled. Medical devices need to fulfill safety requirements according to the United Nations Population Fund (UNFPA). UNFPA evaluates medical devices on the basis of the following criteria: valid marketing licenses, valid ISO 13485 and ISO 9001 certifications, compliance with ISO requirements, certificates of conformity, 'product sampling and testing during the bid evaluation stage' and lastly, product pre-shipment inspections (UNFPA, 2013).

The diagnostic imaging products (DIP) industry belongs to one of the most important sub-segments of the medical devices industry. The DIP industry goes back to 1895 when Wilhelm Roentgen discovered the X-rays. Within a couple of months after the discovery of the X-rays the German company Siemens started to sell X-ray machines for commercial purposes. Over the years, other industry pioneers such as General Electric (USA), Philips from the Netherlands and Japanese companies like Toshiba and Hitachi have entered the DIP industry. Since its inception the diagnostic imaging industry has been a global industry dominated by rather large enterprises which is regarded as an oligopoly market (Tilly and Handel, 1999; Beyer, 2007).

The reason for that oligopoly is the fact, that the diagnostic imaging industry is a 'high technology industry.' In order to create a new diagnostic imaging device, knowhow of electronical and mechanical engineering has to be combined with a specialized form of engineering (radiation regulation). In addition to the high level of expertise, that is needed to produce these enormously complex instruments, magnetic resonance imaging (MRI) and computed tomography (CT) devices indicate short product life cycles (Tilly and Handel, 1999). Annually a few hundreds of CT scanners are produced in the United States. A single high-end MRI or CT machine usually costs more than one million dollars. Such costs indicate financial barriers for smaller companies to enter the market, and therefore, the market is controlled by large multinational enterprises. The ten biggest producers, among them Siemens, General Electric, Philips, and Toshiba indicate a combined worldwide market share of more than 90 percent (EvaluateMedTech, 2014).

The Japanese DIP market is the largest in Asia indicating a market volume of USD 3.6 billion in 2012 (MHLW, 2012). The DIP market which has grown by 1.9 percent each year is dominated by X-ray equipment, followed by CT and MRI equipment (PR Newswire, 2013). Around 60 percent of the DIP demand in Japan is met by local production—the other half of the Japanese DIP (about 40 percent) is met by imports. X-ray and CT equipment is mostly produced in Japan, while the majority of MRI and nuclear medicine equipment is imported from the USA, Germany and China (Gross, 2013a; MHLW, 2012).

During last decades more and more Japanese manufacturers entered the global medical imaging market which was originally dominated by US-American and European companies. Japanese firms increased their market share and establish their brand names not only in Japan but worldwide. Additionally, Japanese firms acted as joint venture partners and suppliers to American and European companies (Tilly and Handel, 1999). In 2014 there were three Japanese companies amongst the top ten best-selling producers of DIP devices worldwide: Toshiba, Hitachi and Konica Minolta (EvaluateMedTech, 2014). Other important Japanese companies in the DIP market niche are Shimadzu, Canon and Fujifilm.

Micro analysis: Siemens Healthcare in Japan

Siemens was established in 1847 under the name Siemens & Halske (S&H), in Berlin, Germany. In 1966, S&H merged with Siemens-Schuckertwerke (SSW) and Siemens-Reiniger-Werke (SRW), which established today's Siemens AG. In 1969, Siemens's medical division was renamed 'Siemens Unternehmensbereich Medizintechnik' and in 2001 'Medical Solutions.' Since 2014, the medical division is known as Siemens Healthcare (Siemens AG, 2015). Since 2015, May 1, the healthcare segment of Siemens AG has become an independent subsidiary company called Siemens Healthcare GmbH (DPA, 2015). The separation of Siemens's healthcare business indicates a strategic decision to allocate resources more efficiently to relevant healthcare research and development activities. Siemens Healthcare is headquartered in Erlangen, Germany (Proval, 2014).

Siemens Healthcare focuses on the development, design, manufacture, and distribution of medical devices. The product portfolio includes vitro diagnostics, medical imaging, and healthcare information technology (MDBR, 2010). Siemens, just like General Electric and Philips, runs its own production facilities for so-called superconducting MRI magnets (Magnetica, 2011). This strategy of vertical integration provides Siemens with a competitive advantage over its Asian competitors.

Siemens serves all price segments of the MRI market—only General Electric does the same. Siemens Concerto and Siemens Magnetom C cover the low-end segment; the midrange price segment is covered by the Symphony Series; and the premium segment is covered by the Siemens Avanto, Siemens Espree, Siemens Essenza, and Siemens Trio (Block, 2012; Rentz, 2012). In 2011, Siemens Healthcare spent USD 1.56 billion on research and development, equaling approximately 9.6 percent of its USD 16.3 billion revenues (FMD, 2012).

Japan is the second most attractive market for Siemens (behind China), which has grown by 7 percent each year between 2009 and 2014. In 2009, Japan was the fourth important market for Siemens with a 6 percent share of total equipment orders. Until 2014, Japan overtook Germany and is now ranked third, with a 9 percent share of total equipment orders, behind the United States (26 percent) and China (14 percent). Siemens has stated that it forecasts further market potential due to Japan's elderly population but worries about increasing price pressure (Requardt, 2014).

Siemens established its Japanese subsidiary Siemens Japan K.K. in 1979. The head office is located in Tokyo. Siemens Japan K.K. includes Siemens Healthcare Diagnostics K.K., Siemens Hearing Instruments K.K., Acrorad Co, Ltd., Siemens Industry Software K.K., Yasukawa Siemens Automation Drive K.K., and Siemens Industry Software Simulation and Test K.K. (Siemens Japan K.K., 2015). Healthcare is by far the most important business for Siemens in Japan. According to Junichi Obata, President and CEO of Siemens Japan K.K., Siemens was able to benefit from its superior technology and gained market access through joint ventures and acquisitions of Japanese companies (Betros, 2012a). One example would be Siemens Kameda Healthcare IT Systems K.K., a joint venture with Kameda Health Informatics Institute Inc., which was established to strengthen Siemens Healthcare information technology business in Japan. Another example is the acquisition of Mochida Pharmaceutical Co., Ltd., formerly a joint venture named Mochida Siemens Medical Systems Co., Ltd., established in 2004. It helped to steadily increase Siemens's market share in the Japanese ultrasound business segment (Siemens 2007a; Siemens 2007b). Siemens Japan K.K. wants to become the leading player in the Japanese medical device market. The company focuses on three market segments: diagnostic imaging; X-ray; and ultrasound equipment. The primary target customers are universities' research laboratories and hospitals. As of 2012, there were 2,200 people working for Siemens in Japan (Betros, 2012a).

Bibliography

AMDD 2011,Comparison of market environment for medical devices in Japan, China, and Korea. *American Medical Device and Diagnostics Manufacturer's Association (AMDD)*, August 2011.

Anzai, M 2010, A Yen for change. *European Medical Device Technology*, vol. 1, no. 7.

Anzai, M 2012, Japan's medical device market is getting better. *European Medical Device Technology*. Available from: www.emdt.co.uk/article/japan%E2%80%99s-medical-device-market-getting-better. [February 20, 2015].

Beaumont, C 2013, Healthcare 2020: Japan's pathfinder role in the global healthcare industry. *Results Healthcare*. Available from: www.resultshealthcare.com/media/84205/healthcare_2020_-_japan_final.pdf. [January 20, 2015].

Betros, C 2012a, Siemens Japan KK. *Japan Today*. Available from: www.japantoday.com/category/executive-impact/view/siemens-japan-kk. [January 20, 2015].

Beyer, M 2007, *Servicediversifikation in Industrieunternehmen: Kompetenztheoretische Untersuchung der Determinantennachhaltiger Wettbewerbsvorteile* [Service diversification in industrial companies: Competence theoretical study of the determinants of sustainable competitive advantage]. Deutscher Universitäts-Verlag, Wiesbaden.

Block, J 2012, MRI machine cost and price. *Block imaging*. Available from: https://youtu.be/LxhB2qGnXU4. [May 23, 2015].

DPA 2015, Siemens gliedert Medizintechnik aus [Siemens spins medical technology off]. *Berliner Zeitung*, 6. March 6, 2015.

Duscha, W, Hundt, T, Jacobi, S, Jaensch, R, Ehman, W, Kemper, W, Mauer, J, von Meien, S, Pasvantis, K, Rohde, R, Rohman, B & Schaaf, B 2014, *Gesundheitswirtschaft in Asien-Pazifik. Special zur Asien-Pazifik Konferenz 2014* [Brochure] [Healthcare industry in Asia Pacific. Asia Pacific Conference 2014]. Germany Trade and Invest, Berlin.

Emergo 2015, Global medical device industry outlook for 2015 [Brochure]. *Emergo*. Emergo, Austin, USA.

Epsicom 2015, Asia reports.*Epsicom*. Available from: www.espicom.com/asia. [April 10, 2015].

EvaluateMedTech 2014, *World preview 2014, outlook to 2020* [Brochure]. Evaluate, London.

FMD 2012, Top 10 medical device R&D budgets Available from: www.fiercemedicaldevices.com/special-reports/top-10-medical-device-rd-budgets/top-10-medical-device-rd-budgets. [February 20, 2015].

Friedrich, M 2012, Siemens ends fiscal 2012 with revenue growth and strong profit. Available from: www.siemens.com/press/en/pressrelease/?press=/en/pressrelease/2012/corporate/2012-q4/axx20121104.htm [March 9, 2015].

Goto, O 2013, *Energy situation in Japan* [Brochure]. Agency for Natural Resources and Energy, Tokyo.

Gross, A 2013a, Asia in the spotlight: diagnostic market in Asia seen growing at unprecedented levels. *Medical Device Daily*. Available from: www.medicaldevicedaily.com/servlet/com.accumedia.web.Dispatcher?next=bioWorldHeadlines_article&forceid=83837. [February 5, 2015].

Gross, A 2013b, The fight is heating up for China's burgeoning medical device market. *Medical Device Daily*. Available from: www.medicaldevicedaily.com/servlet/com.accumedia.web.Dispatcher?next=bioWorldHeadlines_article&forceid=81776. [March 23, 2015].

Hitachi, Ltd. 2015, About Hitachi, Ltd. Available from: www.hitachi.com/corporate/about/history/index.html. [February 21, 2015].

Hitachi Medical Systems 2015a, Corporate information. *Hitachi Medical Systems*. Available from: www.hitachi-medical.co.jp/english/corporateinfo/index.html. [February 21, 2015].

Hitachi Medical Systems 2015b, Products and services: product categories: medical and healthcare equipment. *Hitachi Medical Systems*. Available from: www.hitachi.co.id/eng/products/product_categories/medical_healthcare_equipment/#Milestones. [February 21, 2015].

Innervision Research 2012 Innabinetto 'ModaritiNabi' karawakarugazōshindasōchi no dōnyūjōkyō [Understand the adoption of the diagnostic imaging apparatus from In-Navi-Net's "Modality Navigator"]. *Innervision Research*. Available from: www.innervision.co.jp/01inner/2012/pdf/iv201207_036-039.pdf. [February 26, 2015].

Israel. Ministry of Economy 2007. Overview of pharmaceutical and healthcare in Japan. *Economic department Israeli embassy-Tokyo*. Available from: www.moital.gov.il/NR/rdonlyres/061BE5FC-DA0A-4A84-B90F-0778E7A53301/0/PharmaceuticalandMedicalCareReport.pdf. [January 10, 2015].

Japan. Health Policy Bureau, Ministry of Health, Labour and Welfare (MHLW) 2008, *Annual report on statistics of production by pharmaceutical industry in 2008*, Statistics Section, Economic Affairs Division.

Japan. Health Policy Bureau, Ministry of Health, Labour and Welfare (MHLW) 2009, *Annual report on statistics of production by pharmaceutical industry in 2009*, Statistics Section, Economic Affairs Division.

Japan. Health Policy Bureau, Ministry of Health, Labour and Welfare (MHLW) 2010, *Annual Report on Statistics of Production by Pharmaceutical Industry in 2010*, Statistics Section, Economic Affairs Division.

Japan. Health Policy Bureau, Ministry of Health, Labour and Welfare (MHLW) 2011, *Annual report on statistics of production by pharmaceutical industry in 2011*, Statistics Section, Economic Affairs Division.

Japan. Health Policy Bureau, Ministry of Health, Labour and Welfare (MHLW) 2012, *Annual report on statistics of production by pharmaceutical industry in 2012*, Statistics Section, Economic Affairs Division.

Japanmarkt, 2013, Kampf den Verzögerungen [Fight the delays]. Available from: www.japan.ahk.de/fileadmin/ahk_japan/JM_Artikel/JM_Artikel2013/Kampf_den_Verzoegerungen_Pages_from_JM012013.pdf. [February 17, 2015].

Japan Patent Office 2003, Iyōgazōshindasōchinikansurutokkyoshutsugangijutsudōkōchōsahōkoku [The patent application technology trends survey report in relation to medical diagnostic imaging devices]. *Japan Patent Office*. Available from: www.jpo.go.jp/shiryou/pdf/gidou-houkoku/iyou_gazou.pdf. [March 23, 2015].

Magnetica 2011, Today's MRI market. *Magnetica*. Available from: www.magnetica.com/page/innovation/todays-mri-market/. [February 24, 2015].

Maplecroft 2013, World: Socio-economic resilience index 2013. *Reliefweb.com*. Available from: http://reliefweb.int/map/world/world-socio-economic-resilience-index-2013 [February 20, 2015].

MarketsandMarkets 2012, New product launches with technological advancements, a key strategy adopted by leading market players to foster their growth in the global diagnostic imaging market. *MarketsandMarkets*. Available from: www.marketsandmarkets.com/ResearchInsight/diagnostic-imaging-market.asp. [February 26, 2015].

MDBR 2010, Diagnostic imaging companies.*medicaldevices-business-review.com*. Available from: http://diagnosticimaging.medicaldevices-business-review.com/companies. [January 10, 2015].

MDDI 2014, Top 40 medical device companies.*mddionline.com*. Available from: www.mddionline.com/article/top-40-medical-device-companies. [January 10, 2015].

NPA 2015, Damage situation and police countermeasure associated with 2011 Tohoku district—off the pacific ocean earthquake, *National Police Agency of Japan*. Available from: www.npa.go.jp/archive/keibi/biki/higaijokyo_e.pdf. [February 20, 2015].

OANDA 2015, Average exchange rate, *Oanda.com*. Available from: www.oanda.com/currency/average. [January 10, 2015].

Orlanes, JE 2014, Health check: the cost of medical care in Japan, *tokyoweekender.com*. Available from: www.tokyoweekender.com/2014/12/health-check-the-cost-of-medical-care-in-japan/. [February 20, 2015].

Perkowski, J 2014, Healthcare: a trillion dollar industry in the making, *Forbes*. Available from: www.forbes.com/sites/jackperkowski/2014/11/12/health-care-a-trillion-dollar-industry-in-the-making/. [January 7, 2015].

PR Newswire 2013, Asia pacific medical imaging industry outlook to 2017—driven by rising lifestyle diseases and public healthcare expenditure, *PR Newswire*. Available from: www.prnewswire.com/news-releases/asia-pacific-medical-imaging-industry-outlook-to-2017-driven-by-rising-lifestyle-diseases-and-public-healthcare-expenditure-212163121.html. [February 8, 2015].

PR Newswire 2015, US MRI systems market (magnetic resonance imaging) analysis and forecasts to 2020. Available from: www.bizjournals.com/prnewswire/press_releases/2015/01/02/MN99477. [February 20, 2015].

PR Web 2014, Global positron emission tomography market: industry analysis, size, share, growth, trends and forecast, 2014–2020. Available from: www.prweb.com/releases/2014/08/prweb12079108.htm. [February 20, 2015].

Proval, C 2014, Siemens healthcare to operate as independent unit, *Radiology Business*. Available from: www.radiologybusiness.com/topics/leadership/siemens-healthcare-operate-independent-unit. [May 20, 2015].

Rentz, S 2012, MRI Machine cost and price guide [2015 Update], *Block Imaging*. Available from: http://info.blockimaging.com/bid/92623/MRI-Machine-Cost-and-Price-Guide. [May 20, 2015].

Requardt, H 2014, *Healthcare—solid performance, strong perspectives* [Brochure]. Siemens AG, Berlin.

Sauermost, M 2014, *Branche kompakt: Japan—Medizintechnik (Dezember 2014)* [Industrycompact: Japan—Medical Technology (December 2014)] [Brochure]. Germany Trade and Invest, Tokyo.

Siemens 2007a, Siemens Japan acquires majority stake of Mochida Siemens Medical Systems. *Siemens*. Available from: www.siemens.com/press/en/pressrelease/?press=/en/pr_cc/2007/10_oct/medbv200709069_1464404.htm&content[]=HIM&content[]=HCIM. [May 15, 2015].

Siemens 2007b, Siemens medical solutions increases presence in Japan, *Siemens*. Available from: www.siemens.com/press/en/pressrelease/?press=/en/pr_cc/2007/10_oct/medbv200709068_1464321.htm&content[]=CC&content[]=Corp. [May 12, 2015].

Siemens AG 2015, History. Available from: www.siemens.com/history/en/history/. [March 22, 2015].

Siemens Japan K.K. 2015, About Siemens in Japan: company profile (as of October 1, 2014), *Siemens Japan K.K.* Available from: www.siemens.co.jp/english/Pages/AboutSiemensJapan.aspx. [February 26, 2015].

Sudo, A 2012, *Toshiba group R&D strategies* [Brochure]. Toshiba Corporation, Tokyo.

Tanaka, H 2014, *Toshiba healthcare business—introduction* [Brochure]. Toshiba Corporation, Tokyo.

Tilly, C & Handel, M 1999, What prognosis for good jobs? The medical diagnostic imaging equipment industry, *Corporate Governance and Sustainable Prosperity*, pp. 141–183.

Tokyo Metropolitan Government 2011, Healthcare sector: the Japanese market, *Tokyo Metropolitan Government*. Available from: www.seisakukikaku.metro.tokyo.jp/invest_tokyo/english/why-tokyo/industries/medical.html. [February 12, 2015].

Totsuyuka, T 2012, Iryōkkimēkā no seichōsenryaku [Growth strategy of medical device manufacturers]. *Mizuho Industry Focus*, vol. 111, pp. 1–23.

UNFPA 2013, UNFPA technical requirements for medical devices. Available from: www.unfpa.org/resources/unfpa-technical-requirements-medical-devices [May 17, 2015].

USPTO 2014, Medical devices: all classified utility patents (OR/XR), *United States patent and trademark office*. Available from: www.uspto.gov/web/offices/ac/ido/oeip/taf/meddev.htm. [March 6, 2015].

Verisk Maplecroft 2015, Latest products and reports: natural hazards risk atlas 2015. Available from: https://maplecroft.com/portfolio/new-analysis/2015/03/04/56-100-cities-most-exposed-natural-hazards-found-key-economies-philippines-japan-china-bangladesh-verisk-maplecroft/. [March 20, 2015].

Wada, Y 2015, 2015 healthcare outlook Japan, *Deloitte*. Available from: www2.deloitte.com/content/dam/Deloitte/global/Documents/Life-Sciences-Health-Care/gx-lshc-2015-health-care-outlook-japan.pdf. [April 12, 2015].

Walsh, CF 2012, Country report: the healthcare market in Japan, *Pharmaceutical Market Europe (PME)*. Available from: www.pmlive.com/pharma_intelligence/country_report_the_healthcare_market_in_japan_379354. [January 10, 2015].

WHO 2014, Global health expenditure database. *World Health Organization. Available from:* http://apps.who.int/nha/database/QuickReports/Index/en. [January 10, 2015].

WHO 2015, Medical device—full definition. *World Health Organization. Available from:* www.who.int/medical_devices/full_deffinition/en/. [June 10, 2015].

Wirtschaftswoche 2011, Standort in der Nähe von Fukushima. Boehringer gibt Japan-Werk auf [Location near Fukushima, Boehringer abandons Japan-plant], *Wirtschaftswoche.* Available from: www.n-tv.de/wirtschaft/Boehringer-gibt-Japan-Werk-auf-article3007916.html. [February 16, 2015].

4.5 Case study: Alphabet

Gaining market dominance through external knowledge resources

Mario Glowik

Case review questions

1 How would you review the advantages and disadvantages of acquisitions? Which major business fields has Alphabet launched through acquisitions in recent years?
2 How would you compare the total debt of Greece against the financial assets of Alphabet? Do you know other multinational enterprises with similar resource assets?
3 In terms of fair and equal competitive forces on the global markets, is there a reason to worry for the future if multinational enterprises such as Alphabet continue to grow excessively as witnessed in recent years?
4 Which business fields will Alphabet develop in the future? Provide reasons why you believe so.

About the company

The resource-based view claims that the firm achieves competitive advantage through resources that are rare, valuable, and difficult to imitate by others. If the required resources are not available inside the firm, one of the methods for obtaining them is through external paths, such as strategic alliances and joint ventures, equity participation, mergers, or acquisitions. The case of Alphabet, the parent company of Google, exemplifies how to gain desired resources mainly through external paths, such as acquisitions, instead of developing them in-house, which is time consuming.

Google, the biggest search engine in the world, was founded in 1998 by Larry Page and Sergey Brin and is headquartered in Mountain View, California. In 2000, Google launched its first 10-language versions of Google.com: French, German, Italian, Swedish, Finnish, Spanish, Portuguese, Dutch, Norwegian, and Danish. The first public acquisition of Google was in 2001, when it acquired Deja.com's Usenet Discussion service (Google, 2016a). An important step occurred in 2000, when Google entered a strategic alliance with Yahoo and later with AOL in 2002. Both partnerships did not last and ended in 2004 and 2015, respectively (Zhao, 2005; 147; Peterson, 2015).

The success of Google motivated the company to launch its initial public offering (IPO) in 2004. Just two years later, in 2006, Google announced the acquisition of You-Tube (Google, 2016a). In 2015, the management has declared the formation of a holding company called 'Alphabet Inc.' where Google became a major part of it (Google, 2016b). Presently, Google is rather less known under the name of Alphabet. The mission of Google as cited on its website is 'to organize the world's information and make it universally accessible and useful' (Google, 2016c).

As shown in Figure 4.5.1, Google organizes a wide range of products and services, which include websites, information and data services, and apps better known under

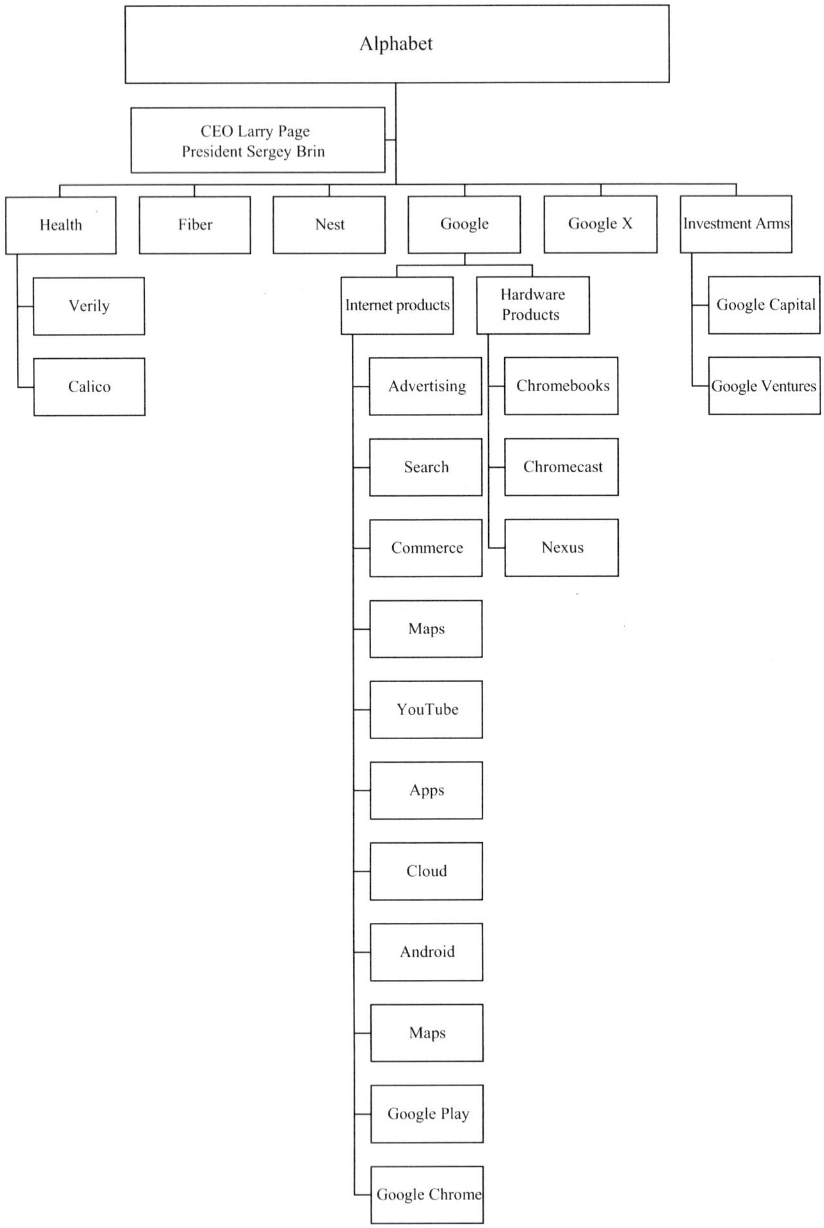

Figure 4.5.1 Organization of Alphabet (2016d).

its various brand names, such as Google Search, Google Maps, Google Shopping, and YouTube (Google, 2016d). Moreover, Google offers advertising and marketing programs, such as AdWords and AdSense. Google provides software and technology devices, for example, Google Chrome and Nexus Phone (Google, 2016a). In addition, the company has established its own research laboratory named Google X, which develops research and development projects, such as Google Glasses, autonomous car driving, and the Loon Project (Stone, 2013; Google, 2016a). Recently, the firm has introduced its healthcare business, which targets to generate, store, and mutually link data and, thus, provide information between hospitals, pharmaceutical companies, medical device companies, insurance companies, and patients. The healthcare business indicates promising market growth rates for the future. When considering the current power of Alphabet in terms of its global data collection and storage facilities, the firm's launch of the healthcare business is not without risks.

Recently, Google has managed to increase its asset values to overtake one of its biggest competitors, Apple Inc., and, thus, has become one of the most financial-rich companies in the world. The total stock market value of Alphabet, beginning 2016, was USD 568 billion, whereas the value of Apple was 'only' USD 535 billion (Bowers, 2016). In comparison, the total national debt of Greece in 2014 was approximately USD 360.18 billion (Statista, 2016). Against the background of such data, the financial power and influence of multinational enterprises such as Alphabet should be critically reviewed. To understand the market dominance of Alphabet, which reached a certain level, it is worthwhile to take a look inside the firm's major business segments.

Business segments

In 2015, Google generated approximately USD 75 billion of total revenues (Alphabet, 2016a), whereas the net income of Google amounted to USD 16.3 billion (Alphabet, 2016c). Within five years, the revenues and profits doubled. The margin (net income as a ratio of net revenues) is approximately 20 percent, which mirrors the extraordinary high profitability of the firm. Google's business segments include basic Internet application products, such as searching machine, advertisement, video streaming like YouTube, Google Maps, Google Apps, cloud computing, Chrome browser, e-mail correspondence named Gmail, smartphone operating software called Android, commercials like Google Play, and hardware products, such as Nexus, Chromecast, and Chromebooks. In addition, there are other, less-known segments, such as Google Nest and Google Fiber, Calico, Verily, Google Capital, and Google X (Alphabet, 2016b).

Advertising, which indicates the firm's most important business field, accounts for 90 percent of overall Google's revenues. Therefore, it is obvious that Google still heavily depends on its advertisement business (Alphabet, 2016b).

Google is mainly competing with other large digital business companies. In its website business, Google competes with Yahoo and the media corporation AOL. Microsoft is also considered to be a serious competitor as well as LinkedIn (which, since 2016, belongs to Microsoft) as a business and social networking social site. In the advertising sector, Google competes with Expedia, Media Company Scripps Interactive, and eBay as well as with social media companies, such as Facebook and Twitter. In the software and technology sectors, Google faces rivals, such as PTC, IBM, and Microsoft (Investopedia, 2016).

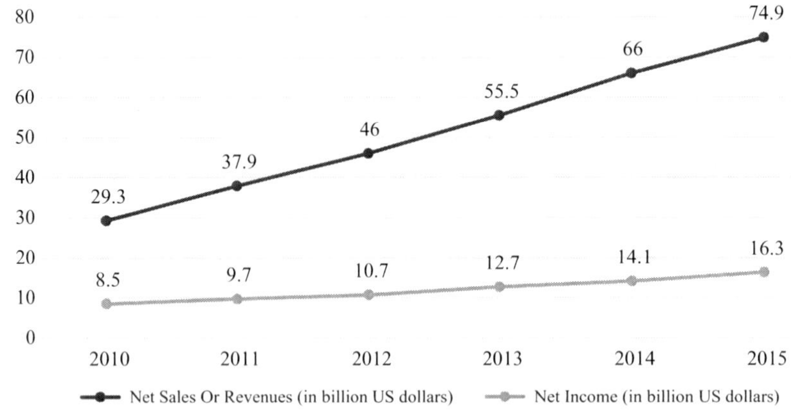

Figure 4.5.2 Google—net revenues versus net income 2010–2015 in billion US dollars.
Source: Author based on annual reports of Google (2016e) and Amigobulls (2016).

Alphabet's access to external knowledge resources through acquisitions

Since Google's establishment in 1998, the firm succeeded to acquire more than 170 companies. The most important acquisitions of Google are listed as follows (D'Onfro, 2015):

1 Acquisition of **Motorola in 2011** for **USD 12.5 billion**
  - The purpose behind this acquisition was to use Motorola's patents.
  - However, in 2013, Google sold Motorola to Lenovo for USD 2.91 billion because it became unprofitable but Google keeps most of the patents.

2 Acquisition of **Nest Labs in 2014** for **USD 3.2 billion**
  - Google acquired Nest Labs, which produces smart thermostats and smoke detectors.
  - The aim was to expand its presence in consumer homes.

3 Acquisition of **DoubleClick in 2007** for **USD 3.1 billion**
  - Google has gained prominence in the advertising world by purchasing DoubleClick.
  - Google was able to access web publishers, agencies, and advertisers.

4 Acquisition of **YouTube in 2006** for **USD 1.65 billion**
  - Google managed to acquire YouTube, the successful video sharing platform.
  - YouTube became the second largest search engine in the world after Google.

5 Acquisition of **Waze in 2013** for **USD 966 million**
  - Google acquired the Israeli mapping service Waze (Cohan, 2013).
  - Waze provides a mapping program, which includes information on traffic and police presence, and enables users to report on accidents.
  - By this acquisition, Google obtained new features that Google Maps did not previously include.

6 Acquisition of **AdMob in 2009** for **USD 750 million** (D'Onfro, 2015)
- Google acquired a mobile ad platform and obtained presence in the mobile advertising market.

7 Acquisition of **ITA Software in 2010** for **USD 700 million**
- ITA is an important stakeholder in the travel industry and enabled Google to launch Google flight search.

8 Acquisition of **Postini in 2007** for **USD 625 million**
- Postini is an email and web security service, which was transferred into Google Apps.

9 Acquisition of **Dropcam in 2014** for **USD 555 million**
- Dropcam offers video monitoring and security technology. This acquisition assisted Nest Labs, also acquired by Google, to increase its home automation products.

10 Acquisition of **SkyBox Imaging in 2014** for **USD 500 million**
- Google achieved up-to-date and accurate imagery of Google Maps with the satellite technology of SkyBox.

Additionally, costly acquisitions have turned Google into a powerful company; some 'cheaper ones' have provided the firm with valuable patents and leading technology. For example, in 2005, the acquisition of Android for an estimated USD 50 million was perceived to be one of the most successful investments that still generates billions of dollars in revenues. Presently, Android is one of the leading mobile operating platforms worldwide (Vasanth, 2014).

Furthermore, strategic alliances and joint ventures are methods to gain valuable knowledge—as successfully applied by Google. Below is a list of strategic alliances and joint ventures that represent an abstract of Alphabet's entire network building dynamics in recent years.

Alphabet's access to external resources through strategic alliances and joint ventures

1 **Google and LG** signed on strategic alliance in 2007, which enabled Google to install its products into LG's mobile devices (Googlepress, 2007). The two companies extended their relationship in 2014 by signing a 10-year global patent license agreement, which enhanced their ability to develop new products and technologies (LG, 2014).

2 **Google and Sony** signed a strategic alliance in 2010, which 'combines Google's open-source Android platform with Sony's expertise in technology product design.' Sony and Google aimed to enhance their technological expertise by providing access to compelling content. Sony Internet TV was incorporated with Google TV platform (Sony, 2010).

3 **Google and Salesforce.com** signed a strategic alliance in 2007, and aimed to provide new business platforms to attract new customers. The result of this alliance resulted in Salesforce Group Edition featuring Google AdWords (Salesforce.com, 2007).

4 **Google and PwC** signed a strategic alliance in 2014; the joint business relationship between the companies aimed to improve the Google Cloud platform.

This alliance combined the power of PwC's analytical acumen and Google Cloud Platform (PwC, 2014).

5 **Alphabet Inc.** and **American Heart Association (AHA)** entered a 5-year joint research venture. The cooperation included a USD 50 million investment from both parties (USD 25 million each), with the purpose of researching new ways for tackling heart diseases (Gupta, 2015).

In recent years, Google has established additional partnerships with data- and technology-driven companies, such as NASA (2005), eBay (2006), NBC Universal (2008), Facebook (2013), Luxottica (2014), Samsung (2014), and Twitter (2015) (NASA, 2005; eBay, 2006; Reuters, 2008; Protalinski, 2014; Luxottica, 2014; Samsung Newsroom, 2014; Patel, 2015).

The above-mentioned records indicate that Alphabet's in-house knowledge generation through research and development is rather out-placed by various acquisitions and cooperative agreements, which provide the firm with innovative ideas and the desired fresh knowledge to secure competitive advantage. Advertisement serves as the most important cash generator for Alphabet. Because Alphabet is a very cash-rich company, they have the optimal prerequisites to proceed and implement their acquisition strategies in the future, thus allowing them to continuously attain valuable technological knowledge and new business concepts from external stakeholders.

The key strengths of Alphabet obviously are that they have the right 'instinct' for promising future businesses. The firm's daily business deals with collecting, evaluating, and storing data stemming from around the world. Having first-hand and privileged access to these valuable data provides the most optimal surroundings to figure out promising future businesses before other firms with less-informative database.

Bibliography

Alphabet 2016a, *Alphabet announces fourth quarter and fiscal year 2015 results*. Available from: https://abc.xyz/investor/news/earnings/2015/Q4_google_earnings/index.html. [April 18, 2016].

Alphabet 2016b, *Alphabet Inc. and Google Inc. Form 10-K for the fiscal year ended December 31, 2015*. Available from: https://abc.xyz/investor/pdf/20151231_alphabet_10K.pdf. [April 18, 2016].

Alphabet 2016c, *Alphabet Inc. quarterly consolidated statements of income*. Available from: https://abc.xyz/investor/pdf/2016_historical_financial_statements.pdf. [April 24, 2016].

Alphabet 2016d, *Financial statements glossary*. Available from: https://abc.xyz/investor/other/additional-financial-information.html. [April 26, 2016].

Amigobulls 2016, Alphabet Inc-C income statement—annual (NASDAQ:GOOG). Available from: http://amigobulls.com/stocks/GOOG/income-statement/annual#. [April 26,2016].

Bowers, S 2016, *Google overtakes Apple as world's most valuable listed company*. The Guardian. Available from: www.theguardian.com/technology/2016/feb/02/google-overtakes-apple-as-worlds-most-valuable-listed-company. [April 18, 2016].

Cohan, P 2013, *Four reasons Google bought Waze*. Forbes. Available from: www.forbes.com/sites/petercohan/2013/06/11/four-reasons-for-google-to-buy-waze/#4d76a2671433. [April 18, 2016].

D'onfro, J 2015, *Google's ten biggest acquisitions*. Business Insider. Available from: www.businessinsider.com/googles-ten-biggest-acquisitions-2015-1?IR=T. [April 18, 2016].

eBay 2006, *Google and ebay sign multi-year agreement to connect users, merchants, and advertisers around the globe*. Available from: https://investors.ebayinc.com/releasedetail.cfm?releaseid=209064. [April 18, 2015].

Glowik, M 2009, *Market entry strategies*, Oldenbourg, Munich.

Glowik, M & Bruhs, SM 2014, *Business-to-business: a global network perspective*, Routledge, Abingdon.

Glowik, M 2016, *Market entry strategies. Internationalization theories, concepts and cases of Asian high-technology firms: Haier, Hon Hai Precision, Lenovo, LG Electronics, Panasonic, Samsung, Sharp, Sony, TCL, Xiaomi*, 2nd ed., De Gruyter, Berlin/Boston.

Google 2016a, *Our history in depth*. Available from: www.google.de/about/company/timeline/. [April 18, 2016].

Google 2016b, *Finance*. Available from: www.google.com/finance?cid=694653. [April 18, 2016].

Google 2016c, *About Google*. Available from: www.google.de/about/company. [April 17, 2016].

Google 2016d, *About Google products*. Available from: www.google.de/about/products/. [April 17, 2016].

Google 2016e, *Financial statements for Alphabet Inc—Google Finance*. Available from: www.google.com/finance?q=NASDAQ:GOOG&fstype=ii. [April 24, 2016].

Googlepress 2007, *LG Electronics and Google team up to enhance the mobile experience*. Available from: http://googlepress.blogspot.de/2007/03/lg-electronics-and-google-team-up-to_28.html. [April 17, 2016].

Gupta, N 2015, *Alphabet Inc (NASDAQ:GOOG), American Heart Association enter $50 million joint research venture*. Invest Correctly. Available from: http://investcorrectly.com/20151110/alphabet-inc-nasdaqgoog-american-heart-association-enter-50-million-joint-research-venture/. [April 18, 2016].

Investopedia 2016, *Who are Google's (GOOG) main competitors?* Available from: www.investopedia.com/ask/answers/120314/who-are-googles-goog-main-competitors.asp. [April 18, 2016].

LG 2014, *Google and LG enter into global patent license agreement*. Available from: www.lg.com/au/press-release/google-and-lg-enter-into-global-patent-license-agreement. [April 24, 2016].

Luxottica 2014, *Google and Luxottica announce strategic partnership for Glass to develop innovative iconic wearable devices*. Available from: www.luxottica.com/en/google-and-luxottica-announce-strategic-partnership-glass-develop-innovative-iconic-wearable-devices. [April 18, 2016].

Morschett, D, Schramm-Klein, H & Zentes, J 2010, *Strategic international management*. Gabler, Wiesbaden.

NASA 2005, *NASA takes Google on journey into space*. Available from: www.nasa.gov/centers/ames/news/releases/2005/05_50AR.html. [April 18, 2016].

Patel, N 2015, *Everything you need to know about the Google-Twitter partnership*. Available from: http://searchengineland.com/everything-need-know-google-twitter-partnership-216892. [April 18, 2016].

Peterson, T 2015, *Microsoft, AOL sign 10-year search, display deal to rival Google's ad dominance*. Available from: http://adage.com/article/digital/microsoft-aol-sign-10-year-deal-rival-google-s-ad-dominance/299276/. [April 18, 2016].

Protalinski, A 2014, *Google partners with Facebook to help its clients buy retargeted ads via the social network's FBX platform*. Available from: http://thenextweb.com/google/2013/10/18/google-partners-facebook-help-clients-sell-ads-via-social-networks-fbx-platform/#gref.

PwC 2014, *PwC and Google announce joint business relationship*. Available from: http://press.pwc.com/News-releases/pwc-and-google-announce-joint-business-relationship/s/091c203d-1de7-466c-8574-f0ac96593edc. [April 18, 2016].

Reuters 2008, *NBC Universal in pact for Google to sell its TV ads*. Available from: www.reuters.com/article/us-google-nbc-idUSWEN786020080908. [April 18, 2016].

Salesforce.com 2007, *Salesforce.com and Google form strategic global alliance*. Available from: www.salesforce.com/company/news-press/press-releases/2007/06/070605.jsp. [April 18, 2016].

Samsung Newsroom 2014, *Samsung and Google sign global patent license agreement*. Available from: http://news.samsung.com/global/samsung-and-google-sign-global-patent-license-agreement. [April 18, 2016].

Sony 2010, *Sony and Google establish strategic alliance to deliver compelling new Cloud-based products and services with the Android platform*. Available from: www.sony.net/SonyInfo/News/Press/201005/10-0521E/. [April 18, 2016].

Statista 2016, Greece: national debt from 2010 to 2015 (in billion U.S. dollars). www.statista.com/statistics/270409/national-debt-of-greece/. [August 31, 2016].

Stone, B 2013, *Inside Google's secret lab*. Bloomberg. Available at: http://www.bloomberg.com/news/articles/2013-05-22/inside-googles-secret-lab. [April 18, 2016].

Vasanth, R 2014, *Google Inc. (GOOG) purchased Android for US$50 million in 2005, now generates revenue in billions: the nature of technology acquisitions [Infographic]*. Available from: http://dazeinfo.com/2014/05/08/google-purchased-android-us50-million-technology-acquisitions-infographic/. [April 18, 2016].

Zhao, F 2005, *Maximize business profits through e-partnerships*. Available from: https://books.google.de/books?id=NgMHzxDZF4oC. [April 18, 2016].

4.6 Case study: Philips

Diversification strategy in practice

Mario Glowik

Case review questions

1 How would you describe the diversification strategy of Philips in the recent two decades? Where do you see Philips's core competence for the future?
2 Reviewing the case study of Philips, how would you discuss the advantages and disadvantages when gaining knowledge through external paths, such as acquisitions and joint ventures, compared to the firm's internal knowledge development?
3 Taking the management perspective, how would you develop a SWOT analysis related to Philips's business activities in the healthcare industry?

About the company

Koninklijke Philips N.V., headquartered in Amsterdam, is the parent company of Philips Group and was founded in 1891 by Frederik Philips and his son Gerard Philips, who established an electric incandescent light bulbs factory named Philips & Co. in Eindhoven, The Netherlands. In 1895, Anton Philips, Gerhard's brother, joined the company and together they managed to turn Philips into one of the leading companies of light bulbs (Philips, 2016a). In 1918, Philips introduced a medical X-ray tube and gained international recognition by founding sale organizations abroad in countries such as Brazil, Australia, and China. An important step was marked in 1927, when Philips started producing radios and became, within a few years, the largest manufacturer of radios worldwide. Following the success of the radio, Philips displayed its first television and electric shaver.

During the 1980s, Philips launched its compact disc, which has been developed together with Sony. Since that time, Philips became mainly known as a leading consumer electronics company offering a wide range of products including television sets, audio and video devices, mobile phones, and others (Philips, 2016b). However, during the second half of the 1990s, Philips increasingly faced emerging competition from emerging countries in Asia, such as South Korea (e.g. Samsung and LG Electronics), China and Taiwan (e.g. Lenovo, TCL, and Foxconn). As a result, Philips incrementally reduced its stake in the consumer electronics industry. Today, we can still buy consumer electronics products, such as television sets with a Philips brand on it. However, the television set itself is manufactured, for example, by Funai (Japan) based on a licensing agreement with Philips. Philips receives 2.2 percent license fee based on the sales price for each television sold by Funai (Reuters, 2014). Instead of consumer electronics, Philips has intensified its diversification strategy towards lightning and healthcare businesses in the recent decade.

As a result, in 2011, Philips was engaged in three main sectors: lighting, consumer lifestyle, and healthcare. Philips gained recognition in the lighting industry through its business segments named, for example, Consumer Luminaires and Professional Lighting Solutions (Philips, 2016b). In 2015, the lighting business employed approximately 34,000 people worldwide (Philips, 2015: 56; Philips, 2016c).

Similarly, the healthcare business gained firm internal importance, which has been structured by the Philips management in major business divisions named Imaging Systems, Patient Care and Monitoring Solutions, Customer Services and Health Informatics, Solutions and Services. As of 2015, the healthcare division of Philips employed approximately 40,000 people worldwide (Philips, 2015: 48). Finally, the third sector of Philips is named 'consumer lifestyle,' which provides 'relaxing solutions' to customers, and therefore is indirectly linked to the conventional healthcare business of Philips. The consumer lifestyle business division of Philips is segmented in Personal Care, Domestic Appliances and Health and Wellness. It offers products such as shavers, electric toothbrushes, dental devices also in addition to coffee machines and audio and display devices (e.g. Philips' Ambilight). Philips Consumer Lifestyle employs approximately 16,000 people worldwide (Philips, 2016d; Philips, 2015: 52).

New organization

Since 2015, Philips's activities are segmented in divisional business divisions (Figure 4.6.1). The main divisions are Healthcare, Consumer Lifestyle, Lighting and Innovation, Group and Services (Philips, 2015: 46). According to Philips's annual report (2015), the Dutch company operated 95 production sites in 25 countries, in addition to sales and services outlets in approximately 100 countries. Philips contracted a total of 112,959 employees worldwide in 2015.

In 2015, the total revenues of Philips amounted to Euro 24.2 billion, whereas the net income was Euro 0.6 billion (Figure 4.6.2) (Philips, 2015).

The financial data of Philips indicate that the firm performs rather marginally (e.g. profit ratio 0.2 percent in 2015). As shown in Figure 4.6.3, Philips's net sales in the healthcare division amounted to Euro 10.9 billion in 2015 and reached nearly half (45 percent) of the firm's total turnover (Philips Group net sales Euro 24.2 billion in 2015). The United States is considered to be the most important healthcare business market and represents 43 percent of the global sales in 2015 (Philips, 2015: 48). In the same year, the sales of the lighting division amounted to Euro 7.4 billion (Philips, 2015: 56). The Consumer Lifestyle business generated sales of Euro 5.3 billion in 2015 (Philips, 2015: 52).

To achieve its organizational goals, Philips launched 'Accelerate Transformation' program to deliver innovation to customers by expanding its global positions, initiating new growth, and addressing underperformance problems to be solved (Philips, 2015: 14).

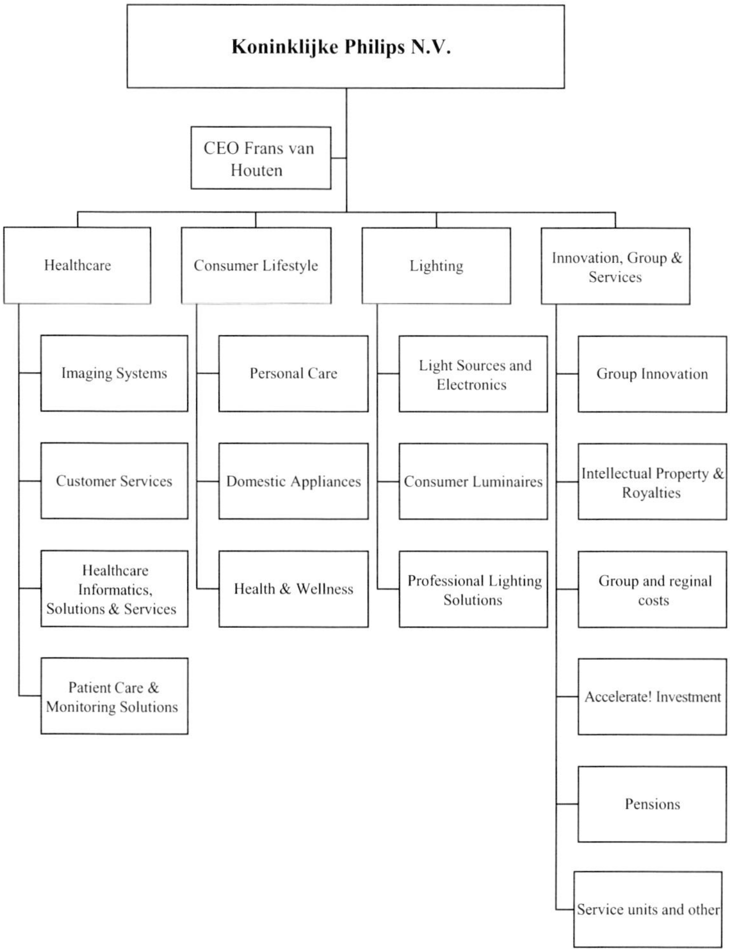

Figure 4.6.1 Organization of Koninklijke Philips N.V. (Philips, 2015).

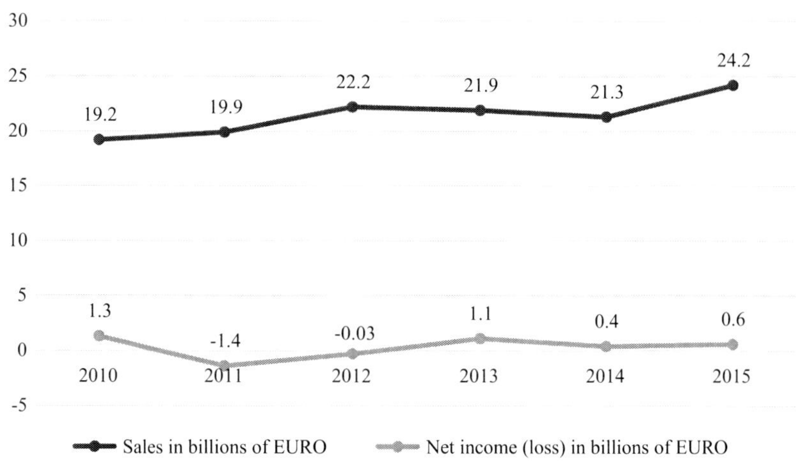

Figure 4.6.2 Net sales versus net income (in billions of Euro) of Philips Group for the period 2010–2015.

Source: Author based on annual reports of Philips (2014a, 2015).

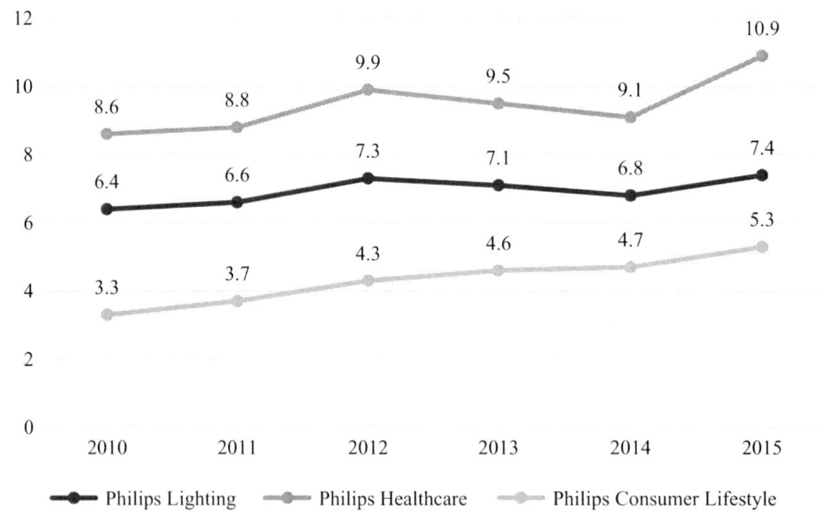

Figure 4.6.3 Sales by business for the period of 2010–2015 (in billions of Euro).
Source: Author based on annual reports of Philips (2014a, 2015).

Philips's lighting

As a result of the firm's reorganization, Philips Lighting became a stand-alone company and is listed at Euronex in Amsterdam (Philips, 2016). Philips's technological competence in lighting has been developed, in addition to its own research and development activities, mainly through acquisitions.

1 Acquisition of Color Kinetics in 2007
   - Color Kinetics is a leader in marketing innovative lighting systems based on Light Emitting Diode (LED).
   - Philips acquired the US firm for Euro 592 million.
   - This acquisition enhanced Philips position in the LED and Solid State Lighting (SSL) market (Philips, 2007a).

2 Acquisition of NCW Holdings, Ltd. in 2010
   - NCW, headquartered in Hong Kong, was considered to be the leading manufacturer and distributor of LED, which provided entertainment lighting solutions worldwide.
   - Philips managed to extend its global position by this purchase, which enabled the company to provide lighting entertainment solutions (Philips, 2010).

3 Acquisition of Teletrol Systems Inc. in 2009
   - Teletrol Systems Inc. is a leading supplier of integrated solutions for simultaneous multi-site management of lighting and energy usage.
   - This acquisition strengthened Philips's stake in lighting solutions in a wide range of areas: institutional customers, networked management of lighting and environment facilities (Philips, 2009a).

4 Acquisition of Dynalite in 2009
- Dynalite is a leading maker of lighting controls headquartered in Sydney, Australia.
- The company has become part of the Lighting Electronics within the Philips Lighting segment.
- Philips continued to expand its presence in the lighting controls business (Philips, 2009b).

5 Acquisition of Selecon in 2009
- The New Zealand-based company indicates a prominent global holder of professional theatrical and architectural lighting fixtures.
- Philips accessed new lighting sectors, such art centers, churches, and hotels.
- Selecon became part of the Entertainment Group within the Philips Professional Luminaires business (Philips, 2009c).

In 2014, Philips entered into a joint venture and invested 51 percent of General Lighting Company (GLC), a major lighting company in the Kingdom of Saudi Arabia. This cooperation strengthened Philips's footprint in the Middle East, while GLC benefited from lighting innovations and was enabled to create sustainable solutions to its customers (Philips, 2014b). In December 2015, Philips entered into lighting partnerships with Cisco, Sap, and Bosch; these three influential companies would enhance Philips's reach in different lighting areas: office buildings, city lighting, and networked homes (Sterling, 2015).

In recent years, Philips has faced increased competition within the lighting sector, such as Siemens, Samsung, General Electric, and OSRAM AG, and various newly emerging competitors from China, such as from Guangzhou (Philips, 2012a). Prices started to erode and negatively contributed to Philips's net revenue performance. In mid-2016, Philips retains 71.23 percent shares of its lighting business and has intensified searching for external investors (Philips, 2016h). After a decade of acquisitions, it has become obvious that, similar to its consumer electronics business, the Dutch firm is incrementally reducing its stake in its lightning business and concentrating mainly on healthcare and medical devices.

Philips Healthcare

Philips strengthened its role in the global healthcare industry but there are other prominent competitors in this sector, such as GE Healthcare, Siemens Healthcare, and Toshiba Medical Systems (MBDR, no date). According to Philips, the firm addresses the challenges of an increasing need for integrated healthcare systems, such as healthcare informatics, wearable patient monitoring devices, and digital pathology. HealthTech business division within Philips organization compromises the Healthcare and Consumer Lifestyle sectors (Philips 2016f, 2015: 46). In recent years, Philips has gained technological knowledge and expertise in advanced healthcare products mainly through external paths, namely, acquisitions.

1 Acquisition of Agilent Healthcare Solutions Group in 2000
- The company is a leading maker of analysis equipment with a portfolio of over 400 products and services, which include patient monitoring, ultrasound imaging, and resuscitation.
- The acquisition made Philips one of the most important suppliers of medical equipment (Philips, 2000; Dorsey, 2000).

2 Acquisition of Respironics in 2007
   - The company based in the USA is a leading provider of innovative solutions for the global sleep therapy and respiratory market.
   - Philips enhanced its position in the sector of home healthcare (Philips, 2007b).
   - Respironics is the most expensive acquisition of Philips Healthcare with a total purchase price of USD 5.1 billion.

3 Acquisition of Unisensor in 2014
   - Unisensor is a Danish healthcare company, which is considered to be an innovator in the field of optical analysis of fluids for diagnostic applications in healthcare.
   - Philips strengthened its capabilities in the field of patient sample analysis (Philips, 2014c).

4 Acquisition of Volcano in 2015
   - The US-American corporation is a technological leader in catheter-based imaging solutions for cardiovascular applications.
   - This acquisition enabled Philips to strengthen its position in the growing image-guided therapy market (Philips, 2015: 49).
   - Volcano is the largest acquisition since 2007, with a total equity purchase price of USD 1.2 billion (Escritt, 2004).

5 Acquisition of Blue Jay Consulting in 2015
   - Blue Jay Consulting is a leading provider of hospital emergency room consulting services in the USA.
   - This purchase helped Philips to improve clinical care and operational effectiveness across the healthcare continuum (Philips, 2015: 49).

Philips strengthened its competitive position by establishing strategic alliances and joint ventures in the healthcare business. Philips and Salesforce.com signed a strategic alliance in 2014, which enabled Philips to build a cloud-based platform for medical equipment. This collaboration resulted in new digital health platforms named Philips eCareCompanion, which is used as a service portal to patients at home. The second platform called eCareCoordinator is used by medicine doctors and nurses to prioritize patient needs and adjust them to suitable care plans (Salesforce.com, no date; Philips, 2014d).

Philips and IBA signed a strategic alliance in 2014. IBA is a leading supplier of proton therapy solutions for the treatment of cancer. This collaboration aimed to provide advanced diagnostic and therapeutic solutions for the treatment of cancer. The alliance compromised cooperation in sales, marketing, R&D of imaging and therapeutic solutions in oncology. In 2015, Philips India and IBA signed an agreement to enhance the access to proton therapy in India (Philips, 2014e; Consilium, 2015).

Moreover, Philips formed various partnerships with universities and hospitals to gain access to research data helping to develop new medical systems. Philips established partnerships with Westchester Medical Center Health Network in New York, Karolinska University Hospital in Sweden, Augusta University Health System in Georgia, Banner Health in the US, and others (Philips, 2016g).

Philips entered into a joint venture in 2012 with Al Faisaliah Medical System (FMS). The purpose of this partnership was to combine Philips's clinical expertise with FMS knowledge concerning local customer needs that aimed to contribute to the healthcare services in the region (Philips, 2012b). In addition, Philips and Teva Pharmaceutical

Industries established a joint venture called Sanara Ventures in 2015. The collaboration included investment by both parties up to NIS 100 million (approximately USD 26.5 million) over eight years in medical device and health technology start-ups in Israel (Reuters, 2015).

The global medical electronics market is expected to reach USD 4.41 billion by 2022, growing at a compound annual growth rate (CAGR) of 5.4 per cent between 2016 and 2022 with North America holding the largest market shares while monitoring application is expected to grow at the highest rate during the forecast period. The key players in the medical electronics market are Philips Healthcare (The Netherlands), Siemens Healthcare (Germany), Medtronic Plc. (Ireland), Analog Devices, Inc. (US), NXP Semiconductors N.V. (The Netherlands), STMicroelectronics N.V. (Switzerland), GE Healthcare, Inc. (US), and Texas Instruments (US) (Tiwari, 2016).

The medical electronics market is expected to grow rapidly owing to factors such as rising ageing population and growing lifestyle diseases; increasing demand for personalized, easy-to-use, and advanced healthcare devices, and increasing adoption of wearable electronics. The major restraint that acts as a barrier for the growth of medical electronics market includes stringent regulatory process for product approval and high maintenance and refurbishment costs. The medical electronics market is highly affected by the legislation and initiatives, such as increasing clinical trial requirements for new products from the governments and regulatory authorities. Over the years, the medical device approval guidelines and regulations across the world have become more stringent to minimize errors associated with medical devices. The medical electronics market has been segmented on the basis of application into diagnostics and monitoring. The monitoring devices market is expected to grow at the highest rate because of the increasing use of patient monitoring devices in outpatient care departments, ambulatory care centers, and home care settings. Factors such as increasing market penetration rates of the portable medical devices, which are used in home healthcare establishments, and an increasing trend towards remote patient monitoring are also expected to contribute to the growth of the medical electronics market for patient monitoring applications in the future. Among all of the geographic regions, North America is considered to be the largest market for medical electronics (Tiwari, 2016).

In the US, Philips Healthcare is the second leading firm in terms of patient monitoring market shares. The company is the leader in the multi-parameter vital sign monitoring market, wireless telemetry and fetal/neonatal monitoring markets. Philips has one of the most extensive product lines of any company in the patient monitoring market. Their IntelliVue™ and SureSigns™ product lines range from low- to high-acuity and have flexible product designs ranging from extremely compact to portable bedside units. Additional competitors in the US patient monitoring device market include Masimo, GE Healthcare, Edwards Lifesciences, Mindray Medical, Natus Medical, Welch Allyn, Omron Healthcare, Honeywell Life Sciences, Nihon Kohden, Spacelabs Healthcare, St. Jude Medical, Nonin Medical, and Boston Scientific, among others (Cidamon, 2016).

Bibliography

Cidamon, M 2016, Medtronic, Phillips Healthcare lead high demand billion dollar U.S. patient monitoring market. The U.S. patient monitoring market is expected to grow over the next several years to reach over USD 6 billion by 2023. Available from: www.marketwired.com/press-release/medtronic-phillips-healthcare-lead-high-demand-billion-dollar-us-patient-monitoring-2162315.htm. [October 12, 2016].

Consilium 2015, *IBA and Philips India to introduce proton therapy cancer.* Available from: www.consilium-comms.com/news-detail.aspx?news=34. [May 1, 2016].

Dorsey, JM 2000, Philips Electronics to purchase medical-products unit of Agilent. *The Wall Street Journal.* Available from: www.wsj.com/articles/SB974469397436822066. [May 1, 2016].

Ericsson 2014, *Ericsson and Philips unite to brighten cities and provide mobile broadband connectivity through smart street lighting.* Available from: www.ericsson.com/news/1763971. [April 30, 2016].

Escritt, T 2014, *Philips expands in medical devices with $1.2 billion Volcano deal.* Available from: www.reuters.com/article/us-volcano-m-a-philips-idUSKBN0JV0G120141217. [May 1, 2016].

MBDR no date, *Philips Healthcare.* Available from: www.medicaldevices-business-review.com/companies/philips_healthcare. [May 1, 2016].

Philips 2000, *Philips to acquire Agilent Technologies' Healthcare Solutions Group for US$ 1.7 billion.* Available from: www.newscenter.philips.com/main/standard/about/news/press/archive/2000/article-2276.wpd. [May 1, 2016].

Philips 2007a, *Philips to acquire Color Kinetics to strengthen leading position in Led lighting systems, components and technologies.* Available from: www.newscenter.philips.com/main/standard/about/news/press/article-15801.wpd. [April 30, 2016].

Philips 2007b, *Philips to make public offer for all shares of US-based Respironics; a major step forward for Philips Healthcare.* Available from: www.newscenter.philips.com/main/standard/about/news/press/20071221_pressrelease_respironics.wpd. [May 1, 2016].

Philips 2009a, *Philips strengthens position in lighting controls with acquisition of US-based Teletrol Systems.* Available from: www.newscenter.philips.com/main/standard/about/news/press/20090716_lighting_controls.wpd. [April 30, 2016].

Philips 2009b, *Philips acquires lighting controls company Dynalite in Australia.* Available from: www.newscenter.philips.com/main/standard/about/news/press/20090325_dynalite.wpd. [April 30, 2016].

Philips 2009c, *Philips acquires Selecon; a key provider of professional theatrical and architectural lighting solutions.* Available from: www.newscenter.philips.com/main/standard/about/news/press/20090401_selecon.wpd. [April 30, 2016].

Philips 2010, *Philips acquires NCW Holdings LTD in China to expand global leadership position of professional lighting entertainment solutions.* Available from: http://www.philips.com/a-w/about/news/archive/standard/news/press/2010/20101206_ncw.html#.U6JhhJSSyTv. [April 30, 2016].

Philips 2012a, *Annual report 2012.* Available from: www.annualreport2012.philips.com/annual_report_2012/en/sector_performance/lighting/about_philips_lighting.aspxwww.annualreport2012.philips.com/annual_report_2012/en/sector_performance/lighting/about_philips_lighting.aspx. [April 30, 2016].

Philips, 2012b, *Philips and Al Faisaliah Medical Systems enter Healthcare joint venture in the Kingdom of Saudi Arabia.* Available from: www.philips.com/a-w/about/news/archive/standard/news/press/2012/20120929-philips-and-al-faisaliah-medical-systems-enter-healthcare-joint-venture.html. [May 1, 2016].

Philips 2013, *New partnership between Philips and US Conference of Mayors.* Available from: http://applications.nam.lighting.philips.com/blog/index.php/2013/01/22/new-partnership-between-philips-and-us-conference-of-mayors/. [April 30, 2016].

Philips 2014a, *Annual report 2014.* Available from: www.2014.annualreport.philips.com/#!/interactive-charts/iac=graphid:chartstatementsofincome3/. [April 30, 2016].

Philips 2014b, *Philips enters into joint venture to create leading lighting player in the Kingdom of Saudi Arabia.* Available from: www.philips.com/a-w/about/news/archive/standard/news/press/2014/20140317-Philips-enters-into-joint-venture-to-create-leading-lighting-player-in-the-Kingdom-of-Saudi-Arabia.html. [April 30, 2016].

Philips 2014c, *Philips to expand technology platforms for near patient diagnostic testing with acquisition of Unisensor.* Available from: www.philips.com/a-w/about/news/archive/standard/news/press/2014/20140724-Philips-to-expand-technology-platforms-for-near-patient-diagnostic-testing-with-acquisition-of-Unisensor.html. [April 30, 2016].

Philips 2014d, *Philips secures 510(k) clearance to market the first clinical applications for its new digital health platform*. Available from: www.philips.com/a-w/about/news/archive/standard/news/press/2014/20141001-Philips-secures-510k-clearance-to-market-the-first-clinical-applications-for-its-new-digital-health-platform.html. [May 1, 2016].

Philips 2014e, *IBA and Philips join forces to advance diagnosis and treatment of cancer*. Available from: www.philips.com/a-w/about/news/archive/standard/news/press/2014/20140911-IBA-and-Philips-join-forces-to-advance-diagnosis-and-treatment-of-cancer.html. [May 1, 2016].

Philips 2015, *Annual report 2015*. Available from: www.philips.com/corporate/resources/annualresults/2015/PhilipsFullAnnualReport2015_English.pdf. [April 30, 2016].

Philips 2016a, *Philips Company: introduction*. Available from: www.philips.com/a-w/about/company/introduction.html. [April 26, 2016].

Philips 2016b, *More than a century of innovation and entrepreneurship*. Available from: www.philips.com/a-w/about/company/our-heritage.html. [April 29, 2016].

Philips 2016c, *Management*. Available from: www.philips.com/a-w/about/company/our-management/executive-committee.html. [April 29, 2016].

Philips 2016d, *About Philips*. Available from: www.buy.philips.co.in/AboutUs. [April 29, 2016].

Philips 2016e, *Annual report* 2014. Available from: www.2014.annualreport.philips.com/#!/performance-highlights/http://www.2014.annualreport.philips.com/#!/performance-highlights/. [April 29, 2016].

Philips 2016f, *Addressing global challenges*. Available from: www.philips.com/a-w/about/company/our-strategy/addressing-global-challenges.html. [April 30, 2016].

Philips 2016g, *Partnerships*. Available from: www.usa.philips.com/healthcare/about/partnerships. [May 1, 2016].

Philips, 2016h, *Philips 2016 Q2 quarterly report*. Available from: www.philips.com/corporate/resources/quarterlyresults/2016/Q2_2016/philips-second-quarter-results-2016-report.pdf. [September 4, 2016].

Reuters, 2014, Konkurrenz aus Asien: Philips steigt komplett aus dem TV-Geschäft aus. Available from: www.spiegel.de/wirtschaft/unternehmen/philips-steigt-komplett-aus-dem-tv-geschaeft-aus-a-944556.html. [September 4, 2016].

Reuters 2015, *Teva and Philips to jointly to invest in Israeli medical device firms*. Available from: www.reuters.com/article/philips-teva-pharm-ind-jointventure-idUSL8N0ZH2DZ20150701. [May 1, 2016].

Saleforces.com no date, *Philips and Salesforce.com announce a strategic alliance to deliver cloud-based healthcare information technology*. Available from: www.salesforce.com/company/news-press/press-releases/2014/06/140626.jsp. [May 1, 2016].

Sterling, T 2015, Philips in lighting partnerships with Cisco, Sap and Bosch. *Reuters*. Available from: www.reuters.com/article/us-philips-lighting-partnerships-idUSKBN0TS14420151209. [May 2, 2016].

Tiwari, R 2016, Global medical electronics market. 5.4 per cent CAGR for 2016–2022. Available from: www.pharmiweb.com/pressreleases/pressrel.asp?ROW_ID=184370. [October 12, 2016].

4.7 Case study: Starbucks

You may think it is franchising only but it is not

Mario Glowik

Case review questions

1. How would you review the business concept and corresponding chances and risks of franchising? How would you explain the reasons regarding why Starbucks obviously prefers market entry modes other than franchising?
2. Do you suppose Starbucks may change their entire business concept towards franchising? What are the potential opportunities and risks when doing so?
3. How would you develop a SWOT analysis for Starbucks? What would you recommend to the management concerning Starbucks's strategical positioning for the future?

Company profile

Starbucks, a global coffee roaster and retailer, was founded in 1971, when the first store was opened in Seattle's 'Pike Place Market.' Howard Schultz joined the company in 1982 as director of retail operations and marketing. During this time, Starbucks began to deliver coffee to restaurants and expresso bars. In 1985, Schultz opened a coffee bar of his own named Il Giornale. Two years later, he purchased Starbucks and changed its name to Starbucks Corporation. Moreover, he launched a growth strategy for Starbucks and opened stores in Chicago and Vancouver, Canada (Starbucks, 2016a).

In 1992, Starbucks has gained popularity with 165 stores worldwide and became a public company, when it launched its initial public offering (IPO). An important milestone occurred in 1996, when Starbucks opened its first store in Japan, the first store outside North America. The company continued expanding globally and opened another store in Asia, namely, in Singapore. In 1998, Starbucks established a joint venture with 'Magic Johnson.' One year later, the company acquired Hear Music, a San Francisco-based music company. The company continued to execute its global growth strategy and purchased Ethos Water in 2005. In 2016, the coffee company had more than 10,000 stores worldwide (Starbucks, 2016a).

In 2008, Starbucks launched My First Starbucks Idea, its first online community, and opened its business page on Facebook and Twitter (Starbucks, 2016a). Chairman since 2000, Howard Schultz resumed the position of president and chief executive officer of

Starbucks in 2008, which he still holds today (Starbucks, 2016d). In 2014, the company managed to strengthen its digital positioning in the markets and launched Starbucks Mobile Order & Pay (Starbucks, 2016a).

Presently, Starbucks is international coffeehouse chain, which offers a wide range of products including coffee, tea, and other beverages and also food. The company mission of Starbucks is 'to inspire and nurture the human spirit—one person, one cup, and one neighborhood at a time.' The company is one of the leading coffee businesses in the world and has more than 24,000 stores around the world (Starbucks, 2016c). Starbucks has gained a leading position in the coffee serving industry. However, it has various competitors like small regional coffee house providers, which are common in Brazil, Italy, and Austria, or larger ones like Tim Hortons from Canada (Woolf, 2014).

Business segments

As shown in Figure 4.7.1, Starbucks has launched a matrix organizational structure, which is a hybrid structure that includes elements from the basic types of organizational structure, such as functional and regional-divisional structures (Meyer, 2015). Starbucks's organizational structure includes geographic division by regions, which is considered to be the operating segments: The first segment belongs to 'Americas,' which consists of the US, Canada, and Latin America. The second segment includes China and Asia Pacific (CAP), and the third segment covers Europe, Middle East, and Africa (EMEA). The last segment is named Channel Development, which compromises roasted whole bean and ground coffees, a variety of ready-to-drink beverages, and other branded products. Moreover, other segments include Teavana, Seattle's Best Coffee, Evolution Fresh, and Digital Ventures business, as well as other developing businesses, such as tea, which is common in China and India (Starbucks, 2015a).

In 2015, the total net revenues of Starbucks amounted to USD 19.2 billion, whereas the net income was USD 2.7 billion, which indicates a margin of approximately 14 percent (Figure 4.7.2).

The revenues of Starbucks originated from the following business segments: company-operated stores, consumer packaged goods (CPG), foodservice operations, and licensed stores. 'Licensed stores' as categorized by Starbucks equals the business concept of franchising. The revenues from the company-operated stores in 2015 generated the largest amount with 79 percent of the total net revenues (Starbucks, 2015) (Figure 4.7.4).

According to Starbucks's annual report (2015a), the America's market represents the largest market and 69 percent from the total net revenues. The other revenues were as follows: China/Asia Pacific (13 percent); Channel Development (9 percent); Europe, Middle East, and Africa (EMEA) (6 percent); and all other segments (3 percent) (Figure 4.7.3).

Furthermore, Starbucks's revenues can be differentiated by product type, which consists of beverages, food, packaged and single-serve coffees and teas, and others (Starbucks, 2015a). The products include coffee products with more than 30 blends, handcrafted beverages such as smoothies and teas, hot and iced espresso beverages, 'Frappuccino' drinks, and others. Starbucks offers not only beverages but also fresh food, such as baked pastries, sandwiches, salads, and yogurt. The successful brand offers merchandise such as coffee and tea brewing equipment, mugs and accessories, packaged goods, books, and gifts (Starbucks, 2016b) (Figure 4.7.5).

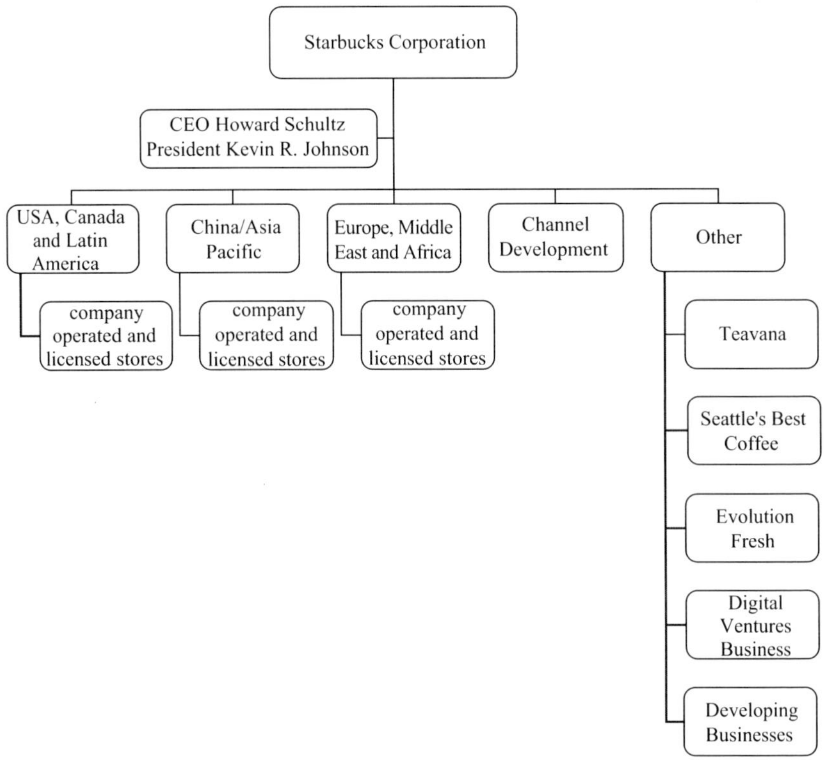

Figure 4.7.1 Organization of Starbucks (2015a).

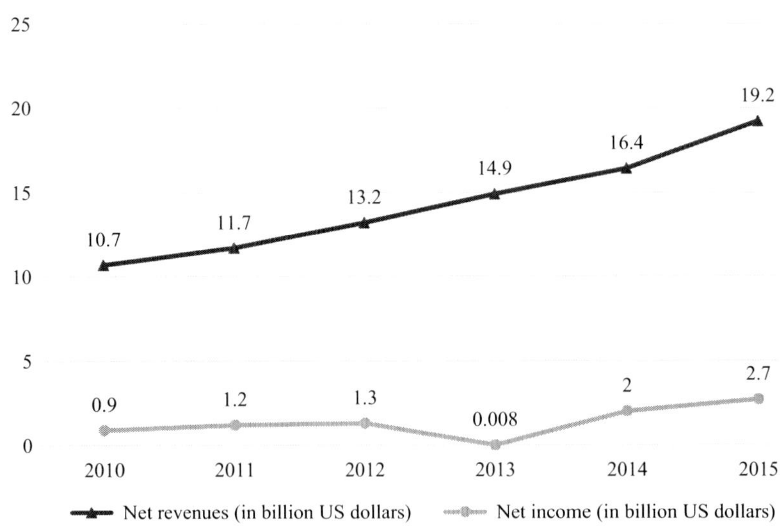

Figure 4.7.2 Starbucks: net revenues versus net income in the period 2010–2015 in billion US dollars.

Source: Author based on annual reports of Starbucks (2014a, 2015a).

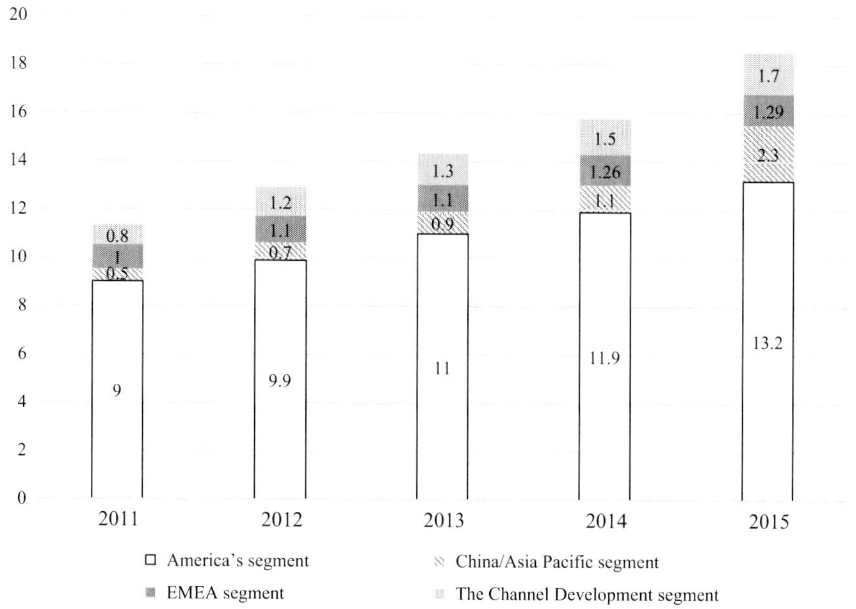

Figure 4.7.3 Starbucks: revenues by business segment for the period 2011–2015 in billion US dollars.

Source: Author based on annual reports of Starbucks (2012a, 2014a, 2015a).

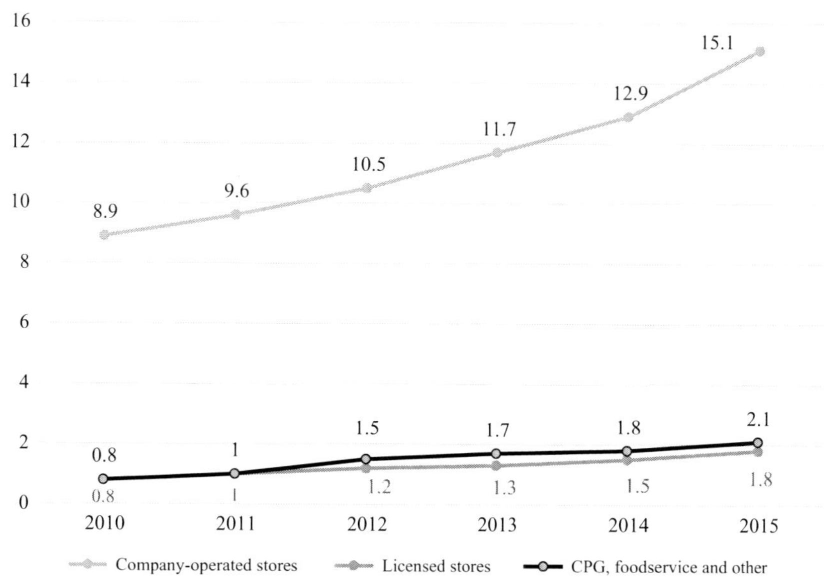

Figure 4.7.4 Starbucks: revenues by business division for the period 2010–2015 in billion US dollars.

Source: Author based on annual reports of Starbucks (2014a, 2015a).

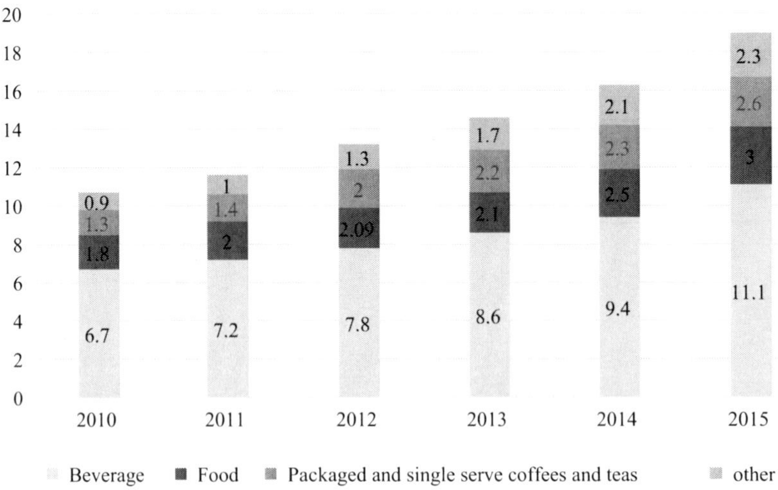

Figure 4.7.5 Revenues by product type for the period 2010–2015 in billion US dollars.
Source: Author based on annual reports of Starbucks (2012a: 87, 2015a: 85).

Mission and strategy

In 2014, Starbucks presented its '5-year growth strategy,' which includes the following 7 steps:

1 Be the employer of choice—invest in partners who would be able to provide superior customer experience;
2 Lead in coffee—strengthen the leadership position in the coffee industry;
3 Grow the store portfolio—increase the scale of Starbucks's stores;
4 Create new occasions—provide new product offers;
5 Extend consumer-packaged goods (CPG) to brand growth globally;
6 Build 'Teavana'—advance its position as a second major business in tea; and
7 Extend digital engagement—build brand awareness through mobile commerce platforms (Starbucks, 2014b).

Starbucks uses market entry and penetration strategies, which include joint ventures, strategic alliances, and acquisitions to expand its product mix and achieve sustainable advantage over its competitors (Geereddy, 2013). The most important acquisitions during the period 1999 until 2012 can be summarized as follows:

1 Acquisition of **Tazo** in 1999
   - Tazo was founded in Portland, Oregon, and produces premium packaged tea and herbal tea products.
   - Starbucks purchased Tazo for more than USD 8.1 billion.
   - Tazo pouches are sold in Starbucks stores, grocery stores, and other retailers around the world (Carpenter, 2015).

2 Acquisition of **Hear Music** in 1999
   - Starbucks expanded into the entertainment and music industry by purchasing Hear Music.

- In 2004, Starbucks formed its own record label, which aimed to develop records for sale in its coffee shops and through traditional music retailers.
- In 2015, Starbucks stopped selling CDs (Kornhaber, 2015) among other reasons, due to emerging cloud and streaming music business, which became more 'stylish and lifestyle' than buying CDs.

3 Acquisition of **Seattle's Best Coffee** in 2003
- The company was established in 1970 as a coffee roaster and retailer outside of Seattle, Washington.
- In 2015, Seattle's Best Coffee was the second-largest coffee roaster behind Starbucks.
- It has a variety of distribution points, such as Burger King, Subway restaurants, Chevron service stations, AMC movie theaters, and Safeway grocery stores.

4 Acquisitions of **Torrefazione Italia Coffee** in 2003
- Torrefazione Italia Coffee was founded as a coffee roaster and retailer in Seattle, Washington.
- Starbucks bought the company as part of the acquisition of Seattle's Best Coffee (Carpenter, 2015).

5 Acquisition of **Ethos Water** in 2005
- Ethos Water is a privately held bottled water company based in Santa Monica.
- Starbucks acquired Ethos Water as part of its sustainable practices, aimed to provide clean water for children around the world (Starbucks, 2005).
- 'Each bottle of Ethos Water sold in the US adds 5 cents to the Ethos Water Fund.' In 2014, the fund distributed more than 3.3 million US dollars in grants to six nongovernmental organizations in Nicaragua, Tanzania, Indonesia, Guatemala, and Colombia (Carpenter, 2015).

6 Acquisition of **Evolution Fresh** in 2011
- This acquisition enabled Starbucks to rapidly grow beyond the coffee bean product.
- Evolution Fresh manufactures bottled fruit juices and vegetable and fruit juice blends.
- The company operates three retail locations in Seattle and Bellevue, Washington.

7 Acquisition of **Teavana** in 2012
- Teavana is a retail chain offering more than 100 varieties of premium teas and other tea-related products.
- The acquisition supported Starbucks growth strategy and strengthened its position in the tea industry (Starbucks, 2012b).

In addition, Starbucks established two important joint ventures.

In 1994, Starbucks formed a joint venture with PepsiCo, one of the world's largest food and beverage companies (PepsiCo, 2016). The joint venture, North American Coffee Partnership (NACP), aimed to build the ready-to-drink (RTD) coffee category in the US (Starbucks, 2015b). Since then, the companies have expanded its cooperation. In 2007, Starbucks and PepsiCo extended the companies' relationship beyond North America and entered into the Chinese market (The Wall Street Journal, 2007). Moreover, in 2015, a new agreement was signed between the two companies. The purpose of this agreement was to bring Starbucks's ready-to-drink coffee beverages to the first Latin American markets in 2016 (Starbucks, 2015b).

In 2012, Starbucks established a joint venture with Tata Global Beverages Limited, the second largest branded tea company in the world, which is based in India. The 50/50 joint venture, Tata Starbucks Limited, aimed to introduce Starbucks's products to Indian consumers (Starbucks, 2012c).

Business opportunities and challenges

Undoubtedly, Starbucks can rely on a strong brand recognition and strong market position. Starbucks has a significant global presence, with more than 24,000 stores in 70 countries (Starbucks, 2016c). However, the firm is very dependent on the United States, with a clear focus on Western markets. Customers are emerging in countries like China, Vietnam, or India where tea is preferred rather than coffee. Thus, it remains questionable whether Starbucks is able to transfer its valuable coffee brand reputation from its Western hemisphere towards the East. The coffee provider pays enormous attention to quality and a comfortable and charming atmosphere at the shop where the coffee is sold. Starbucks shops are usually located at highly frequented and optimally visible locations in expensive town areas. Aesthetics and a wide product range of its shops are defined as Starbucks's strengths (Geereddy, 2013). However, all of these Starbucks shop features are not costless and its products are already perceived to be relatively expensive. Thus, it remains questionable how Starbucks can further develop in emerging markets with comparatively lower purchasing power than in the US, increasing local competition and how the firm will maneuver in times of economic downturns as experienced during the last subprime crisis (Geereddy, 2013).

Although Starbucks has managed very well its global growth strategy, it has not managed to successfully enter all of their target markets. Starbucks failed to penetrate the Israeli market, and although there was a remarkable launch at the beginning, Starbucks was forced to close its operations in Israel only after two years. The explanation for this unsuccessful experience is a lack of peripheral vision (Barnea, 2011). Peripheral vision refers to the ability to 'detect and act on signals from the periphery before others' (Day and Shoemaker, 2005: 3). In this respect, Starbucks failed to scan the Israeli market signals appropriately, particularly in terms of local customer characteristics (Barnea, 2011: 87).

Starbucks failed to recognize the consumption behavior of the Israeli customers. Furthermore, the senior management lacked experience running a coffee shop chain. In fact, many customers did not like the taste of Starbucks's products and perceived it as lower quality compared to local Israeli brands. Another important factor, which influenced Starbucks's poor performing business, was that the local competitors were prepared when Starbucks was supposed to enter the market and they managed to improve their businesses' presence by offering new products and opening new locations (Barnea, 2011). This combined local customer reaction can be interpreted as a (non-tariff) market entry barrier for Starbucks in Israel.

Germany serves as another example of less successful developing markets for Starbucks. Starbucks entered the German market in 2002 and operated 158 stores across the country. However, in April 2016, Starbucks announced the sellout of Starbucks business in Germany to AmRest, a Polish restaurant operator. AmRest received the license approval to operate and develop Starbucks brand in Germany. This licensing agreement aimed to improve the foothold of Starbucks within the German market (Starbucks, 2016e), which has performed far below expectations. 'Drinking coffee' is rather understood as a pragmatic activity (e.g. enjoy the taste, 'become awake') and is not perceived as a prestigious lifestyle activity by many local German consumers. Consequently, the majority of German customers are not willing to pay higher prices for Starbucks coffee than market average—as long as the quality is equal. Additionally, the competition in the German market is intense. Various local coffee shops exist, and some small bakeries offer tasty coffee in a more personalized and familiar atmosphere compared to what is offered at Starbucks's metropolitan shops. Nevertheless, the Starbucks's coffee shop located at the Brandenburg Gate in Berlin is always crowded ... mainly by tourists.

Bibliography

Barnea, A 2011, Lack of peripheral vision—how Starbucks failed in Israel, *African Journal of Marketing Management*, vol. 3, no. 4, pp. 78–88.

Carpenter, JW 2015, *Top 6 companies owned by Starbucks* (SBUX, Investopedia. Available from: /www.investopedia.com/articles/markets/101415/top-6-companies-owned-starbucks.asp. [July 18, 2016].

Day G & Schoemaker P 2005, *Scanning the periphery, Harvard Business Review*. Available from: www.researchgate.net/profile/Paul_Schoemaker/publication/7468632_Scanning_the_periphery/links/0c9605325c14116199000000.pdf. [July 20, 2016].

Geereddy, N 2013, *Strategic analysis of Starbucks corporation. Harvard University*. Available from: http://scholar.harvard.edu/files/nithingeereddy/files/starbucks_case_analysis.pdf. [July 18, 2016].

Kornhaber, S 2015, *Starbucks's failed music revolution*. Available from: www.theatlantic.com/entertainment/archive/2015/02/starbuckss-failed-music-revolution/385937/. [July 18, 2016].

Meyer, P 2015, *Starbucks coffee company's organizational structure*, Panmore Institute. Available from: http://panmore.com/starbucks-coffee-company-organizational-structure. [July 16, 2016].

PepsiCo 2016, *Timeline*. Available from: www.pepsicobeveragefacts.com/home/timeline. [July 18, 2016].

Starbucks 2005, *Financial Release*. Available from: http://investor.starbucks.com/phoenix.zhtml?c=99518&p=irol-newsArticle&ID=694216. [July 18, 2016].

Starbucks 2012a, *Fiscal 2012 annual report*. Available from: http://investor.starbucks.com/phoenix.zhtml?c=99518&p=irol-reportsAnnual. [July 16, 2016].

Starbucks 2012b, *Starbucks announces agreement to acquire Teavana to globally transform tea industry*. Available from: https://news.starbucks.com/news/starbucks-announces-agreement-to-acquire-teavana-to-globally-transform-tea-. [July 18, 2016].

Starbucks 2012c, Tata Global Beverages and Starbucks form joint venture to open Starbucks cafes across India. Available from: https://news.starbucks.com/news/tata-global-beverages-and-starbucks-form-joint-venture-to-open-starbucks-ca. [July 18, 2016].

Starbucks 2014a, *Fiscal 2014 annual report*. Available from: http://investor.starbucks.com/phoenix.zhtml?c=99518&p=irol-reportsAnnual. [July 16, 2016].

Starbucks 2014b, *Starbucks details five-year plan to accelerate profitable growth at investor conference*. Available from: https://news.starbucks.com/news/live-blog-starbucks-path-for-growth-outlined-at-2014-biennial-investor-day. [July 16, 2016].

Starbucks 2015a, *Fiscal 2015 annual report*. Available from: http://investor.starbucks.com/phoenix.zhtml?c=99518&p=irol-reportsAnnual. [July 16, 2016].

Starbucks 2015b, *Starbucks and PepsiCo to bring Starbucks RTD beverages to Latin America*. Available from: https://news.starbucks.com/news/starbucks-and-pepsico-agreement-for-rtd-beverages-in-latin-america. [July 18, 2016].

Starbucks 2016a, *Starbucks Company timeline*. Available from: www.starbucks.com/about-us/company-information/starbucks-company-timeline. [July 15, 2016].

Starbucks 2016b, *Starbucks Company profile.* Available from: www.starbucks.com/about-us/company-information/starbucks-company-profile. [July 15, 2016].

Starbucks 2016c, *Starbucks Coffee International.* Available from: www.starbucks.com/business/international-stores. [July 18, 2016].

Starbucks 2016d, *Executive team.* Available from: https://news.starbucks.com/leadership/howard-schultz. [July 19, 2016].

Starbucks 2016e, *Starbucks extends licensing agreement with AmRest to grow stores in Germany.* Available from: https://news.starbucks.com/news/starbucks-extends-licensing-agreement-with-amrest. [July 19, 2016].

The Wall Street Journal 2007, *Starbucks, PepsiCo expand venture to China.* Available from: www.wsj.com/articles/SB119094839219742364. [July 18, 2016].

Woolf, Nicky 2014, *Starbucks faces growing rivals as coffee wars reach boiling point.* Available from: www.theguardian.com/lifeandstyle/2014/dec/12/starbucks-faces-growing-rivals-as-coffee-wars-reach-boiling-point. [July 15, 2016].

4.8 Case study: Fresenius

Concentration strategies in healthcare business

Mario Glowik

Case review questions

1 How would you describe the advantages of the concentration strategy as implemented by Fresenius?
2 Are there potential risks related to the vertical integration strategy from Fresenius's point of view and from the patient's perspective?
3 Do you believe Fresenius is positioned in promising business segments or is it worthwhile to think about considering a diversification strategy? Would you also consider the current margin of Fresenius?

Company profile

Fresenius offers dialysis products and services for hospitals and local patient treatment. The company's origin goes back to Hirsch Pharmacy located in Frankfurt am Main, which was established in 1462. In 1912, Dr. Eduard Fresenius took over ownership of the business and established the pharmaceutical company named Dr. E. Fresenius. He expanded the activities into small manufacturing operations. The main products were special pharmaceutical products, such as injection solutions, serologic reagents, and Bromelain nasal ointment. In 1933, the manufacturing company separated from Hirsch Pharmacy and moved to Bad Homburg. In 1952, the foster daughter of Dr. Fresenius, Else Fernau, took charge of the company (Fresenius, 2016a).

An important milestone in 1966 occurred when Fresenius started to sell dialysis machines. As a result, the company gained substantial market shares. During the 1980s, the company was converted into a joint stock company, and the supervisory board was headed by Else Kröner. In 1996, the merger of Fresenius's dialysis business with the US dialysis provider National Medical Care led to the creation of Fresenius Medical Care, the world's leading dialysis provider. After three years, Fresenius Kabi was established, which operates in nutrition and infusion therapy with subsidiaries and distributors worldwide (Fresenius, 2016a). Throughout the 2000s, Fresenius Group gained recognition and acquired several companies. In 2012, Fresenius celebrated its 100th anniversary; the company employed 160,000 employees in 100 countries. After two years, Fresenius Helios completed the purchase of 41 hospitals and 13 outpatient facilities from Rhön-Klinikum AG (Fresenius, 2016a).

Presently, the company operates in four business segments, all of which are positioned in promising growth markets within the healthcare industry. First, Fresenius Medical Care is involved in treating patients who suffer from chronic kidney failure. Second, Fresenius Helios in Germany is one of the largest hospital operators. Third, Fresenius Kabi supplies essential medications, clinical nutrition products, medical devices, and services to help patients suffering from chronic illnesses. Finally, Fresenius Vamed plans and develops healthcare facilities. As of 2016, the company, which is headquartered in Bad Homburg, contracts approximately 200,000 employees in more than 100 countries worldwide (Fresenius, 2016b). In accordance with the above-mentioned business areas, Fresenius operates as a functional organization (Figure 4.8.1). Fresenius's main competitors are DaVita, Baxter International Inc., and Dialysis Clinic. DaVita HealthCare Partners Inc. provides a variety of healthcare services to patients throughout the US. In 2013, DaVita announced an agreement to provide selected pharmacy services to Fresenius Medical Care (DaVita, 2013).

Organization and business segments

In 2015, the sales of Fresenius Group amounted to Euro 27.6 billion, while the net income reached Euro 1.4 billion, which equaled to an operating margin of 5 percent (Figure 4.8.2).

Fresenius Medical Care is considered to be the largest sector within the company generating Euro 15 billion in 2015 (Fresenius, 2016b). Fresenius Medical Care provides

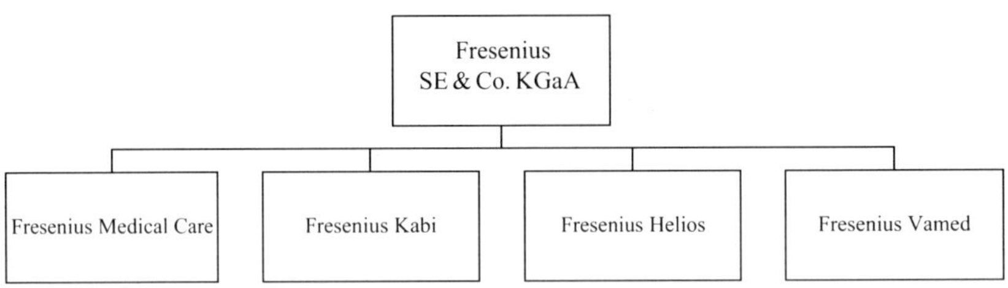

Figure 4.8.1 Functional organization of Fresenius (2016g).

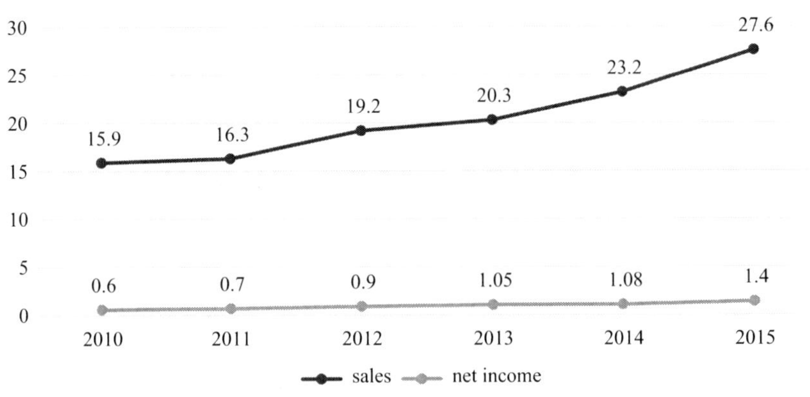

Figure 4.8.2 Fresenius: sales versus net income for the period 2010–2015 (in billion Euro).
Source: Author based on annual reports of Fresenius (2014, 2015).

treatments to 2.8 million patients worldwide, who receive routine dialysis. Dialysis is a vital blood cleaning procedure that substitutes the function of the kidney in the event of kidney failure (Fresenius, 2016c).

Fresenius Kabi specializes in medications and technologies for infusion, transfusion, and clinical nutrition. The company offers products for the collection and processing of blood components and for the therapeutic treatment of patients' blood using apheresis systems. The total sales of Fresenius Kabi amounted to Euro 5.9 billion in 2015 (Fresenius, 2016d).

Fresenius Helios, headquartered in Berlin, which generated sales of Euro 5.5 billion in 2015, is Germany's largest hospital group. The Helios Kliniken Group provides expertise in various areas of clinical care. The Helios Kliniken operates 112 hospitals in Erfurt, Berlin-Buch, Duisburg, Wuppertal, Schwerin, Krefeld, and Wiesbaden. The hospitals provide inpatient care for more than 1.3 million patients every year. The sub-division of Fresenius employs more than 67,000 people (Fresenius, 2016e).

Fresenius Vamed is responsible for managing healthcare projects and provides services for hospitals and other healthcare facilities worldwide. The portfolio ranges along the entire value chain from project development and turnkey construction, via technical management to operational management. In general, turnkey operations are attractive for firms, such as Fresnius Vamed, that have specific industry knowledge and complex managerial, operational, and technological process know-how. Turnkey describes a market entry mode where a firm sells complete operations and supply and distribution chain services: material procurement, assembly, testing, and aftersales service, including warranty support (Henning, 2013). Turnkey operations are usually used in large investment initiatives, such as the design, planning, construction, and building of larger operational facilities. Turnkey operations include the start-up of operations as well as necessary training, qualification, and consulting of the personnel who will operate the facility in the future (Glowik, 2016).

According to the firm's annual report, Fresenius Vamed manages projects and provides services for hospitals and other healthcare facilities worldwide. The portfolio ranges throughout the entire value chain: from project development, planning, and turnkey construction, via maintenance and technical management, to total operational management. This expertise enables Fresenius to support complex healthcare facilities efficiently and successfully at each level of their life cycle (Fresenius Vamed, 2013). The company is also engaged in public-private partnership (PPP) models for hospitals and other healthcare facilities. Up to the end of 2013, 21 of these models had been or are being implemented. In Europe, the focus was on Austria and Germany. Three new rehabilitation facilities in Austria launched operations in 2013. The new building for the 'Hofheim am Taunus' hospital and the turnkey construction of the new examination and treatment center at Cologne's University Hospital (UB West) have been projects in Germany. In Bosnia and Herzegovina, Fresenius Vamed completed the turnkey construction of the 220-bed Bijeljina General Hospital. In Russia, the healthcare firm continued the renovation and expansion of Sochi's Municipal Hospital (Fresenius Vamed, 2013).

In Africa, Fresenius Vamed launched the turnkey construction of five polyclinics in Gabon as well as projects in Nigeria and Ghana; and in Latin America, Fresnius Vamed completed its first project in Honduras; and in Trinidad and Tobago, the company modernized the San Fernando General Hospital. In China, Fresnius Vamed was able to enter the private hospital sector with the construction of an acute care and rehabilitation

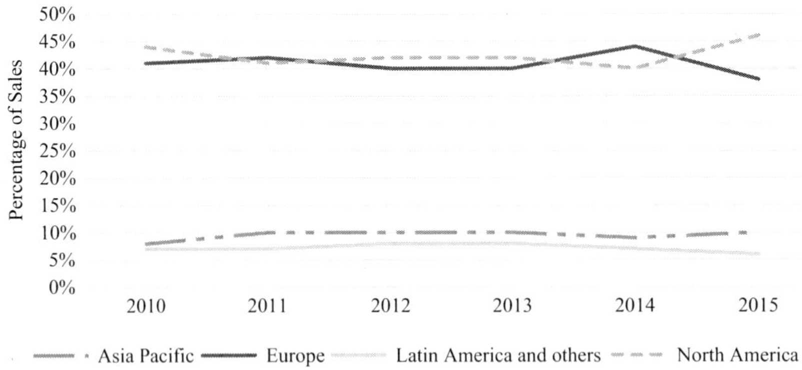

Figure 4.8.3 Fresenius: sales contribution (in percentage) by region for the period 2010–2015.
Source: Author based on annual reports of Fresenius (2010, 2011, 2012a, 2013, 2014, 2015).

hospital in Haikou, located in southern China. Fresenius Vamed was responsible for the total operational management of 43 healthcare facilities on three continents with approximately 5,000 beds in 2013. Worldwide, Vamed provides technical operation services to more than 380 hospitals with approximately 110,000 beds (Fresenius Vamed, 2013).

In Austria, Vamed continued its partnership with Vienna's General Hospital and University Hospital (AKH), one of the largest hospitals in Europe. They have been responsible for its technical management since 1986. With the start-up of hospitals in Kitzbühel and Vienna-Baumgarten, Vamed is now responsible for ten facilities, making it the largest private rehabilitation provider in Austria. A consortium led by Vamed in Germany has been responsible for all technical and infrastructural services at Berlin's Charité Hospital since 2006. In the Czech Republic, Vamed acquired three clinics and expanded its portfolio to seven locations with approximately 1,000 beds. In Gabon, Vamed is responsible for the overall management of seven regional hospitals and for the technical management of three hospitals in Libreville (Fresenius Vamed, 2013).

With its comprehensive range of services and as a worldwide-acting provider of a full line of services for the healthcare industry, Fresenius Vamed holds a unique position and completed during its entire existence approximately 650 projects in 72 countries. In 2015, the sales of Fresnius Vamed amounted to Euro 1.1 billion. The company already completed more than 700 projects in approximately 80 countries (Fresenius, 2016f).

Fresenius operates in Europe, Asia-Pacific, North America, Latin America, and other regions. North America is considered to be the largest market of Fresenius and has approximately 45 percent of the total sales in 2015. Europe serves as the second most important market, reaching 38 percent of the total sales in 2015. Ten percent of the company sales are generated in the Asia-Pacific region and 6 percent are contributed from Latin America.

Concentration strategy of Fresenius

According to their company mission statement, the aim of Fresenius is to strengthen its position as a leading global provider of products and therapies for chronically ill people (Fresenius, 2016h). In the context of horizontal concentration, the firm focuses on its current value added activities and expands its corresponding product and services offerings. A concentration strategy through vertical integration means that a firm utilizes an internal transfer within the organization of intermediate parts that a firm produces for its own use, such as materials, components, semi- or completely assembled products, and services (Glowik, 2016). Fresenius applies a concentration strategy through horizontal and vertical integration strategy, which is unique in the healthcare business. The advantages of vertical integration of Fresenius are quality and sensitive knowledge control, quick supply to its patients, specialized research, and development knowledge (Fresenius, 2012b). Important milestones related to the realization of Fresenius concentration strategy are described below.

Fresenius Medical Care

- The strategy of Fresenius Medical Care is to capture the firm's vertically integrated value added activities using the advantages that arise from covering the complete value chain of dialysis (Fresenius Medical Care, 2016).
- In 1979, Fresenius opened a plant in Schweinfurt and started producing dialysis machines.
- In 1996, the takeover of the American company National Medical Care helped to further develop Fresenius's dialysis business. The takeover serves as an example of horizontal concentration.
- In 2006, Fresenius acquired US dialysis provider Renal Care Group. This acquisition enabled the company to strengthen the provision of dialysis treatment around the globe (Fresenius, 2016a).
- In 2014, the acquisition of Cogent Healthcare, which is a provider of specialist physicians to hospitals, offers hospitalist and intensivist services to more than 80 hospitals throughout the United States. This acquisition helps Fresenius to augment their network of dialysis, cardiac, and vascular care centers (Fresenius Medical Care, 2014).
- In 2016, Fresenius Medical Care purchased from a group of investors 85 percent of the equity interest in the Indian dialysis company Sandor Nephro Services. Sandor Nephro Services is India's second largest dialysis care provider. Fresenius Medical Care significantly increased its market share of dialysis products in India (Fresenius, 2016i).

Fresenius Kabi

- In 1963, Fresenius launched the production of plastic bottles for infusion solutions (Fresenius, 2016a).
- In 2012, the acquisition of Fenwal from Illinois, which is a medical device firm focusing on transfusing medications using specialized expertise in blood separation, collection, filtration, storage, and transfusion. This purchase provided Fresenius Kabi the opportunity to expand its medical devices transfusion technology segment and get access to the US transfusion technology market (Fenwalin, 2012; Reuters, 2012).
- With the acquisition of business assets from Becton Dickinson: Fresenius Kabi expanded its business portfolio to include a pharmaceutical manufacturing plant in Wilson, NC, and seven medications in ready-to-administer prefilled glass syringes (Fresenius, 2016b).

Fresenius Helios

- In 2016, Fresenius Helios acquired the largest private Spanish hospital group named Quirónsalud for a total equity price of Euro 5.67 billion. The Spanish hospital group consists of 43 hospitals and 39 outpatient centers and approximately 300 occupational risk prevention (ORP) centers (Fresenius, 2016j). It is the first acquisition outside of Germany by Fresenius Helios (Bray, 2016).

Through its various acquisitions, Fresenius significantly increased its global presence. The business outlook of Fresenius is promising. In mid-2016, Fresenius had indicated that it expected 2016 adjusted net profit to increase between 11 percent and 14 percent over the 2015 figure. Fresenius confirmed its 2016 sales growth target between 6 percent and 8 percent. Fresenius Kabi, the group's clinical technology provider, also raised its full-year outlook for sales. It expects sales in constant currency to grow between 3 percent and 5 percent. Fresenius Kabi reported a net profit rise of 7 percent to Euro 180 million during the second quarter in 2016.

Fresenius Group's quarterly adjusted net profit increased to Euro 393 million. Earnings before interest and taxes increased by 8 percent to Euro 1.05 billion and sales went up by 2 percent to Euro 7.1 billion during the second quarter in 2016. All four business divisions of Fresenius contributed to the business performance improvements. Fresenius's largest business unit, Medical Care, the world's largest provider of dialysis products and services, reported a 22 percent increase in net profit (Dauer, 2016).

Value added chain of Fresenius

As shown in Figure 4.8.3, Fresenius implemented a concentration strategy through vertical integration. The healthcare firm owns and controls relevant and important value added activities ranging from dialysis-focused research and development (Fresenius Medical Care), to medical devices and dialysis and infusions treatments (Fresenius Kabi), to the company's owned hospitals in Germany and Spain (Fresenius Helios). Fresenius Vamed specializes in planning and management of small and large healthcare facility projects for other firms, which are, among others, also organized as turnkey projects. Reports on the patients' illnesses collected at the firm-owned hospitals can be used for the company's own research and development. Altogether, this concentration strategy contributes to make Fresenius globally a leading firm in dialysis treatments. Undoubtedly, patients suffering from illnesses requiring dialysis benefit from the firm's specialized expertise, which is unique in the global healthcare markets. However, are there any potential drawbacks for either Fresenius or the patients or other stakeholders with regard to the concentration strategy of Fresenius?

Table 4.8.1 Vertical integration strategy of Fresenius

Fresenius Medical Care	**Fresenius Kabi**	**Fresenius Vamed**	**Fresenius Helios**
Research and development dialysis products	*Infusion equipment*	*Planning and management of healthcare projects and facilities around the world*	*Hospitals e.g. in Germany and Spain (patient treatment)*

Bibliography

Bray, C 2016, Fresenius to buy Spain's largest private hospital operator, *The New York Times*. Available from: www.nytimes.com/2016/09/07/business/dealbook/fresenius-quironsalud-deal.html. [September 12, 2016].

DaVita 2013, DaVita announces partnership with Fresenius Medical Care. Available from: http://phx.corporate-ir.net/phoenix.zhtml?c=76556&p=irol-newsArticle_print&ID=1772476. [September 12, 2016].

Dauer, U 2016, *Fresenius boosts profit outlook*. Available from: www.marketwatch.com/story/fresenius-boosts-profit-outlook-2016-08-02. [September 27, 2016].

Economist 2009. Idea: vertical integration, *Economist*. Available from: www.economist.com/node/13396061. [September 12, 2016].

Fenwalinc 2012, Fresenius to acquire Fenwal. Available from: www.fenwalinc.com/PressReleases/Pages/News/Fresenius-to-acquire-Fenwal.aspx. [Accessed 12 September 2016].

Fresenius 2010, Annual report 2010. Available from: www.fresenius.com/media/FSE_GB_2010_final_eng(1).pdf. [September 12, 2016].

Fresenius 2011, Annual report 2011. Available from: www.fresenius.com/media/F_GB11_2011_e_Internet.pdf. [September 11, 2016].

Fresenius 2012a, Annual report 2012. Available from: www.fresenius.com/financial_reporting/GB_englisch_USGAAP_2012.pdf. [September 11, 2016].

Fresenius 2012b, Fresenius 100 years. Available from: www.fresenius100.com/files/100Years_Fresenius_s.pdf. [September 12, 2016].

Fresenius 2013, Annual report 2013. Available from: www.fresenius.com/financial_reporting/GB_englisch_US_GAAP_2013.pdf. [September 11, 2016].

Fresenius 2014, Annual report 2014. Available from: www.fresenius.com/media_library/GB_US_GAAP_2014_englisch.pdf. [September 11, 2016].

Fresenius 2015, Annual report 2015. Available from: www.fresenius.com/financial_reporting/Fresenius_GB_US_GAAP_2015_englisch.pdf. [September 11, 2016].

Fresenius 2016a, History. Available from: www.fresenius.com/history. [September 11, 2016].

Fresenius 2016b, Group overview. Available from: www.fresenius.com/Group-Overview. [September 11, 2016].

Fresenius 2016c, Fresenius Medical Care. Available from: www.fresenius.com/fresenius-medical-care. [September 11, 2016].

Fresenius 2016d, Fresenius Kabi. Available from: www.fresenius.com/fresenius-kabi. [September 11, 2016].

Fresenius 2016e, Fresenius Helios. Available from: www.fresenius.com/fresenius-helios. [September 11, 2016].

Fresenius 2016f, Fresenius Vamed. Available from: www.fresenius.com/fresenius-vamed. [September 11, 2016].

Fresenius 2016g, Group structure. Available from: www.fresenius.com/group-structure. [September 12, 2016].

Fresenius 2016h, Goals and strategy. Available from: www.fresenius.com/goals-and-strategy. [September 12, 2016].

Fresenius 2016i, Fresenius Medical Care acquires dialysis service provider Sandor Nephro Services in India. Available from: www.fresenius.com/5081. [September 12, 2016].

Fresenius 2016j, Fresenius Helios acquires largest private Spanish hospital group Quirónsalud. Available from: www.fresenius.com/5095. [September 12, 2016].

Fresenius Kabi 2016a, IV Drugs. Available from: www.fresenius-kabi.co.uk/4518.htm. [September 12, 2016].

Fresenius Kabi 2016b, History. Available from: www.fresenius-kabi.com/sites/global/Pages/company/History.aspx. [September 12, 2016].

Fresenius Medical Care 2014, Fresenius Medical Care announces agreement to acquire Cogent Healthcare. Available from: www.freseniusmedicalcare.com/en/news/details/title/fresenius-medical-care-announces-agreement-to-acquire-cogent-healthcare/. [September 12, 2016].

Fresenius Medical Care 2016, Strategy. Available from: www.freseniusmedicalcare.com/en/investors/at-a-glance/strategy/. [September 12, 2016].

Fresenius Vamed 2013, *Annual report 2013*. Available from: http://geschaeftsbericht2013.fresenius.de/reports/fresenius/annual/2013/gb/English/105040/fresenius-vamed.html?printDoc=1. [October 9, 2016].

Glowik, M 2016, *Market entry strategies: internationalization theories, concepts and cases of Asian high-technology firms*, second ed., De Gruyter Oldenbourg, Berlin and Boston.

Henning, G 2013, Choosing between turnkey and consignment manufacturing, *Surface Mount Technology*, vol. 28, no. 1, pp. 18–24.

Reuters 2012, Update 3: Fresenius buys Fenwal for $1.1 bln-sources. Available from: www.reuters.com/article/fresenius-fenwal-idUSL6E8IKGSD20120720. [September 12, 2016].

4.9 Case study: Boehringer Ingelheim

License-driven market entry

Mario Glowik

Case review questions

1. Taking the case of Boehringer Ingelheim, how would you describe the meaning of licensing and corresponding varieties, advantages and disadvantages from the licensor's and the licensee's points of view?
2. Considering the background of Boehringer Ingelheim, can you describe how market entry strategies through licensing, strategic alliances and joint ventures differ in terms of opportunities and risks?

Company profile

The family-owned Boehringer Ingelheim is one of the leading pharmaceutical companies in the world. The company was founded in 1885 by Albert Boehringer in Ingelheim am Rhein. In 1893, Boehringer's discovery that lactic acid can be produced in mass quantities by means of bacteria led the company to become the leading manufacturer of large-scale biotechnologies. In 1895, the company registered its first patent for a new process to manufacture lactic-acid-based baking powder (Boehringer Ingelheim, 2016a).

Following the death of the founder, Albert Boehringer, his sons took over the management of the company. An important milestone occurred in 1948, when the first foreign subsidiary, Bender & Co. GmbH in Vienna, was established followed by various additional subsidiaries in Europe and overseas. The expansion and the success of Boehringer Ingelheim included bringing innovative products into the markets, including respiratory agents and products for treating diseases of the cardiovascular system. In 1987, 'Actilyse' was launched and considered to be a significant step for leading the company into the future. 'Actilyse' serves as the first thrombolytic treatment for severe heart attacks, manufactured at biopharmaceutical production sites of Boehringer Ingelheim (Boehhringer Ingelheim, 2016b).

In 1992, Erich von Baumbach, the son-in-law of Albert Boehringer, was appointed chairman of the shareholders' committee. In fact, in 1993, the German company had two sites under common management—one in Ingelheim and one in Biberach. In 1995, the pharmaceutical business achieved additional market shares through global research and development initiatives exceeding Deutsche Marks one billion (approximately

Euro 511 million). The company employed a total of 23,277 people (Boehhringer Ingelheim, 2016c). Today, Christian Boehringer is the chairman of the shareholders' committee. The company operates 145 affiliates and a total of approximately 47,500 employees worldwide. Boehringer Ingelheim focuses on the therapeutic areas, research and development, and manufacturing and marketing of medications for human and veterinary medicine (Boehhringer Ingelheim, 2016d).

Business segments

As shown in Figure 4.9.1. Boehringer Ingelheim generated net sales of Euro 14.8 billion in 2015, which makes the firm one of the world's top 20 pharmaceutical companies. The net income in 2015 reached Euro 1.5 billion, which equals a margin related to the net income of approximately 10 percent (Boehringer Ingelheim, 2015a).

Boehringer Ingelheim's business activities are organized on an industry sector basis, which is divided into five business units: prescription medicines; consumer healthcare; animal health; biopharmaceuticals; and industrial customers. Prescription medicine is the main business of the company activities and generated in 2015 the largest amount of sales reaching Euro 11.2 billion, which is approximately 2/3 of the total revenues. According to Boehringer Ingelheim's annual report (2015a), the promising sales growth was realized by launching several newly developed products resulting from extended clinical trials.

Consumer healthcare serves as the second main sales generator of Boehringer Ingelheim and amounts to Euro 1.5 billion. In 2015, the largest contributor in this sector was DULCOLAX, which demonstrated a sales record of Euro 225 million. Animal health is considered to be the third most important sector. In 2015, the revenues from the animal health products amounted to Euro 1.4 billion. As a part of animal health, sales of products for so-called 'livestock' accounted for the biggest share reaching Euro 979 million. The sales in biopharmaceutical contract manufacturing generated Euro 576 million. Finally, the industrial customer business, which compromises several third-party businesses, generated sales of Euro 145 million in 2015 (Figure 4.9.2) (Boehringer Ingelheim, 2011, 2012, 2013a, 2014a, 2015a).

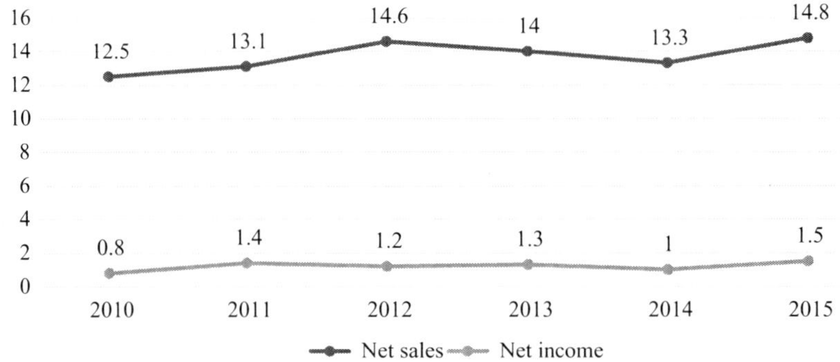

Figure 4.9.1 Boehringer Ingelheim: net sales versus net income (in billion Euro) during the period 2010–2015.

Source: Author based on annual reports of Boehringer Ingelheim (2011, 2012, 2013a, 2014a, 2015a).

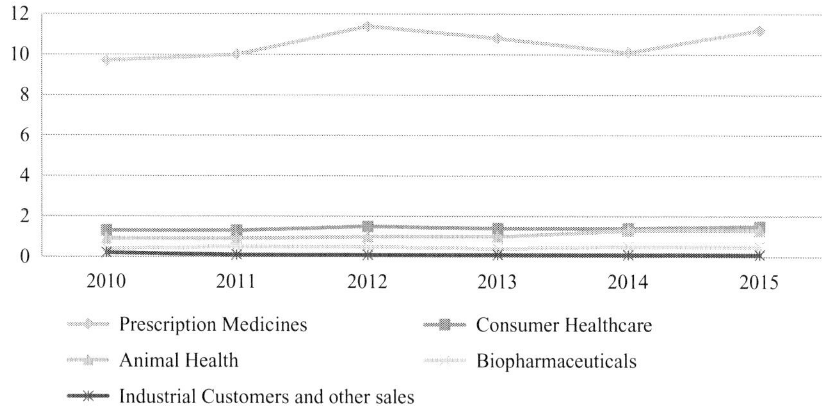

Figure 4.9.2 Boehringer Ingelheim: net revenues (in billion Euro) by business segment during the period 2010–2015.

Source: Author based on annual reports of Boehringer Ingelheim (2011, 2012, 2013a, 2014a, 2015a).

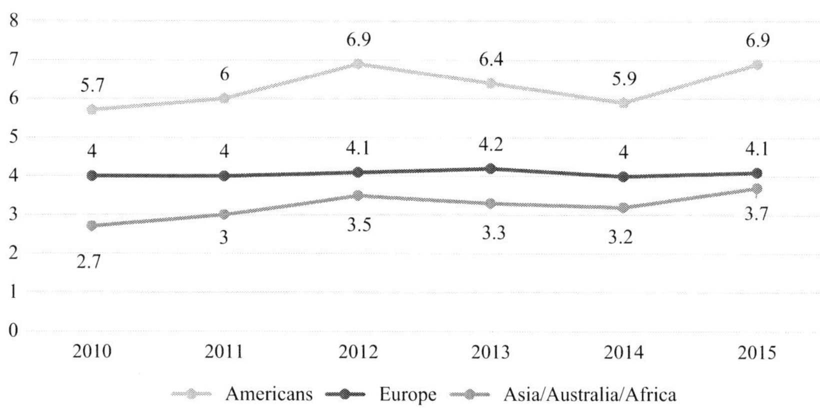

Figure 4.9.3 Boehringer Ingelheim: net revenues (in billion Euro) by sales region during the period 2010–2015.

Source: Author based on annual reports of Boehringer Ingelheim (2011, 2012, 2013a, 2014a, 2015a).

Boehringer Ingelheim's activities can be also divided by geographical sales regions. The company achieved the majority of its sales from America (47 percent) and Europe (28 percent) (Figure 4.9.3). The revenues from areas such as Asia/Australia/Africa (AAA) in 2015 amounted to approximately 25 percent of the total net sales. The three largest sales markets for Boehringer Ingelheim are USA, Japan, and Germany, which generate approximately 57 percent of the total sales in 2015 (Boehringer Ingelheim 2011, 2012, 2013a, 2014a, 2015a).

As shown in Figure 4.9.4. Boehringer Ingelheim, due to its extended international business activities, is organized according to its sales regions within an international matrix organization.

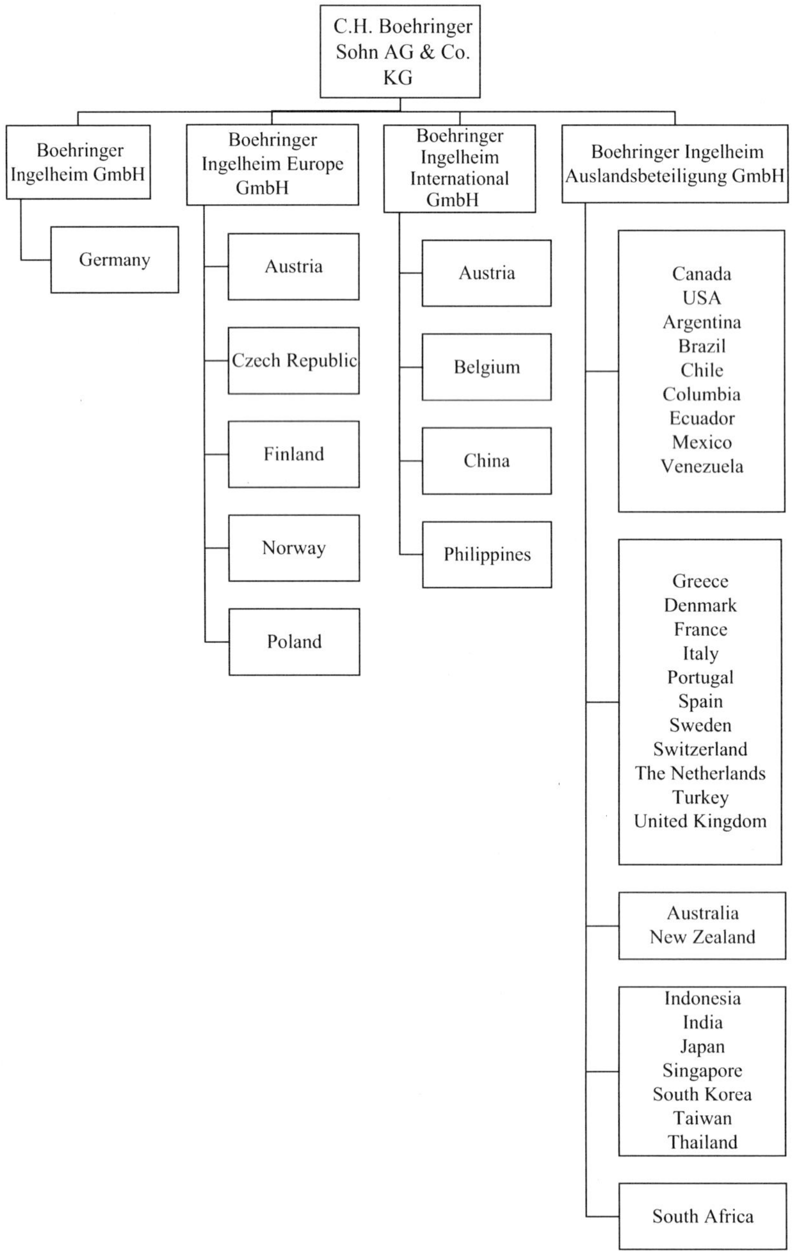

Figure 4.9.4 Organization chart (international matrix organization) of Boehringer Ingelheim in 2015 (2015a).

Bilateral relationships

The mission of Boehringer Ingelheim, as cited on their website, is described as 'value through innovation' (Boehringer Ingelheim, 2016e). The primary goal aims to research and develop innovative medicines and therapies for diseases and respond to the need in areas in which there is no adequate treatment currently available (Boehringer Ingelheim, 2015a). As the main business areas of Boehringer Ingelheim are prescription medicines, consumer healthcare, and animal health, the company particularly expanded their product portfolio in these segments by establishing partnership agreements and systematic licensing.

The discovery of pharmaceutical medications is costly and time-consuming, taking approximately ten years and easily accumulating one billion Euros of resources (Morgan et al., 2011; DiMasi et al., 2016). Additionally, the process comes with a high risk originated by the so-called attrition rate: As a result, the vast majority of medication candidates never reach a pharmacy store (Waring et al., 2015). The process is usually divided into several steps, from preclinical discovery to early clinical research followed by late-stage clinical development (Drews, 2000). Any project can fail at any of these stages. Therefore, pharmaceutical companies manage their portfolio of R&D projects by selling and buying assets, mergers, and acquisitions, and quite often, via in- and out-licensing.

Licensing describes a contractual relation where the owner of intellectual property sells the right to use this knowledge to the licensee who, in return, pays royalties to the licensor. In other words, a license describes the transfer of intangible resources for a defined purpose. The licensee takes the entrepreneurial business risk and undertakes financial investments in its own operating capacities. The licensor does not give up its ownership of the knowledge for the entire time of the license agreement (Glowik, 2016).

There are in-licensing and out-licensing activities that are important for pharmaceutical companies. In many cases, a pharmaceutical company (licensee) acquires intellectual knowledge property through in-licensing from another firm (licensor) targeting to fill a gap in its own research and development value chain (Reepmeyer, 2008). The in-licensed innovation can originate at academic institutions, biotech startups, or midsized or global pharmaceutical companies.

In contrast, out-licensing at pharmaceutical companies concern improving research and development returns on investments by commercializing the firm's research and development results. Pharmaceutical companies use out-licensing agreements with often young, small, and highly specialized firms, which indicate at the time of the deal closure no track record that proves their ability through internal resource allocation to successfully develop the licensed knowledge (Reepmeyer, Gassmann, and Rüther, 2011). The deal structure (usually a kick-off payment, followed by later payments when milestones are reached [which is, a project has 'survived' a test phase successfully and is ready to enter the next development phase], and royalties to participate in the market success) reflects the risks of the corresponding projects (Villiger and Bogdan, 2009; Havenaar and Hiscocks, 2012). It is thus comparable to a convertible bond where the specifications of the bond issue also reflect the uncertainty of the future financial performance of the bond issuer.

Boehringer Ingelheim, which is heavily involved in licensing, has agreed to the following important license contracts in recent years.

License contracts

1 In 2014, Boehringer Ingelheim and CureVac announced an exclusive global license agreement.

- CureVac is a clinical stage biopharmaceutical company from Tübingen, Germany. It was founded in 2000 and its most advanced project is in the middle of clinical development.
- Boehringer Ingelheim obtained exclusive global rights for the development and commercialization of CureVac's investigational therapeutic cancer vaccine, so-called CV9202.
- The in-licensing of this investigational cancer compound added a highly innovative new approach to Boehringer Ingelheim's lung cancer development portfolio (Boehringer Ingelheim, 2014b).

2 In 2015, Boehringer Ingelheim entered into a license agreement with Hanmi Pharmaceutical.

- Hanmi Pharmaceutical is a South Korea-based global pharmaceutical company focused on the development and commercialization of new pharmaceutical products.
- In July 2015, Hanmi signed an 850 billion won (USD 773.1 million) agreement with the German pharmaceutical giant to jointly develop and sell the new treatment, HM61713.
- HM61713 is a novel third-generation tyrosine kinase inhibitor for lung cancer patients who have developed a resistance to previous EGFR targeting agents.
- Hanmi received an initial (upfront) payment of USD 65 million and is entitled to potential milestone payments of USD 680 million plus tiered double-digit royalties on future net sales.
- This in-licensing agreement strengthened Boehringer Ingelheim's lung cancer portfolio and enabled the company to provide more patient tailored treatment options (Boehringer Ingelheim, 2015b).
- The deal effective outside of South Korea, China, and Hong Kong included initial and milestone payments as well as double-digit royalties on future net sales.
- In the summer of 2016, the new drug was approved by the regulatory authorities of South Korea.
- On September 30, 2016, Hanmi Pharmaceutical Co. announced that its license deal on a lung cancer treatment with Boehringer Ingelheim had terminated.
- In a regulatory filing, the Korean firm said Boehringer decided not to proceed with the clinical tests and return the license. But Hanmi does not need to return USD 65 million it received as upfront and milestone payments.
- Apparently, two cancer patients participating in a clinical trial of the new compound had died. The death could be related to the mechanism by which similar agents typically work.
- After a reevaluation of available clinical data and the competitive landscape, Boehringer concluded that it should cut its losses and focus on other pipeline programs.
- Rather than start clinical trials of olmutinib, Boehringer will return development rights and responsibilities to Hanmi, which is currently testing the agent in three Phase I/II and Phase II trials. Boehringer came on board as a co-sponsor of those trials, but only ran a Phase I pharmacokinetic study itself. That Phase I

trial in healthy volunteers is the only study listed on ClinicalTrials.gov as having started or finished in the brief period in which Boehringer was involved with olmutinib (Taylor, 2016).
- The announcement came one day after Hanmi signed a USD 910 million deal with Zentec Pharmaceuticals of Canada to export the technology for its self-developed anti-cancer substance (Yonhap, 2016).

3 In 2016, Boehringer Ingelheim and Arena Pharmaceuticals signed an agreement to advance research in patients with schizophrenia.
- Arena Pharmaceuticals focuses on discovering, developing, and commercializing agents to address so-called unmet medical needs.
- Arena is a California-based biotech company, which has licensed a marketed agent to the Japanese pharmaceutical company Eisai and has several projects under clinical development.
- The companies signed the agreement to conduct joint research to identify medication candidates targeting an undisclosed G protein-coupled receptor.
- Arena provided Boehringer Ingelheim the rights to its internally discovered, novel compounds and intellectual property for an orphan CNS receptor.
- The collaboration enabled Boehringer Ingelheim to accomplish its commitment to research and develop new and more effective treatments for psychiatric diseases and their symptoms.
- Arena receives payments up to USD 262 million in success milestones in the case of full commercial success of multiple medication products, including an upfront payment and research funding (Boehringer Ingelheim, 2016f).

4 In 2016, AbbVie and Boehringer Ingelheim announced global collaboration on promising immunology compounds.
- AbbVie and Boehringer Ingelheim share responsibility for future clinical development and they establish a joint steering committee.
- AbbVie is a global, research-based biopharmaceutical company formed in 2013 when former Abbott Laboratories split itself into two companies.
- Under the terms of the license agreement, AbbVie makes an initial upfront payment of USD 595 million.
- AbbVie will be solely responsible for the commercialization of BI 655066 (an anti-IL-23 monoclonal biologic antibody in the Phase 3 development for psoriasis) while Boehringer Ingelheim will retain an option to co-promote the compound in asthma (Boehringer Ingelheim, 2016g).

Cooperative agreements

In addition, Boehringer Ingelheim established cooperative agreement as shown below.

1 Boehringer Ingelheim and Micromet
- In 2010, the companies entered into a collaboration agreement for the research, development, and commercialization of a new BiTE antibody for the treatment of multiple myeloma.
- Micromet is a biopharmaceutical company focused on the discovery, development, and commercialization of antibody-based therapies for the treatment of

cancer. Micromet is a biopharmaceutical company focused on the discovery, development, and commercialization of antibody-based therapies for the treatment of cancer. Their proprietary technology is the development of so-called bispecific T-cell engagers (BiTE antibodies). Here, one half of the drug always attracts immune cells; the other half is custom-made for each medication project. Once such medication is already approved and marketed, several others are under development.
- In 2012, Amgen acquired Micromet. Amgen is a global biotech company, founded in California in 1980.
- Microment received an upfront cash payment of Euro five million, and additional milestone and royalty payments depending on the products' business performance are agreed on (PR Newswire, 2010).

2 Boehringer Ingelheim and Lilly
- The aim of the collaboration in 2011 was to develop and commercialize a portfolio of diabetes compounds, which are currently positioned in mid- and late-stage development processes.
- Lilly is developing a growing portfolio of pharmaceutical products by applying the latest research from its own worldwide laboratories and from collaborations with eminent scientific organizations, primarily based in Indianapolis. Lilly is also a global pharmaceutical company (Lilly, 2011).
- In 2014, the companies revised the operational structure of diabetes alliance in certain countries (Boehringer Ingelheim, 2014c).
- In 2016, Boehringer Ingelheim and Lilly announced clinical trial collaboration in metastatic breast cancer (Boehringer Ingelheim, 2016h).

3 Boehringer Ingelheim and Sanofi
- The companies entered into alliance in 2015 to extend Sanofi's manufacturing capacity network for therapeutic monoclonal antibodies.
- Sanofi is a French company, considered to be a global healthcare leader, that discovers, develops, and distributes therapeutic solutions focused on patients' needs. Sanofi was created in 2004 when Sanofi Synthelabo acquired Aventis, which had been created in the fusion of German Hoechst AG with French Rhone-Poulenc (Sanofi, 2015).
- Boehringer Ingelheim's cell culture operations provides contract manufacturing capacities to support the production of Sanofi's biologics pipeline (Boehringer Ingelheim, 2015c).
- In 2016, Boehringer Ingelheim and the French pharmaceutical company, Sanofi, signed an 'asset swap' agreement. The contract was signed after six months of intense negotiations. The strategic agreement includes an exchange of Sanofi's animal health business ('Merial') and Boehringer Ingelheim's consumer healthcare business. The strategic swap provides the basis for both companies to realize economies of scale in highly attractive pharmaceutical market niches (Boehringer Ingelheim, 2016i).

4 Boehringer Ingelheim and Taizhou China Medical City
- In 2013, Boehringer Ingelheim established an international joint venture with Taizhou China Medical City.
- The international joint venture includes operating joint manufacturing of veterinary vaccine products.

- The partnership included a total investment of Euro 58 million aiming to strengthen the position of Boehringer Ingelheim in China in the animal health sector (Boehringer Ingelheim, 2013b).

In autumn of 2016, Boehringer joined some of its larger rivals in shrinking its sales and administration operations to save money and divert more cash towards research and development. For example, AstraZeneca already announced in early 2016 that it would cut jobs and manufacturing to save USD 1.1 billion, much of which it plans to invest in developing medications.

'Following a careful examination of our human pharmaceuticals business, we made the difficult decision to eliminate (the positions),' Boehringer spokeswoman Erin Crew said in a statement. 'Many of those given pink slips will have the chance to apply for jobs elsewhere in the company,' she added.

'The actions we are taking now will help us reinvent the way we serve the needs of our patients, and enable us to continue to make significant investments' in research and development, Crew said.

Boehringer's latest cuts come as the company struggles with patent-cliff losses—its blockbuster blood pressure medication Micardis took a big hit from the generic brands last year—and pricing pressures in the US market. The company announced layoffs of approximately 900 in 2014 as part of a drive to cut costs by 15%. Last summer, it announced it would sell its US generics operation, Roxane Labs, to Jordan's Hikma Pharmaceuticals for USD 2.65 billion, saying it needed to focus on medication development and branded drug sales—hence, the need to up spending on research and development.

One bright spot for Boehringer has been in diabetes, where revenue shot up by 49 percent in currency-adjusted terms last year to Euro 1.1 billion (USD 1.24 billion). The company sees its diabetes portfolio—consisting of six medications the company shares with partner Eli Lilly—as having now 'established itself as a long-term growth driver' that Boehringer expects will keep revenues flowing (Staton, 2016).

To summarize, the pharmaceutical industry is known for intense research and development efforts necessary to secure the firm's sustainable competitive survival. Medical devices and medicine-related knowledge proprieties, usually protected through patents over long periods of time, play a crucial role for the firm's sustained business success. The records clearly indicate Boehringer Ingelheim's preference towards license contracts followed by cooperative agreement, such as strategic alliances and joint ventures, which come along with various opportunities (e.g. fast global market entry) but also risks (e.g. limited control of knowledge proprieties), just to mention some.

Bibliography

Boehringer Ingelheim 2011, Annual report 2011. Available from: http://us.boehringer-ingelheim.com/content/dam/internet/opu/us_EN/documents/Media_Press_Releases/2011/BoehringerIngelheim_Annual_Report_2011_complete.pdf. [September 3, 2016].

Boehringer Ingelheim 2012, Annual report 2012. Available from: http://annualreport.boehringer-ingelheim.com/fileadmin/downloads/alte_berichte/bi_gb2012_annual_report_en_04.pdf. [September 3, 2016].

Boehringer Ingelheim 2013a, Annual report 2013. Available from: http://annualreport.boehringer-ingelheim.com/fileadmin/downloads/alte_berichte/annual_report_2013_complete.pdf. [September 3, 2016].

Boehringer Ingelheim 2013b, Boehringer Ingelheim takes a further step to establish Animal Health business in Asia. Available from: www.boehringer-ingelheim.com/press-release/

boehringer-ingelheim-takes-further-step-establish-animal-health-business-asia. [September 10, 2016].

Boehringer Ingelheim 2014a, Annual report 2014. Available from: http://annualreport.boehringer-ingelheim.com/fileadmin/downloads/alte_berichte/annual_report_2014_complete.pdf. [September 3, 2016].

Boehringer Ingelheim 2014b, Boehringer Ingelheim and CureVac announce collaboration to develop next generation lung cancer immunotherapy. Available from: www.boehringer-ingelheim.com/press-release/boehringer-ingelheim-and-curevac-collaboration. [September 10, 2016].

Boehringer Ingelheim 2014c, Boehringer Ingelheim and Lilly revising operational structure of diabetes alliance in certain countries. Available from: www.boehringer-ingelheim.com/press-release/boehringer-ingelheim-and-lilly-revising-operational-structure-diabetes-alliance. [September 8, 2016].

Boehringer Ingelheim 2015a, Annual report 2015. Available from: http://annualreport.boehringer-ingelheim.com/fileadmin/downloads/boehringer_ingelheim_annual_report_2015.pdf. [September 1, 2016].

Boehringer Ingelheim 2015b, Boehringer Ingelheim enters into an exclusive license agreement with Hanmi Pharmaceutical to develop 3rd generation EGFR targeted therapy in lung cancer. Available from: www.boehringer-ingelheim.com/press-release/boehringer-ingelheim-and-hanmi-developing-egfr-tki. [September 10, 2016].

Boehringer Ingelheim 2015c, Boehringer Ingelheim and Sanofi enter into a strategic contract manufacturing alliance to produce biopharmaceuticals. Available from: www.boehringer-ingelheim.com/press-release/boehringer-ingelheim-and-sanofi-enter-strategic-contract-manufacturing-alliance. [September 7, 2016].

Boehringer Ingelheim 2016a, 1885–1948: Innovative beginnings. Available from: www.boehringer-ingelheim.com/history/history-milestone/1885–1948. [September 1, 2016].

Boehringer Ingelheim 2016b, 1948–1988: Going global. Available from: www.boehringer-ingelheim.com/history/history-milestone/1948-1988. [September 1, 2016].

Boehringer Ingelheim 2016c, 1988–2015: Value through innovation. Available from: www.boehringer-ingelheim.com/history/history-milestone/1988–2015. [September 1, 2016].

Boehringer Ingelheim 2016d, A successful and independent corporation. Available from: www.boehringer-ingelheim.com/who-we-are/our-company. [September 1, 2016].

Boehringer Ingelheim 2016e, Vision. Available from: www.boehringer-ingelheim.com/who-we-are/vision. [September 9, 2016].

Boehringer Ingelheim 2016f, Boehringer Ingelheim and Arena Pharmaceuticals collaborate to advance research in schizophrenia. Available at: www.boehringer-ingelheim.com/press-release/boehringer-ingelheim-and-arena-pharmaceuticals-collaborate-advance-research. [September 10, 2016].

Boehringer Ingelheim 2016g, AbbVie and Boehringer Ingelheim announce global collaboration on promising immunology compounds. Available from: www.boehringer-ingelheim.com/press-release/abbvie-boehringer-ingelheim-immunology-compounds. [September 10, 2016].

Boehringer Ingelheim 2016h, Boehringer Ingelheim and Lilly announce clinical trial collaboration in metastatic breast cancer. Available from: www.boehringer-ingelheim.com/press-release/boehringer-ingelheim-and-lilly-announce-clinical-trial-collaboration-metastatic-breast. [September 10, 2016].

Boehringer Ingelheim 2016i, Sanofi and Boehringer Ingelheim have reached definitive agreements to swap Sanofi's Animal Health and Boehringer Ingelheim's Consumer Healthcare businesses. Available from: www.boehringer-ingelheim.com/press-release/sanofi-and-boehringer-ingelheim-have-reached-definitive-agreements-swap-sanofi-s. [September 10, 2016].

DiMasi JA, Grabowski HG & Hansen RW 2016, Innovation in the pharmaceutical industry: new estimates of R&D costs, *Journal of Health Economics*, vol. 47, pp. 20–33.

Drews, J 2000, Drug discovery: a historical perspective, *Science*, vol. 287, no. 5460, pp. 1960–4.

Glowik, M 2016, *Market entry strategies: onternationalization theories, concepts and cases of Asian high-technology firms*, second ed., De Gruyter Oldenbourg, Berlin and Boston.

Havenaar, M & Hiscocks P 2012, Strategic alliances and market risk, *Drug Discovery Today* vol. 17, issue 15–16, pp. 824–7.

Lilly 2011, Lilly and Boehringer Ingelheim announce strategic alliance to bring new diabetes treatments to patients worldwide. Available from: https://investor.lilly.com/releasedetail.cfm?ReleaseID=542971. [September 10, 2016].

Morgan S, Grootendorst P, Lexchin J, Cunningham C & Greyson D 2011, The cost of drug development: a systematic review, *Health Policy*, vol. 1, pp. 4–17.

PR Newswire 2010, Boehringer Ingelheim and Micromet announce global collaboration for multiple myeloma BiTE Antibody. Available from: www.prnewswire.com/news-releases/boehringer-ingelheim-and-micromet-announce-global-collaboration-for-multiple-myeloma-bite-antibody-92850644.html. [September 10, 2016].

Reepmeyer, G 2006, *Risk-sharing in the pharmaceutical Industry: the case of out-licensing*, Physica Verlag. Heidelberg.

Reepmeyer, G, Gassmann, O & Rüther F 2011, Out-licensing in markets with asymmetric information: the case of the pharmaceutical industry, *International Journal of Innovation Management*, vol. 15, no. 4, pp. 755–95.

Sanofi 2015, Sanofi enters strategic manufacturing collaboration with Boehringer Ingelheim to produce biologics Available from: http://en.sanofi.com/Images/38190_20150115_Sanofi_BI_IA_agreement_en.pdf. [September 10, 2016].

Staton, T 2016, *Boehringer slashes 724 jobs off U.S. sales payroll to boost research and development spending* [Online]. Available from: www.fiercepharma.com/pharma/boehringer-slashes-724-jobs-off-u-s-sales-payroll-to-boost-r-d-spending. [October 7, 2016].

Taylor, NP 2016, *Boehringer backs out of USD730M lung cancer pact with Hanmi following data review* [Online]. Available from: www.fiercebiotech.com/biotech/boehringer-backs-out-730m-lung-cancer-pact-hanmi-following-data-review. [October 7, 2016].

Villiger, R & Bogdan, B 2009. Licensing: pros and cons for biotech, *Drug Discovery Today*, vol. 14, no. 5–6, pp. 227–30.

Waring, MJ, Arrowsmith, J, Leach, AR, Leeson, PD, Mandrell, S, Owen, RM, Pairaudeau, G, Pennie, WD, Pickett, SD, Wang, J, Wallace, O, & Weir, A 2015, An analysis of the attrition of drug candidates from four major pharmaceutical companies, *Nat Rev Drug Discov*, vol. 14, no. 7, pp. 475–86.

Yonhap 2016, *Hanmi Pharmaceutical says license deal with Boehringer ended* [Online]. Available from: http://english.yonhapnews.co.kr/news/2016/09/30/62/0200000000AEN20160930007400320F.html. [October 7, 2016].

Index